Praise for *END OF THE ROPE*

"Climbing mountains becomes a source of both joy and loss for Jan Redford—as she finds her own gutsy route through that other wilderness, of marriage and motherhood. Cheryl Strayed, move over: *End of the Rope* is a rambunctious, funny, heartstopping memoir that carries us along on an electric current of risk and courage."

Marni Jackson, Senior Faculty, The Mountain and Wilderness
Writing Program, Banff Centre, and author of *The Mother Zone*

"A hair-raising triumph—my heart raced on every page, wondering if Jan Redford would seize her lost courage or plummet to physical and psychological annihilation." Kathleen Winter, author of *Lost in September* and *Boundless*

"Jan Redford is a badass. She is also a born storyteller, and this one—the mountains she has climbed, the men she has loved—and survived—is gritty, funny, tragic, and ultimately victorious. Women's voices are a conspicuous rarity in the mountaineering world, and tobacco-chewing mother's voices are even rarer; Redford's is a bracing and refreshing corrective—intimate, affectionate, loud and clear."

John Vaillant, author of *The Tiger* and *The Golden Spruce*

"*End of the Rope* is a riveting journey of surviving loss, finding love, and summoning the courage to keep climbing. Jan Redford takes us inside the male-dominated world of climbing, where missteps can mean death, and mental grit is as important as physical strength. A beautifully written and breathtakingly honest book."

Carol Shaben, author of *Into the Abyss* and *The Marriott Cell*

"Jan Redford's debut is beautifully crafted, fierce and uncompromising. Her cathartic book pivots around the moment she learned that her boyfriend Dan Guthrie had perished in an avalanche. With a 'take no prisoners' style she recounts the freewheeling years leading up to her relationship with Dan, how his loss sent her life into a tailspin and how she finally found balance. Jan writes with blistering honesty; she is fearless in relating the conflicts of family life and mountaineering, a disastrously co-dependent marriage, and her struggles with her father, her ex-husband and herself. *End of the Rope* is a compelling and often unsettling read."

Maria Coffey, author of *Where the Mountain Casts Its Shadow*

"Jan Redford is my new favourite feminist anti-heroine: a potty-mouthed, tobacco-chewing, take-no-shit mountain climber who is at once strong-minded and insecure, fierce and vulnerable, loveable and flawed. Redford's voice pulsates with immediacy and vitality, and she writes her story with a bull's eye precision and unflinching honesty. Inspiring, funny, heartbreaking, and bold, *End of the Rope* is a book about survival and courage, about letting go of old dreams and finding new ones. I couldn't put it down."

Ayelet Tsabari, author of *The Best Place on Earth*

"Move over, boys—I have a new favourite adventure writer! *End of the Rope* tells the mountain story I've been longing to read. Surrounded by death, Jan Redford must learn to live. In a world dominated by powerful men, she fights for the courage and confidence to lead rather than follow. I love Redford's grit, her fallibility, her physicality, her honesty. I want to put this memoir into every mountain woman's hands, every mother's hands, and the hands of every woman struggling to take charge of her own future. A hearty welcome to a new voice that's sometimes tough, sometimes vulnerable, but always brave."

Angie Abdou, author of *The Bone Cage* and *In Case I Go*

"Jan Redford shows us that there are many types of bravery required, not just in the wilderness, but in surviving day to day life. *End of the Rope* is at times funny, but always compassionate and courageous."

Tanis Rideout, author of *Above All Things*

"Rowdy, raw, even raucous at times, *End of the Rope* is a heartbreakingly vulnerable memoir. Through her story, Jan Redford exposes contradictions within the climbing community that test the hearts and souls of the tribe she calls her own." Bernadette McDonald, author of *Art of Freedom: The Life and Climbs of Voytek Kurtyka*

"*End of the Rope* is a rare thing, an at once thrilling and thoughtful book. Readers will make their way up perilous slopes and across daunting ridgelines. They will dangle from cliffs in their harnesses and carabineers. But at the end of this book about daring, about doing, about defining oneself in the face of the steepest challenges, readers will also summit with author Jan Redford, exhilarated and moved."

Timothy Taylor, author of *The Rule of Stephens* and *Stanley Park*

END OF THE ROPE

Mountains, Marriage, and Motherhood

JAN REDFORD

RANDOM HOUSE CANADA

PUBLISHED BY RANDOM HOUSE CANADA

www.penguinrandomhouse.ca

Random House Canada and colophon are registered trademarks.

Library and Archives Canada Cataloguing in Publication

Redford, Jan, author
End of the rope : mountains, marriage and motherhood / Jan Redford.

Issued in print and electronic formats.
ISBN 978-0-345-81231-5
eBook ISBN 978-0-345-81233-9

1. Redford, Jan. 2. Redford, Jan—Marriage. 3. Redford, Jan—Divorce.
4. Women authors, Canadian (English)—21st century—Biography. 5. Women
Mountaineers—Canada—Biography. 6. Self-actualization (Psychology).

I. Title.

CT310.R42A3 2018   305.4092   C2017-905413-9

All photos, except those credited, courtesy of Jan Redford

Text design by Five Seventeen
Cover design by Five Seventeen

Cover images: courtesy of Jan Redford;
(background mountains) © Hero Images / Getty Images

Printed and bound in the United States of America

2 4 6 8 9 7 5 3 1

Penguin
Random House
RANDOM HOUSE CANADA

Time gives us a whirl. We keep waking from a dream we can't recall, looking around in surprise, and lapsing back, for years on end. All I want to do is stay awake, keep my head up, prop my eyes open, with toothpicks, with trees.

ANNIE DILLARD, *PILGRIM AT TINKER CREEK*

You've got to jump off the cliff and build your wings on the way down.

RAY BRADBURY

For Dan Guthrie, Ian Bult and Niccy Code,
who will forever be part of my story.

And for Jenna and Sam.
My wildest, most meaningful adventure was having you.

And for Dan,
who has always believed in me.

CONTENTS

AUTHOR'S NOTE

The events in this memoir happened a long time ago and the people you'll meet in these pages have all matured. We now all behave much more appropriately. Just in case that caveat is not enough, I've changed several names to protect people's privacy. I've also recreated conversations and events to the best of my ability based on my elephantine memory, multiple boxes of letters, and passages from the angst-ridden journals I've kept since I was eleven.

PROLOGUE: FIRST CLIMB

"Load me up."

I stretched out my arms and my father passed me a liquor-store box marked Bacardi from the back of the station wagon. We were hauling our third load of gear a whole mile on foot to our cabin. We'd already dropped off sleeping bags, boxes of food, propane stoves, paint, tools and building materials. My little sister, Susan, and my mother had decided they'd had enough physical exertion for one day. They'd stayed at the cabin to clean.

My parents, in cahoots with my two uncles, had recently bought a dilapidated little shack on Crown land in the Laurentians. Finally, they'd done something right. A cabin in the woods was my dream come true. Three years earlier, in 1972, we'd moved from the Yukon to Ontario, and I still yearned for the snowy mountains, pink fire-weed and wild rivers of the north. I was fourteen and counting down the years until I could escape, throw a pack on my back and hitch across Canada, all the way back to the Yukon to live off the land.

"Drop this box and I'll have to thump you," my father said, then made a rumbly, Donald Duck–like noise in the back of his throat to show he was just joking. This noise signalled a good mood, something of a rarity with him since we'd left the north.

As the weight settled into my arms I admired the bulge of my biceps. I was the only girl in gym class who could do the flexed-arm hang. My physical strength was one of the few things about me that impressed my father, though he *had* gone ballistic when I tried to show him I could do ten pull-ups on the shower curtain rod. On the drive here, he'd promised I could help repair the siding and replace a few missing cedar shakes on the roof, saying I was handier with my hands than my mother's nincompoop brothers.

Dad threw a full pack on his back, scooped up a large plastic box, and we headed up the trail with me in the lead.

It was quiet in the woods. Just the sound of our feet shuffling through the leaves and pine needles, and the muffled *clink, clink* of the bottles in the box. The maple, beech and birch trees were just turning colour, crimson and gold against the deep green of the conifers. This was a real forest, so unlike the flat fields of hay and corn surrounding the bland, unincorporated town of Munster Hamlet, Ontario, where we now lived. The only wilderness I could find there was a scruffy clump of deciduous trees by the sewage lagoon where I'd sit on my favourite boulder surrounded by bulrushes, composing restless poems and writing in my diary while trying to ignore the smell.

My uncles Steve and Dunk wound through the trees ahead carrying the cooler between them. I didn't want to catch up to them; it would break the spell of this special camaraderie I was feeling with my father. Moments like these were scarce. At home we walked on eggshells. Here in the Laurentians, I wanted to enjoy walking on a soft path of decaying maple leaves as long as I could. I wanted to enjoy my "nice" father.

I had two very distinct dads. The one here in the woods with me was my "breakfast" dad, who I could charm and joke around with. My "after-work dad" locked himself in his den with a bottle of Scotch after he got home every night. We had to stay the hell out of that one's way. Suppertime was so explosive that my big brother, Eric, no longer ate with us. My mother took his food down to his bedroom. On the rare occasion he and Dad found themselves in the same room, they ended up screaming obscenities, even shoving each other around. Eric had refused to come this weekend, saying he'd rather have his toenails pulled out with pliers.

When we arrived at the cabin, I placed my load on the picnic table where my uncles were settling in beside the cooler. My father unshouldered his pack and leaned it against the table. He looked outdoorsy in his plaid shirt and the boots he'd dusted off from his days of hiking the Chilkoot Trail—just like he did in his Arctic photos, looking out from the hood of a fur-lined parka with miles and miles of white spread out behind him. In the sixties, my father had worked as an "Indian agent," living in Fort Chimo, Frobisher Bay and Inuvik, travelling to all the tiny Inuit outposts by dogsled and Ski-Doo. When I compared the old photos of him in the north to those of my mother sitting indoors on a government-issue sofa with a baby in one hand and a cigarette in the other, it was obvious who was having more fun. I wanted my father's life, not the one my mother led, following her husband from community to community, popping out babies along the way, cleaning floors so cold they froze the mop. I intended to *be* the adventurer, not *marry* one.

Dad opened the cooler and pulled out three beers. Handed two of them to my uncles, lit up a cigarette.

"Go see if your mother needs a hand," he said to me.

"I don't want to help Mom." Through the hazy glass of the cabin window I saw my twelve-year-old sister's blond head bobbing around. My throat tightened. "You said I could help *you*."

"Go see what your mother and sister are doing. This is men's work. You'll just get in the way."

Anger surged through me like adrenalin. "I don't want to see what they're doing."

"Well, just do something, for chrissake." He shooed me like I was a pesky Yukon mosquito. And just like that—*poof!*—his promise was forgotten. Just like always. He never kept his word. Especially with a beer in his hand.

Betrayal closed my throat. Stole my voice. I spun away and stomped over to the cabin, holding back my tears. When I stepped out of the sunshine into the dim light, the musty scent of decaying forest was replaced by the harsh smell of clean. With a Windex bottle in one rubber-gloved hand and paper towel in the other, my mother was scrubbing the layers of grime from the windows, while Susan swept leaves and dirt into a pile by the wood stove.

"I'm going for a walk." I grabbed my daypack full of my father's books on plant identification and wilderness survival, my mother's Robert Service poems, and my diary.

"Can I come?" Susan dropped the broom.

"No, I'm going by myself."

"I want to go for a walk too!" She turned toward our mother.

"Oh, Jan, why can't you take your sister?" With pursed lips, Mom gave me her don't-be-so-dramatic look.

I flipped my pack on my back and pushed open the door. "I need to be alone," I said.

"Don't go too far!" Mom called after me.

I charged into the thick forest, away from the cabin, away from my family, trying to get as much distance between me and *them* as possible. As I zigzagged through the trees, branches etched thin lines of red across my bare legs and arms, but the physical sting was nothing compared to that sting of betrayal that was becoming too familiar. On some days my father would goof around with me, teach me swear words in French, confide in me, telling me all about his hard childhood. On others, he'd turn into a wild-eyed lunatic and chase my sister and me through the house with his father's old cane. Or push my brother into the wall.

Just a few weeks back, in the summer, when my mother was on night shift at the Ottawa hospital where she was a psychiatric nurse, my father had started to cry in front of me, telling me I was the only one he could talk to, the only one who loved him. I told him we all loved him, but I knew Eric had quit school to work at a gas station so he could leave home to get away from him, my sister was too scared to even go *near* him, and sometimes I hated him so much it made my stomach ache. But it was a love-filled hate, or maybe a hate-filled love. I felt sorry for him because he'd grown up in poverty with six siblings and a father who wore a scowl as permanent as the limp he'd acquired from a piece of shrapnel in the war. I suspected Dad's mother had died young just to get away from her husband. My whole life, I'd wanted to protect my father. Love him better. Make him happy.

I knew he *had* been happy. I'd seen photos of him in his twenties, laughing and holding a beer and cigarette, surrounded by friends, a girl on each arm. Before *we* were born.

I wove in and out amongst the trees, swiping branches away from my face, carving my own trail through the woods. But stomping over a forest floor cushioned by thick, spongy moss and rotting maple leaves was like stomping on a camping foamy. Not much drama. I slowed, then paused and looked back, wondering how far I'd gone. I could no longer hear voices, could no longer smell the smoke from the fire my father had started in the ring of rocks. Just the musty scent of decay under my feet. It would serve them right if I disappeared and they never saw me again.

I carried on until, finally, I had to stop—at the base of a cliff about four times as high as my house. I had a strong urge to climb all the way to the top, blow off some of this *fuck you!* anger. I knew I could do it. I'd been told just that summer that I'd make a good *escaladeur*. A rock climber.

It was Jocelyn who had told me that. He was a climbing instructor at the outdoor centre where I'd spent a weekend during a month-long high-school bilingual exchange near Quebec City. A real climber. I kept a photo I took of him in my diary and looked at it every night before I went to bed. There was a wildness to him, with his dark, scruffy beard and ponytail and the red bandana tied around his fore-head. Every part of his body bulged with muscle, his biceps and forearms, his tanned, hairy quads.

He was supposed to take us climbing but it had poured rain so we'd gone caving instead. As we hiked up a hill above the lodge, I'd pretended I was heading up Everest with my climbing boyfriend and three Sherpas. When we came to the cave entrance, a hole in the rock the size of a St. Bernard doggie door, the other kids wouldn't go near it, but I said, "I'll do it!" and Jocelyn said, "Ah, Janeese," making my name sound so exotic. "You are tough, *n'est-ce pas?*"

I stuck my head in the hole and squeezed through, praying my butt wouldn't plug it, then wormed along on my belly through a long dark tunnel toward a dot of light with Jocelyn right behind me. We had to squeeze through an even tinier hole on the other side and when I got stuck and panicked, he said, "If the head, she goes, the body, he follows." And he was right. I finally popped out the hole, and that's when he told me I'd be a good climber.

Then he said, "You come to my room. I show you my mountain climbing equipment." Warm tingles rose through me, like bubbles, starting from my toes. I wondered if maybe he could fall in love with me. But he was old, at least thirty, and had a girlfriend. Why would he want a five-foot-nothing, 110-pound, flat-chested fourteen-year-old anglophone tomboy from Munster Hamlet? After a whole year of high school, even the boys my own age weren't exactly lining up at my locker.

Back at the lodge, Jocelyn led me through a side door and down some dark stairs into the basement, to a room with a narrow cot that took up half the space. The log walls were studded with long nails, and on each nail hung climbing gear: brightly coloured ropes, harnesses, odd-shaped pieces of metal, bunches of shoes with black rubber soles. A photo was pinned into the wood above his bed— Jocelyn clinging to a steep wall of rock, a bright red rope dangling below him. If he could cling to that blank wall, I figured he could do anything.

And now, standing at the base of the cliff among the boulders, I thought of Jocelyn and almost doubled over with longing. This was bigger than the longing I'd had for some of my brother's friends. I didn't just want to marry him. I wanted his life. I wanted his freedom. I wanted to wear grubby clothes and a bandana and hiking boots and not have anyone telling me what to do. I wanted to cling to a rock face like that, in total control. I wanted to *be* him.

I studied the cliff. It wasn't blank like the one in Jocelyn's photo, but broken up. Crumbly. There were lots of places to put my hands and feet. And it wasn't as steep. Narrow ledges, some with stubby, twisted trees, interrupted stretches of smooth rock all the way up.

I placed my hands flat on the rough, grey rock, dotted with black lichen. I could climb *this*. Of course I could. I was a gymnast. And a sprinter. And once, in gym class, I'd rappelled down the brick wall of our school.

I reached up and grabbed two outcrops, stepped up on an edge big enough for half of my sneaker. Step, hold, search for another handhold, like ascending a staircase to the sky. The movement came naturally.

I reached a stubby little tree growing out of a crack in the middle of the cliff. Standing on a ledge about the width of my feet, I held on to a spindly branch and looked down. It was a long way to the ground, maybe thirty feet, but instead of feeling fear, I tingled with excitement. My toes and fingers and skull felt pinpricked by millions of tiny needles, the adrenalin zinging through me. I'd always loved heights. At school in Whitehorse I'd gotten in trouble for going down the boys' slide, instead of the tiny girls' slide beside it. I could climb higher trees than any of the boys, and jump off the tallest cliffs into the quarry not far from Munster. I loved standing on the edge, wide awake, looking down at the water, knowing I was going to jump.

The top was still a long way up, and the rock was smooth and steep right above me, so I shuffled sideways, my chest touching the rock, traversing along the ledge to find an easier way. Then I continued straight up. Higher and higher. My mind was uncluttered. My father's voice gone. I felt graceful and light, the way I felt in gymnastics in that split second during a layout on the vault when my body was fully extended, flat in the air. A moment of flying.

The farther I climbed, the more crumbly the rock became, and a few holds broke off from the cliff face in my hands. I started testing each handhold before I trusted it with my weight. I eventually hoisted myself onto a ledge, two feet deep, that spanned half the width of the cliff. The top was just above me. Reaching high, I groped around for something to hold on to, but all I found was moss, dirt and loose rock. I took a deep breath and looked around. To my left was a pile of rubble, so I shuffled to the right till the ledge narrowed to the depth of my feet. I reached again and tried to pull myself up, but a softball-sized chunk of rock broke away and released a cascade of greenery and dirt, narrowly missing my feet and bouncing off the cliff to the boulders below. I stared at the ground, so far away, and imagined my body splatting like a water balloon.

This wasn't fun anymore. Hugging the rock, I started to hyperventilate. I couldn't go up, I couldn't go down. I wanted Jocelyn to swoop in and save me. I wanted to be back at the cabin, roasting wieners and marshmallows. I closed my eyes and attempted to pray to a god I didn't even believe in. "Please, please, God, just a few more feet." But the sky failed to open and God did not send forth Jocelyn or a team of angels with ropes and climbing gear.

I started to yell. "Dad! Dad! Help!" My anger at him dissolved. He'd know what to do. He'd survived the Korean War. He'd survived a night out in a storm on Ungava Bay with a pregnant Inuit woman, an interpreter and a bunch of chickens. Maybe he'd have a rope in his pack. He could drag me over the lip of this cliff and save me.

Eventually I stopped yelling. My father would be into the Scotch by now. It was just me. Alone. On a steep rock face that didn't give a shit if I could do the flexed-arm hang.

It was getting cold. And late. Goosebumps sprang up on my legs and arms. I had to do *something*. There was a small tree growing out of the grass at the top of the cliff, several more feet to my right. I took a deep breath, forced myself to edge along the ledge until I was directly below it, then reached up and grabbed the trunk. It was about the size of my wrist. I pulled, and rocks and dirt trickled down on me. I pulled harder, watching the roots to make sure they'd stay in the ground. The little tree seemed pretty tenacious, so I started to walk my feet up the wall, kicking moss and loose rock out of my way, my eyes still fixed on the roots. If they popped out, I was screwed. Just as I reached the edge, Uncle Dunk and my sister came out of the trees above me. "What are you doing?" Susan sounded close to hysterics.

I dragged myself over the top, flopping on my chest like a seal with my feet kicking. As I stood up, blood beat against my temples and I could barely breathe. But I pushed out a laugh, raised my fist and flexed like a muscle man.

Dunk looked over the edge, his Leica camera swinging out from his chest. "Good God!" he said.

Susan peeked over, but wouldn't go too close. "Why didn't you just take the trail like we did?"

I rolled my eyes and brushed the dirt off my cut-off jean shorts and T-shirt. I was as proud as if I were standing on the summit of Everest.

Back at the cabin, Dunk told everyone about my rock wall. "Close to a hundred feet," he said.

We all hiked back to the top of the cliff, found my little tree and looked over the edge. Uncle Steve whistled, shook his round bald head. My mother's face crinkled up with worry. "*Aie, Jésus!*" she said, as though swearing in French wasn't really swearing. I knew she wouldn't let me out of her sight for a while.

My father stared at the boulders at the bottom, his black hair flopped over his glasses, then looked back at me.

"Jesus Christ! Did you really climb that?"

That night, still basking in the warmth of my father's approval, I wrote in my diary: *I'm going to be a mountain climber when I grow up.*

1

ON THE ROCKS

There he was, the Beast, my eighty-pound backpack, squatting on the snow-covered parking lot in the Wind River Range of Wyoming. My pack was definitely *he*, not *she*. No *she* would put another *she* through this kind of torture. My skis were on and it was time to go. I just had to get the Beast on my back.

My pack was so heavy that when I pulled it out of the back of the bus after we'd arrived, it fell to the ground like an anchor, dragging me with it, and I lay there on top of it, my hands still gripping the metal frame, with thirteen guys laughing at me. The other three girls in our group weren't laughing. They let the guys unload their packs.

In the Lumberyard, the equipment-issue building back in Lander, Wyoming, I'd practised getting it on and off, but that was before strapping skinny 180 centimetre boards to my feet. I'd only cross-country skied with my outdoor education class in high school, and a couple times near Mont-Tremblant with my Uncle Steve. I wasn't sure how far I could get on skis even *without* the pack.

My mother's voice popped into my head. *You can do anything you set your mind to, Jan. You have so much potential.* But she hadn't seen the Beast. Maybe my training regime of the past three months could have been more rigorous. I should have spent more time running laps around the track at the Ottawa Coliseum and less time reading self-help books and saying affirmations. I should have done more crunches. And I definitely should not have been taking drags on my sister's cigarettes.

Panic washed down my back like a melting snowball. What if I couldn't do this? What if I was too small, too weak, too out of shape, too female? I couldn't go running back to my parents with my tail between my legs, not after they'd paid three thousand non-refundable American dollars for tuition. My father had made it clear that this was it. They would pay for an outdoor school or college, but not both.

And what would I tell my friends? For years I'd been bragging that I was going to hitch-hike across the country, live off the land, climb mountains, be a ski patroller, a photographer, a writer. I was going to have a big life. Everyone thought I was being dramatic, but right after high school, I *had* escaped Munster. I'd joined Katimavik, the nine-month volunteer program for Canada's youth, expecting to be transformed into the muscular, tanned, chainsaw-wielding envi-ronmentalist in a red plaid jacket and hiking boots on the brochure. Instead, after spending all those hours milking cows, picking rocks and weeding gardens in BC, and clearing land with the Dene in 30-below temperatures in NWT, I'd turned into a shaggy-legged, directionless hippie, ten pounds overweight from a vegetarian diet of bread, pasta and beer.

But now here I was. In Wyoming. On my way to becoming a

mountain climber. This was what I'd imagined for six years, ever since climbing that crumbling cliff in the Laurentians. I could not fail.

We were on day one of a three-and-a-half-month semester course with the National Outdoor Leadership School—NOLS. Apparently, this was the best training for outdoor leaders. Better than anywhere in Canada. Three weeks each of ski touring, desert hiking, mountaineering, then two weeks of caving and two of rock climbing. At the end of it all, if I performed well, I would be recommended for the NOLS instructor course.

The orange bus, our only link to civilization, chugged back out to the road belching a cloud of diesel, and the second-last group glided off into the woods with Richie, one of the instructors, in the lead. I wanted to be in his group. He was twenty-two, only two years older than me, and already an outdoor instructor. And he was cute. Blue eyes, blond hair, and cheeks rounded by a wad of Red Man chewing tobacco. He'd hefted his eighty-pound pack as though he were perching a baby on his hip.

That left only six of us in the parking lot: Tony, the instructor, us four girls, and Gunter. Young, gangly Gunter from Europe, with the coordination of an overcooked noodle. He was the only one who wasn't here by choice—his parents had sent him. The rest of us had our own agendas, most of us wanting to push ourselves to our limit in the wilderness. Some were planning to go on to take the instructor training with NOLS, some wanted to escape soul-sucking jobs in New York or Albuquerque for a few months, and for others this course was a rite of passage after graduation from high school or university. My own goal was modest: to emerge from the fires of NOLS transformed, like the phoenix, into a completely different person. One who was in control of her life.

So far, my year and a half out in the big bad world had been anything but controlled. My survival was nothing short of miraculous. During the first Katimavik rotation, near Lund, BC, I'd almost been

lured up Toba Inlet—an area so remote it was accessible only by boat—
by a middle-aged sex-offender hippie; I'd signed up for—and was
saved by friends from—three weeks of fasting and Dianetics indoc-
trination in some Scientology leader's basement in East Vancouver;
and I'd almost moved into a trailer with a mill worker from Powell
River, whom I'd met and necked with at a party. That was just in the
first three months away from home, and just the highlights.

In the second three-month rotation, up in Fort Simpson, NWT, I
fell in love with my guitar-playing, Quebec-separatist group leader,
Guy, and was subsequently dumped by him on my nineteenth birthday at the end of the program. Maybe because I hadn't filled out the
manuscript-sized compatibility questionnaire he'd sent me during
my third rotation in New Brunswick.

After the nine months, I'd set off back to Lund, where I'd felt the
most free, to find a hippie commune. Hitch-hiking alone across BC,
I took a ride from two guys in a windowless van who were on their
way to a dog show, with no dogs. Not wanting to appear rude, I
accepted an invitation up to their hotel room in Kamloops, only to
narrowly escape being raped. After finally making it to Lund alive,
I worked as a cook for four loggers and dodged their advances by
hooking up with the youngest and only unmarried one, Calvin, a
near-albino in a black Stetson hat and grey Stanfields. After a month
of heavy drinking and country music, I escaped by taking a job as a
cook's helper and chambermaid at a fly-in fishing camp on Great
Slave Lake in NWT. I jogged the one bear-infested road to the lake
daily and wrote, *Je suis seule dans ma peau*—I'm alone in my skin—in
the sand, overcome with loneliness, but in reality, I didn't have any
peau. I was skinless. Open and raw and exposed to the world. Maybe
that's why, when I crawled back to my parents' new house in Ottawa
and promptly assumed the fetal position around my self-help books
and journal, they'd been willing to fork out the money for NOLS.
Maybe they knew I had to learn to protect myself.

Either that, or my father was trying to get rid of me. He *had* said, "You can't hang out in my basement reading *I'm OK—You're OK* for the rest of your life."

Nancy from New Jersey had somehow managed to get her pack on her back and was standing rigidly on her skis. Sue, also from New Jersey, was halfway there, eighty pounds balanced on her knee. Gunter was bent over at the waist, recovering from his last attempt, and Tony was trying to comfort our Texan, Laurie, who was crouched beside her pack, almost in tears.

One consolation was that the more we ate, the lighter our packs would become. We'd packed food rations for ten days, enough to get us to our resupply halfway through the three weeks. My tent mates, Dave from Calgary, the only other Canadian, and Vince from California, and I had divvied up the group equipment—the first-aid kit, stove, fuel, cookware and tent—so our packs all weighed the same, even though Dave had at least forty pounds more body weight than me. Vince had about eighty.

Tony coaxed Laurie back to her feet, while Sue, a competitive soccer player for Princeton University who was about my size, somehow got her pack on her back while staying upright on her skis. The duffle bag of gear she'd strapped to the pack's metal frame towered more than a foot higher than her head, and the ten-pound NOLS sleeping bag strapped onto the bottom extended almost to her knees.

With my eyes fixed on my pack, I whispered my worn-out affirmation: *I am strong and fit and emotionally prepared for this.* Widening my stance, I leaned down to grab the straps of the pack. Air whooshed out of my lungs as I heaved it onto my shaky bent knee, where it wobbled dangerously for a few seconds. This wasn't the first time I'd reached this stage, but each time my pack had gone crashing to the ground. I repositioned my hands, slipped an arm through the far strap, then twisted my body sideways to set up for the next shoulder.

My back arched as the weight pulled me backwards, but I ground my teeth and threw my body forward, regaining control.

I can do this. I am in control. I am my own best friend.

A little wiggle and dance as I edged my arm into the second strap. A few feet in front of me, Gunter's skis skidded out and he crashed to the ground, backwards. Tony rushed to help him.

Leaning forward, I inched the pack onto my back until both my arms were in the straps, then straightened up. I locked my knees as the load settled on my back like an apartment-sized, beer-filled fridge. I was still vertical. Nancy and Sue, legs splayed out like newborn moose under the weight of their packs, glanced over in my direction. We all smiled, but not too much.

My ski poles lay on the snow, parallel to my skis. I stepped outward to stabilize myself and get a bit closer to the ground, took a deep breath, and bent forward at the waist. I reached for the poles. My quadriceps muscles strained to hold me in position, my back tightened like a fully loaded slingshot. My fingertips were inches away, almost there. I bent a bit more till my fingers wrapped around the cold metal. Before I could start my ascent, my pack—not yet cinched at the hip—started to shift. Dropping the poles, I grabbed at the hip band, but the Beast was on a roll, like a fully loaded toboggan on a steep, icy slope. He slid up my back, dragging me with him, till the metal frame jammed to a halt on the packed snow of the parking lot and I was doubled in half, my nose almost touching my knees. I spun my arms like windmills, trying to right myself, but my pack had me pinned.

"Help! Tony!"

Within seconds Tony was beside me, hauling me to my feet. I wobbled back and forth, trying to regain my balance, then stared back down at my ski poles. They looked a mountain range away. Tony picked them up and handed them to me. I took them gratefully.

The Beast was on my back, and I was still upright.

We shuffled through the woods. Nancy was in front, then me and Sue, and Tony was bringing up the rear behind Laurie, following the tracks of the thirteen other guys and three instructors who were by now miles ahead of us. Gravity had increased, and my poles were the only things keeping me upright. I tried to keep my eyes fixed on the track in front of me so I wouldn't tip over, but I couldn't resist sneaking quick looks at the white and blue mountains peeking through the trees, way off in the distance. We were heading into the Ramshorn Basin. Today, apparently, we were only covering a few miles of mostly flat terrain, but soon we'd be in the mountains. It was such a relief not to think about what to do with the rest of my life, where to live, how to make money, who to be. All I had to focus on was getting from point A to point B without killing myself.

Sunlight glinted off the snow piled waist-high on either side of our track. It was bright, even with my glacier sunglasses, which had leather sides like blinders on a horse. I slid my skis forward, one then the other, trying to ignore the pain building wherever the pack straps made contact with my body. I stopped to cinch the hip strap to take weight off my shoulders, then a few feet later stopped again to cinch up the shoulder straps to take weight off my hips, but there was nothing I could do to relieve the ache of my vertebrae compressing into my pelvis, or the chafing under the shoulder straps that I was sure was about to draw blood.

"No!" Laurie's voice pierced the quiet, followed by a soft thump. I twisted around to see her lying sprawled on her back on top of her pack, her skis sticking straight up in the air. When I turned back, Sue was falling over sideways in slow motion in front of me. She landed with another soft thump. Nancy and I looked from Sue to each other and burst out laughing. Giggles rose out of Sue's hole in the snow, and Gunter behind us joined in. Only Laurie remained silent. When I bent forward into my laughter, which was now verging on hysteria, my poles plunged deep into the snow and my body followed, till I lay collapsed on my side on the opposite side of the track to Sue, my arms hugging my aching stomach muscles.

"Oh my God. We are so fucked!"

Our laughter petered out as quickly as it had begun. Sue, Laurie and I started wallowing around in the snow, trying to free ourselves from our packs, as Gunter and Nancy watched, bodies rigid, trying not to tip over too. I undid my hip buckle, loosened the shoulder straps, wiggled out to a squatting position, reached for my bindings, released my feet, and stepped off my skis. Immediately I sank over my knees in the snow. I dragged my pack out of its crater and stood it upright, then stepped up out of my hole onto my skis and clamped down the bindings. Planting my poles beside me for support, I reached for my pack. I took three more falls trying to heave it onto my back. Tony had to help. By the time Sue, Laurie and I were ready to go again, half an hour had passed. As we started our slow shuffle, I looked back to see how far we'd come. The parking lot was still within sight.

It was dusk by the time we straggled into camp—seven tents scattered throughout the trees. Our little group was completely silent; the nickname Tony had given us, the Giggly Sisters and Gunter, no longer applied. The past few hours had been full of curses and tears. We'd lost count of how many times we fell, but a safe estimate would have been thirty falls each. Thirty times we had to take off our packs and skis, find a raised area like a stump to set the pack on, or rely on each other's help, then put our skis and pack back on. My last crash occurred as I tried to step over a fallen tree about the diameter of my ankle. I lifted my foot, and there I was again, on my back in a crater, tears of frustration mingling with sweat and melted snow.

It's all in your head, my mother had said about my "imagined" fears of this course. But she was wrong. My fears were all very real. A month shy of my twentieth birthday, I was one of the youngest in the group. At five foot one and a half, I was the smallest, though I was carrying the same weight as the two-hundred-pound guys. I was a walking illustration of the term "the weaker sex," at least from a biological perspective.

"Hey, Jan! Over here!" Dave waved a billy pot over his head, a big metal ketchup can with wire for a handle. He and Vince stood in a dugout snow kitchen in front of our two-man tent. It looked so far away. The aroma of food—sausages, melted cheese and hot chocolate—wafted toward me and my knees almost gave out.

My head down like a starving packhorse, I urged myself forward. Richie looked up from his stove with a big grin as I passed, his face swollen with tobacco. He spat a long brown stream into the snow.

"Way to go, Jan!

Every muscle in my body throbbed, but I smiled at him and straightened up under my load, making it the last few feet to my tent without falling.

Almost two months later, I sat cross-legged in the dirt with my group at the base of a cliff in Sinks Canyon, Wyoming. Mike, our climbing instructor, stood in front of us holding a red climbing rope that was attached to Lonnie, another instructor, who was waiting to lead us up a fifty-foot vertical crack in the rock.

"On belay!" Mike said.

"Climbing!" she responded.

We'd been camped at Bumfuck Butte here in the canyon for almost a week, and half of that time it had rained. It had even snowed one day. In May. So we'd spent hours practising knots and "pretend" belaying each other on horizontal ground till I was ready to pull out clumps of my tangled, overgrown hair. But we'd managed to do a few climbs, bombing between the sandstone and granite cliffs in the NOLS truck we called the Ambulance, and Mike had told me I was a natural. "Like a little piggie in shit." Attributable, possibly, to my years of dabbling in gymnastics.

"Climb on." Mike gave Lonnie the go-ahead.

Lonnie was demonstrating lead climbing. She would head up first, trailing the rope to set up a "top rope" above us. She was on the "sharp end" of the rope, the risky end. If we fell on the "blunt end" the rope would catch us right away. The follower can relax, climb and enjoy the scenery. The leader has to battle her demons because a fall on the sharp end is almost always scary, and sometimes deadly. The leader was what I wanted to be—a real climber, not some climbing groupie.

Lonnie slipped her hands into the crack, then the tip of her rubber-soled climbing shoe, and stepped up. Under her skimpy tank top, the muscles in her back popped. Broad shoulders tapered to a skinny waist. I wanted to look like that—lean and mean.

I looked down at my tanned legs and flexed my quads. I'd rediscovered former muscles from gymnastics and track. It hadn't come easily. I'd just barely survived the three weeks of skiing with eighty pounds, and another three weeks of slogging up and down steep canyons in the deserts of Utah. With only seventy pounds on that trip, and no skis, I'd finally mastered the Beast. For the next two weeks we would be camped here in Sinks Canyon, and then we'd head off to go car camping in South Dakota to spelunk in the Jewel Caves. No more eighty-pound packs until our last section, mountaineering in the Winds.

Lonnie had both feet crammed in the crack now, and long, sinewy calf muscles almost burst through her skin. She moved up, then stopped, rummaged through the jumble of various-sized pieces of protection slung around her neck, decided on a tiny triangular wedge, slipped it into the crack, and clipped the rope so it ran through the carabiner. This protection, or "pro" for short, would catch a fall.

"So at this point, folks, imagine that Lonnie falls." Mike's voice boomed over our heads like a sports announcer. "That little stopper she placed in the crack can withstand a huge force if it's placed correctly. And as long as she evenly spaces her protection she'll never fall far."

"Fuck me! You'd never catch me falling on that tiny thing!" Nancy was my tent partner on this trip. We'd been keeping each other sane by outshining the guys in the crude department.

"How far's 'not far'?" Dave pushed his scraggly blond hair off his face. We were all getting scruffy and smelly again, in spite of our last much-needed showers in Lander after the Canyonlands trip. Three weeks without a shower was a very long time when the school's policy of *no impact on the environment* prohibited the use of toilet paper. At least here and in Canyonlands we could jump in the occasional river or spring if we were willing to freeze our butts and nipples off. On the ski section, with snowballs passing for toilet paper and each of us with only one pair of polypropylene underwear for the whole trip, there'd been no escaping the smell, wedged three to a two-man tent.

"She's about three feet away from her last piece of protection, which means she can fall three feet to the pro, then three feet past it. Allow for rope stretch and this could be an eight-foot fall. Maybe nine. Unless her protection pops out. Then she could hit the deck."

Dave made a face of mock horror at me. We'd just decided we were going to hitch-hike back to Canada together. We would hit the road in five weeks, after the last section, but I couldn't stand the thought of leaving Lander. I wished I were American so I could live here forever, get a job, learn to be an instructor. I had no idea what I was going to do or where I would go once I crossed over the border into Alberta. I had no work lined up and was almost out of money. Dave possibly had a job with Outward Bound in BC, but I had work to do on my navigational skills in the mountains before I dared apply to a program like that.

Lonnie continued up the rock like she was performing an upward dance, dipping hands and feet into the crack, twisting and locking them in place, stopping only to place protection. A few of the guys, including Vince and Dave, were going to get a chance to try a lead this week, but when I asked Mike if I could too, he hemmed and hawed, then finally said, "It takes a lot of judgment and self-control to safely lead. Maybe I'll let you do a mock lead." Which means placing protection in the crack as you climb, but with the security of a top-rope above you in case you fall. In other words, not really leading.

Judgment and self-control. I'd be an eighty-year-old with a walker before I was ready to lead. Even on the winter course I hadn't exhibited an overabundance of leadership qualities. When it was my turn to be group leader of the day, I was so terrified of having to be the responsible one that I couldn't sleep the night before. As a result, I'd slept in and when I finally crawled out of my tent, none of the guys would listen to me. They sat in their snow pits drinking tea and laughing while I tried to get them moving. The instructors glared at me when we finally skied past them three hours late.

Lonnie finally pulled herself onto a ledge fifty feet above us in one fluid motion, like she was mounting a vault horse. She had complete mastery over her body and, it seemed, her life. She had two dogs, Lucy and Willie, and her own pickup truck, and a NOLS instructor boyfriend. Everything I wanted.

"Off belay!" Lonnie yelled down.

"Belay off!" Mike relaxed his grip on the rope, then a few minutes later, lowered Lonnie till she was back on the ground. She left the rope so it was running through the anchor above, like a big pulley, so the rest of us would have a top-rope.

"Who wants to go next?" Mike looked into the crowd of students. My gut seized and my hand didn't shoot into the air. This was the hardest climb yet. What if I couldn't do it? What if I made a total fool of myself? With everyone watching?

Mike's eyes met mine, and he smiled. Or was it a leer? Had Richie told him about what we'd done? Like a bunch of guys in a locker room, bragging about their conquests? My ears and temples tingled with heat. It was strictly forbidden for instructors to "fraternize" with the students, but Richie had said it was okay because we were finished with the winter course, which was the only one he was instructing. I'd been flattered that he wanted me.

"Vince, why don't you go?" Mike said. "You can take a look at how Lonnie placed the protection before you take it out. Good prep for leading."

Vince stood up. My shoulders relaxed.

I studied the crack and tried to visualize myself dancing up it, but I couldn't focus. My mind slipped back to Richie. I'd told him I didn't have any birth control and he'd said, *There are ways around that.* I thought he meant we'd do other stuff. Everything but *that.* So we scaled the fire escape of the Noble Hotel in the dark and snuck into an empty room where he'd produced a condom. Afterward, he fell into a deep coma, while I lay awake, feeling like I'd forced myself into it to avoid admitting I was nervous. Even though I'd turned twenty on the winter course, my sexual curriculum vitae would barely fill a rolling paper: some heavy petting in high school; a debatable loss of virginity at seventeen followed by hours of drunken puking; one sober, and thus painful, session with a broken safe with my next boyfriend, which left no doubt as to the loss of my virginity; then a couple of alcohol-fuelled copulations with that BC albino cowboy logger.

As Vince tied into the rope, I started to squirm. My butt was going numb in the hard dirt and Mike's instructions were starting to sound like the adults in the Charlie Brown cartoons—*wah, wah wah.*

"Could I bum a pinch off you, Nance?" A good hit of tobacco would settle me down. In Canyonlands, we'd started bumming snuff off Gunter just to gross everyone out and to prove girls could do anything guys could, but now we were buying our own.

After Nancy had taken a pinch, she handed me her tin of Copenhagen. As soon as I'd tucked a chew into my lower lip, a familiar buzz spread through my body.

"I can't believe you two chew that shit." Vince looked up from tying his knot. My dark stream of tobacco juice splatted into the rocks near his feet, à la Clint Eastwood, which sent Nancy and me into a fit of giggles. He shook his head and turned his back on us.

Vince had told us he liked his women to be feminine, which just made me want to cram a bigger pinch in my lip. Richie didn't mind that I chewed. He chewed leaf tobacco, which was not as harsh as snuff, but he always had a big wad in his cheek like he'd just gotten his wisdom teeth out. He said he wanted to take me to Yosemite. Said it was the best climbing in the world. Right now he was away climbing Mount McKinley in Alaska, but he'd be back before our last trip.

"On belay," Mike told Vince.

"Climbing."

"Climb on."

Vince climbed, stopping to take the protection out of the crack and clip each one to his harness. It wasn't long before he was grunting with exertion, his feet scrabbling away at the rock. After Lonnie's poetry, he made it look like hand-to-hand combat with gravity. When he finally fell out of the crack, he only dropped about a foot, as much as the rope stretched. He sat back in his harness with his feet on the wall and shook out his arms.

"Notice that you can't drop far when you fall on a top-rope. It's only the leader who risks a longer fall, not the second," Mike said as he strained to hold Vince's weight.

"Vince, use your feet, don't rely on brute force. You've got to finesse your way up," Lonnie coached.

Nancy and I glanced at each other. Vince was ten times stronger than we were. He was a lifeguard and bodybuilder and he'd hired a personal trainer to prepare for this course. On the winter section, when Sue had been pinned under her pack with her face in the snow and was starting to suffocate, Vince had picked both her and her pack up off the ground.

Vince finally made it to the top and got lowered to the ground red-faced and sweaty. He sat back on his rock without a word.

"Okay, who's next?" This time I didn't let myself think. My hand shot up. I wanted to beat Vince.

"I probably won't get up it, but I'll give it a go." Better to put myself down first before someone else did.

"That's the spirit," Lonnie said.

I scooped out my mound of tobacco, flicked it away as Mike handed me the end of the rope. My fingers fumbled with a figure eight follow-through. Tying knots brought out my inner space cadet. The bowline was the worst—the bunny going in the hole and around the tree could be interpreted several different ways. I even screwed up the reef knot, which was the simplest knot of all.

But this time, when I finished, Lonnie turned the knot over and said, "Good job."

"On belay," Mike told me, and pulled his baseball cap lower to shade his eyes.

The wall of grey granite looked steeper when I was standing right beside it. Tiny diamond crystals and black specks sparkled in the sun. The crack headed straight up and there were only a few small edges for rest breaks.

"Climbing?"

"You'll do great. You cruised the boulder problems yesterday."

My neck warmed with Lonnie's words and I took a deep breath, sank my hands in the crack. They fit perfectly. In high school I'd hated my hands—big and square with purple veins like my mother's. For the first time, I appreciated their size. Clenching my teeth against the pain of sharp crystals digging into my skin, I cupped my palms so they could expand once they were in the crack, the way Mike had shown me on the first day. "Jamming," he'd called it. Next, I stuffed my shoe into the crack and twisted, then stepped up.

Mike took in the rope to keep it tight as it ran through the anchor above, and I repeated the hand and foot jams, moving up the rock. The higher I went, the more exhilarated I felt, and the more natural the movement became. This was what I'd come to NOLS for. The rock climbing.

"This is so amazing!" I yelled down to my audience.

"All right! You go, girl!" Nancy shouted.

"You're doing great," said Mike.

"It's because she's small." Vince spoke just loud enough for me to hear. I was tired of being Munchkin, the nickname he'd given me on day one.

"It's because she's using her feet, not relying on her arms," corrected Lonnie.

I twisted around, gave Vince the finger, and almost fell backwards off the little ledge I was standing on.

"Keep going, Jan. The crux is coming up."

The crux! Shit! The crux meant the hardest section, but I thought I'd already gotten over that bit. I took a deep breath and continued, moving steadily up the crack till it started to thin, and only my fingers would fit into it. My feet, smeared on the gritty granite, defied logic and held. When I pulled my fingers out of the crack and reached for another jam, I noticed a dark stain of red on the rock. Blood oozed from under a flap of skin on my knuckle. My first climbing wound! I loved the way climbers' hands were covered in scars.

Strength drained from my arms the farther I went. I paused, looked up. There were no more little ledges to rest on, nothing till I got to the big ledge at the top where the rope ran through the bolts. The ground looked very far away all of a sudden. My feet started to slip, and panic swirled through me.

"Keep your eyes on where you want to go and keep moving," Lonnie shouted up to me. "The worst thing you can do is freeze."

I wasn't afraid of heights. I loved being up high. And with a rope, I knew if I fell I wouldn't go anywhere. My fear now wasn't of falling, it was of failing.

"Don't stop, Jan. Just trust yourself."

Trust myself. This was what my mother had kept telling me, over and over before I left. "*Trust yourself, Jan. You're stronger than you think.*"

Fighting off waves of homesickness, I took a deep breath and focused on the grey granite in front of me. I'd never wanted anything with this much certainty. Right from the first day with NOLS, dancing to John Prine while we packed our food in the Lumberyard, surrounded by mountain people, I knew this was the life I wanted. I wanted to be a gypsy like Jocelyn, with my own pickup truck and dog, travelling from climbing area to climbing area, totally free. For once, I felt like I fully belonged.

"You can do it," I whispered into the rock.

As soon as I started climbing again, my feet stopped slipping and stuck to the sandpapery granite. Panic was replaced with a smooth calm. Lonnie was right. That was the key: keep moving. My body seemed to know what to do if I could get my mind out of the way.

When I got to the ledge at the top, I hoisted myself up, pushing down on the rock with my palms and bringing my knee close to my ear to get my foot flat on the edge beside my hand. Just like Lonnie had done. A mantel, she'd called it. Sitting on the ledge with my back against the rock, I basked in the sun and the cheers from below, felt my heart thudding in my throat. I stared off at the horizon, broken up by jagged mountains. Twists of soft cloud, like smoke, were strewn through the powder-blue sky.

During our three-day solo in the Canyonlands, I'd read Annie Dillard every day, and my favourite quote was: *Time gives us a whirl. We keep waking from a dream we can't recall, looking around in surprise, and lapsing back, for years on end. All I want to do is stay awake, keep my head up, prop my eyes open, with toothpicks, with trees.*

I felt like I'd been sleepwalking through my life, and climbing propped my eyes open. Made me fully alive. *I'll be okay, because I'm okay now.*

When Mike gave the go-ahead, I leaned back off the ledge into space and let myself be lowered gently to the ground.

Mike thumped me on the back, almost knocking me off my feet, and said, "Maybe you *will* be lead climbing on this trip after all."

2

LION'S LAYBACK

"Shit, Niccy! You said these little fuckers couldn't survive up here!" I flicked a tick, the size and shape of a burnt sunflower seed, off my red rope, and it sailed through the air, landing on the grey limestone in front of us. We were in the middle of a rock wall with very little greenery and no other warm-blooded critters around. Slim pickings for ticks.

"What do I know?" Niccy shrugged. "They suck blood. They shouldn't be hanging out up here." A brown curl stuck out from under her white helmet, glommed against her cheek. The sun was beating down on us. Perfect tick weather.

I grabbed a pointy stone, used it to grind the tick. Eight tiny legs wiggled under the rock. "Little bastard won't die."

Wendy leaned in to watch the execution. "Better do a good body search when we get off. Don't want Lyme disease." She felt the back of her neck. She'd just finished a wilderness first-aid course.

"Don't be such wussies," Niccy said. "They're just bugs."

"Right. Bugs that kill," I said. A year ago, during the last three weeks of my NOLS course, the mountaineering section, we'd evacuated four people with Rocky Mountain spotted fever. All had been so violently ill we'd had to carry them out on makeshift stretchers. Lyme disease was worse. You could live out the rest of your days with bizarre neurological symptoms and finally keel over, never even knowing your health had been ruined by a bug.

As though on cue, Wendy and I leaned out from the rock and looked down at the ground. We were tied into two bolts, about two hundred feet up. My brown '67 Dodge Dart was parked near the trailhead, not far from the highway.

"Maybe we should rap down," I said. We were three pitches up Lion's Layback with two more to go. A pitch in climbing parlance is the distance between two belay points.

"No way," said Niccy. "We're finishing the climb. The rock's way too loose to rap."

Rockies limestone was notoriously loose, and this climb on Cascade Mountain, just outside Banff, Alberta, was no exception— one big loose slag heap. We'd been knocking rocks off all morning, and if we did a rappel, the rope could dislodge rocks above us.

"Only two more pitches. Let's get out of here." Wendy handed me my rack of protection. Most of my gear was hand-me-downs from the guys I'd worked with all winter at a climbing store in Calgary. They'd been happy to make a few bucks on their obsolete cast-offs to put toward newfangled gear that was beyond my budget. Even my harness was second-hand. I'd bought it from Jeff, a.k.a. Dr. Risk, who'd assured me he hadn't taken one of his famous hundred-foot falls on this one.

I slipped the webbing over my head and popped an arm through. The gear dangled down my side, almost to my knees. I had a bit more leading experience than Wendy and Niccy, so I got the crux pitch.

The best thing about climbing with other women was we shared the lead, but there were only a handful of us around. Most of my partners were guys who were stronger climbers than me, who liked to *take* me climbing, not just *go* climbing. But following was like being the passenger instead of the driver. Real climbers led.

The three of us were all the same age, twenty-one, and we'd all taken similar outdoor courses. Wendy was a lanky five foot ten and Niccy was somewhere in between us, sturdy as a shot putter. Our common goal was to climb and to eventually become mountain guides. So far, there was only one accredited female guide in all of Canada, Sharon Wood. Or at least she was an assistant guide, which was the first step. She worked for the Yamnuska Mountain School, similar to NOLS, which was where I hoped to work one day, but I needed more mileage in the mountains. In the meantime, I was working on the Kananaskis Country trail crew with Wendy, for $7.50 an hour minus room and board for our tent cabin, and Niccy was working at Camp Chief Hector, a YMCA camp between Calgary and Canmore.

Right after NOLS, I too had worked as a counsellor at Camp Chief Hector. Dave and I had hitch-hiked to Calgary from Wyoming as planned, a thousand miles with four dollars in my pocket and a couple of cans of tuna left over from NOLS. Dave, with a bit more experience and a lot more confidence, continued on to BC to work at Outward Bound, while I moved into a teepee with ten pre-pubescent girls and resigned myself to spending the summer singing "John Jacob Jingleheimer Schmidt" around the fire and making useless shit with Popsicle sticks and clothes hangers. But after the first session, I was promoted to the coveted position of Pioneer counsellor. I got to take the older girls on seven-day hikes, horse packing and canoe trips, and somehow managed to emerge from the bush after each trip with the same number of girls I'd headed in with. But just barely.

My partner Laurel and I spent much of the first hike trying to figure out where we were on the map and how to start the stove. On the second trip we almost lost two girls in a raging creek after they fell off a log crossing. While one clung to a branch, the other went bobbing away with Laurel and me running along the bank after her till we finally pulled her out by her pack. Then there was the five-day canoe trip down the Saskatchewan River. Neither of us had paddled before, except on lakes. On day one, with the tiniest camper as my paddling partner, I launched off and immediately got swept under a fallen tree. We avoided decapitation by lying flat in the canoe.

But eight months of working at a climbing store had given me a whole outdoor community to play with, so my mountain mileage was building: a winter of ski touring in the Rockies, two summers leading on rock, and in the spring my first trip to Yosemite, a climber's mecca. Three weeks of climbing granite every single day in the sunshine.

"Fuckers! Get off!" I flicked two more ticks off my brand-new rope. This was its christening. It had cost me over a hundred dollars, a third of what I'd paid for my Dart. But to climb most routes in the Rockies, especially multi-pitch routes in a team of three, we needed two ropes. Wendy had one, and now I did too.

"Okay. Time to blow this Popsicle stand," Niccy said as she rubbed her hands up and down her arms and legs, feeling for ticks.

When Wendy reached for the rope to put me on belay, I noticed that the scarred, rice-paper-thin skin on the back of her hands had started to bleed again.

"Where's your gloves?"

"I keep wearing through them."

"I can belay if you want," Niccy said.

"I'm fine. Go. Get out of here," Wendy said.

The first time I met Wendy, two years before, she'd marched into the climbing store like a mummy with attitude, swathed in a white face and body mask and white gloves. Two blue eyes stared directly back at me through the slits in the cloth, daring me to recoil with horror, ignore her or, worse, to pity her. I found out later that an experiment at college had blown up in her face. She hadn't lost her eyes because, by some bizarre trick of fate (late for class), she'd worn her glasses that day instead of contacts. Now the mask had been off for several months. The scars were stretched and red across her still beautiful face, her nose had been reconstructed, and her long brown hair had grown back.

I traversed across the crumbling ledge toward a deep corner. The first real "obvious feature" yet. The guidebook description kept instructing us to climb to the "obvious ledge" or the "obvious tree"— it was up to us to figure out which one was obvious. Route finding on Rockies limestone was tricky. When in doubt, traverse.

I continued for twenty feet, trying not to knock off any loose rock, moving up and across while looking for a slot in the rock for a placement. Nothing. I looked back at the girls. If I fell I'd pendulum and end up forty or fifty feet below them. With the highway so close, my rescue would provide the hordes of tourists with more entertainment than the elk wandering down Banff Avenue.

I pulled myself up another ledge system, still twenty feet from the corner I was aiming for. Right in front of my face was a piton hammered deep into a small crack by previous climbers. I almost laughed with relief as I grabbed a sling and two carabiners and clipped in the rope.

When I reached the corner, the vertical rock walls clam-shelled around me on either side. A crack formed where the two walls met. This looked like the crux.

I stepped up on small holds, sized up the crack, then stepped down and chose a small hex—an eight-sided piece of hollow metal—from my rack, stepped up again and tried to squeeze it into the crack. Too big. I stepped back down, chose a wedge-shaped piece of protection, a stopper, and it slipped perfectly into the crack. Hoping it wouldn't pull out as I passed it, I continued climbing.

The first time I did a mock lead with NOLS, two of my pieces popped out and slid down the rope to the belayer, my instructor, Mike, who'd said, "Just so you know, if you were really leading and you fell right now, you'd be toast." My next two pieces on that climb would have held a tank.

Mike's instruction saved me when I took my first fall on lead in Yosemite in the spring, fifteen feet onto a big hex. It had held me, but I'd almost hit the ground. When I got down, I thought, *Glad that's over with,* as though my first leader fall were a rite of passage, like losing your virginity.

With one foot on each wall, my legs were almost in the splits, my arms reaching wide above me. I wanted to go straight up, but I was too spread out, like Wile E. Coyote going splat into a cliff in pursuit of the Road Runner. I couldn't make the moves, couldn't find a good handhold above me. I placed another piece of protection as high in the crack as I could and clipped the rope. There were handholds way above, ones that Wendy would be able to reach, and probably Niccy, but I had a couple more moves to make before I got there.

Lion's Layback. There must have been a reason why it was given that name. I probably had to do a layback to get over this move, and I hated laybacks—pulling with your hands and pushing with your feet till it felt as if you were going to launch yourself backwards. The technique was exhausting and it was hard to stop in the middle of the moves to put in protection—you needed to fully commit and trust. That leader fall I'd taken in Yosemite had been on a layback.

I studied the rock one more time, hoping some other method would reveal itself, but the good holds were out of reach, so a layback it would have to be. I turned sideways, gripped the edge of the crack with my fingers and pulled, creating an opposing force so I could walk my feet up the facing wall.

As I shuffled my hands and inched my feet up, grunting with exertion, my hip scraped painfully against the rock. The trick was to keep the feet high but not too high. Too low and the feet could slip out. After a few moves I was able to face the corner again and get my feet on comfortable holds. I found a permanent piton in the crack above and clipped it.

"That was a grunt!" I yelled down.

The corner deepened as I went higher. I could no longer see the girls. I continued up, testing handholds as I went, but even though I bypassed the ones that wiggled, small rocks ricocheted down the wall below me.

"Fucking limestone!"

I missed the solid granite of Yosemite where the rock didn't come out in your hands every few feet. Where the guidebook said, "Follow the obvious crack" and that's what you did. A single crack that went on and on, instead of traversing sideways for thirty feet, up a sort of crack, and then traversing twenty feet in the other direction. But I didn't have long to wait. Niccy and I were heading to Yosemite in the fall. We just had to find a way to get there.

My rusted-out Dart probably wouldn't make it that far. Some days it barely got me to the highway from the Kananaskis. "Baby Beater" was my freedom machine, but I had to wedge a stick in the choke to get it started and the steering was on its way out.

My spring trip to Yosemite had been with Saul and Geoff, in Saul's car. They were friends I'd met through my boss, Rory, at the climbing store, who became more than just my boss, until his girlfriend visited from back east. In Yosemite Saul and I had shared a tent, since I didn't own one, which had gotten me in trouble with *his* girlfriend, though our only transgression had been a few sexually charged wrestling matches. Clearly, it was time to rid my life of men, especially men with girlfriends.

So Niccy was the perfect partner for Yosemite. She wouldn't hog the lead, and like me she seemed incapable of hanging on to a boyfriend, so there was little chance we'd ditch each other for some guy. She just had to get her parents off her back. They wanted her to stay in school, become a forester, not a mountain guide. Thankfully, my parents didn't have any aspirations for me. I sent postcards from Calgary or Yosemite or Wyoming, describing the ski touring and climbing, and Mom thought I was going for nice hikes in the mountains. Dad didn't care what I did as long as I didn't ask for money, though he *had* paid for my flight to Ottawa at Christmas.

I hadn't seen my family for almost a year, but that eight-day visit cured me of my homesickness. My father was stashing bottles in his desk, the garage, and even the linen closet; my sister was binge-drinking; my brother was planning to wrap his car around a telephone pole at a hundred miles an hour if life still sucked in a year; and my mother had joined Al-Anon. Before I left, Mom had plied me with a collection of pamphlets and books on Adult Children of Alcoholics. At least here, on the other side of Canada, I could pretend I had a normal family.

It was getting harder and harder to move my body upward. It felt as if I were dragging a couple of tires on the end of the rope below me. I set my feet on good holds, one on each wall, looked down at almost three hundred feet of air, seventy feet from the start of the corner. I reached for the rope, pulled.

"Slack!" I pulled harder. "Wendy!" She couldn't hear me with the drone of the traffic, and I knew it wasn't Wendy's belaying that was the problem. It was the rope drag from all the zigs and zags around corners and traverses.

I pulled the rope, held a loop in my hands so I could climb, then did it again until I reached a sloping ledge covered in loose rock. On its edge, a tree leaned like a gnarled old man looking down the whole face of the mountain. I wrapped its trunk with a big sling and tied myself off.

"Off belay!" I shouted. No response. "Wendy! Off belay!" I pulled hard at the rope. Wendy was feeding it out in short jerks. She wouldn't know to take me off belay until the rope went tight. I hauled hand over hand till it came to a stop, then sat with my feet braced against the trunk of the tree and wrapped the rope around my waist in a hip belay. Tugged three times, hoping they'd figure out I was ready.

"On belay!"

No response. I tugged on the rope and finally there was slack. Niccy must have untied from the anchor. I pulled till I felt something solid again. Then more slack. Niccy must be climbing. I belayed, trying to keep the rope away from all the loose rock on the ledge, till Niccy stopped again. Finally, there were a couple of jerks and some rope came up. A couple more jerks. Niccy was on the crux. I kept the rope tight.

A slight tickle on my leg. I ran my free hand down my thigh, felt a bump just above the knee. Like a small, flat scab. Or a tick.

Keeping my brake hand tight around my body, I pulled up the leg of my red rugby pants, which were faded almost to pink, my most hated colour. There was a black tick, its head sunk into the flesh of my thigh.

Just as I dug it out with my nail and flung it away, the rope went tight. Niccy must have peeled off the crux. And now I was falling too, dragged off by her weight. I swung around the tree heading straight down the corner, then jerked to a stop when the rope between me and the tree tightened, like a dog reaching the end of its chain. I hung there, upside down, staring at a few-hundred-foot drop. The rope cinched my waist, digging deep into my flesh, but I clamped my fist, kept my brake hand tight across me, holding on to Niccy. I couldn't see her, but I felt her on the rope, so that meant she hadn't hit the ledge.

A clatter above me. I looked up. A rock the size of a microwave was rolling down the slope, right toward Niccy. With my brake hand still clamped hard, I reached out with my other arm and one leg and deflected the rock just before it rolled past. It landed heavily on the pile of rope.

"Niccy!" Nothing. "Niccy! Are you okay? Fuck!" I grunted, spun my legs, trying to turn myself upright. More weight on the rope, like Niccy was jumping on it. "Niccy! What the fuck are you doing?"

Did she want slack? I eyed the big rock, willing it not to move. If it fell, it would land on top of her.

More weight on the rope. She must want slack. I fed out some rope. As it seared the skin of my waist, I thought of Wendy. Third-degree burns to 30 percent of her body. I gave Niccy more rope. She must be lowering to the ledge. Finally, her weight came off and I could breathe. As I spun upright, rocks and dirt funnelled toward the corner.

"Rock!" I screamed. Those stones would turn to missiles by the time they got to Niccy, seventy feet down. I wedged myself into a sitting position, the rope still tight, and pushed the big rock off my rope, to the side, where there was no chance it would get dislodged again. The white of the rope's innards hung out. I'd chopped my first brand new rope.

When Niccy finally came in sight, she looked up at me, her face wet and red with exertion. "What the fuck? I almost hit the ledge!"

"Sorry," I muttered. "I fucked up."

I knew what I'd done wrong. I'd sat *above* my anchor, the tree, instead of below it Sitting on the ledge would have been better. In my attempt to avoid all the loose rocks, I'd ended up being dragged through them. I'd chopped my rope and I'd almost killed my friend.

Niccy climbed past and tied into the tree. As she flicked ticks off her cotton pants, I gave her a rundown of the near-catastrophe, showed her the rope-wrecking rock.

"Don't sweat it," she said. "I'm still here, aren't I?" But she wouldn't look at me, and I felt her annoyance. She'd never been mad at me before.

Niccy passed me the end of the rope she'd trailed behind her, which was attached to Wendy. I pulled in the slack and got ready to belay. This time I stood on the sloping ledge, with the tree above me, the way I should have belayed Niccy.

"Fuck!" Niccy ripped her shirt over her head, picked a tick off her white tummy and flicked it off the ledge.

"Wussie," I said. "It's just a bug." She grinned at me. We were good.

"You chopped your first rope," Niccy said. "That is not cool."

"Yeah. And I almost killed you. Sorry about that."

"Apology accepted," she said. "You can buy me a cold beer. Or two."

"Fucking limestone. We've got to get to Yosemite."

The rope jerked a few times so I knew Wendy was ready. Holding the rope above the loose rocks, I pulled in the slack, focused on Wendy's every move. One almost-dead friend was enough for the day.

3

THE RESCUE

I stood at the base of El Capitan, straining my neck to stare up three thousand feet of granite. A single line of red rope lay against the blank face and disappeared up out of sight. I was back in Yosemite Valley, twelve hundred miles away from crappy Alberta limestone.

Rik threw his backpack on the ground and started to dig out the gear. He was a member of the Yosemite Rescue Team and we'd met in the spring, on my first trip to the valley. A few days ago, he had offered to take me up some harder routes, routes I couldn't do with Niccy, and I'd accepted, with a twinge of guilt. But Niccy had lots of partners. It seemed half of Alberta's climbers were in Camp 4 with us.

"How many ropes did you guys leave up there?" I asked.

Rik straightened up, his arms crossed over his chest like a teacher, except I'd never seen a teacher with forearms bigger than my calves. Rock climbing half the year in Yosemite and ice climbing the other half in Alaska had turned him into a scruffy, red-bearded, dark-eyed Popeye.

"Six. We should be up and down in a couple of hours."

We weren't here to rock climb, we were here to ascend ropes. Rik and his friend Jake had spent three days climbing a route way off to our left, then traversed over here to descend this featureless wall, which was used as a rappel route. They'd left their ropes "fixed" with plans to go back up and finish the route. But Jake had had to bail and leave the valley, so now the ropes had to come down. All nine hundred feet of them.

I reached into my shorts pocket, pulled out my tin of Copenhagen. A little pinch always calmed my nerves, which was why I couldn't quit. I tucked the black tarry tobacco into my lower lip, tamped it down with the tip of my tongue, spat out a few floaters. The nicotine buzz spread through my body, heating and numbing my mouth.

Rik stopped sorting gear. "You're not going to spit that down on me, are you?"

"Why, am I going first?"

It made no difference, really, who went first. The ropes were already above us, but somehow, following felt safer, even though dead is dead if you fall from almost a thousand feet.

"Yeah, I'll come up behind—clean the anchors and drop the extra ropes," Rik said. "We just need two to get back down."

Rik thought this would be good preparation for my first big wall route, a multi-day climb that involved specialized equipment and techniques, and sleeping on ledges or in hammocks. He thought I could be one of the top female climbers if I set my mind to it. He'd also invited me to move out of Niccy's tent and into his, and I'd declined. Rik was twenty-five, four years older than me, and he was such a good climber that I knew I'd follow him around like a baby duck if I slept with him. So I'd told him I wasn't looking for a boyfriend, that it would interfere with my climbing. I'd considered telling him I already had someone back home, but that would have been stretching it. Rory had never really been my boyfriend, since he already *had* a girlfriend, and a little fling I'd had with a friend the night before I left for California could hardly be considered "a relationship" since I'd fallen asleep in the middle of it. Unfortunately, I'd stored my Dart in the guy's yard in Canmore just east of Banff. It could be a bit awkward upon my return.

I spat a long, dark stream of tobacco juice onto the rocks.

"That's a disgusting habit." Rik sounded irritated, not his normal self. He was usually so agreeable. He handed me a tangled pile of nylon slings and two yellow metal ascending devices. "Here's your jumars. We'd better get going. We've got less than three hours of daylight left."

After I scooped out my tobacco and took a swig of water, I attached my jumars to the rope and clipped an etrier—a six-foot ladder made from webbing—into each. Jumars can slide up the rope, but when you weight them, they lock and won't slide down.

"Okay, I'm ready."

Rik studied me through narrowed eyes. "I thought you said you'd used jumars before."

"I have. Niccy and I jugged up a tree to hang our food."

Rik shook his head. "Shit." He grabbed the two pieces of nylon webbing that were curled up at my feet. "You forgot your daisy chains."

Daisy chains?

He slipped the webbing through my harness in a girth hitch and attached one to each of the jumars hanging from the rope. "That's your lifeline."

Looking down at the mess of gear hanging from my harness, I could see that the daisy chains were the only thing securing me to the rope. Without them, if I were to let go of the jumars, I'd fall to the ground.

"Your harness is doubled back?" He grabbed my harness and jerked it roughly.

"Yeah, yeah." I pulled away.

When Rik turned his back, I checked my buckle, just in case. Right here in Yosemite, a woman had leaned off a ledge to rappel and fallen to her death because she hadn't done her harness up properly. One stupid, split-second mistake.

I slid the top jumar as high up the rope as I could reach, slipped my sneaker into one of the loops of the etrier, and stepped up. The jumar locked and held my weight, but the rope swung me around and I slammed into the rock.

"Fuck!"

"Gotta get the stretch out of the rope. Here, I'll hold it for you."

"I can do it!"

Rik threw up his hands and stepped back to watch me fumble with my etriers.

He was talking to me like I was an idiot, the way I overheard boyfriends talking to their girlfriends at the base of a climb. But I had come to Yosemite to *really* climb, not to follow some hot-shit climber around. When I climbed with guys, it was too easy to give up the sharp end of the rope, and lately, I'd started to feel I was being guided. The best thing I could have done was to swear off men altogether. But given my track record, it didn't look like there was much chance of that happening. And given my latest impulsive, drunken lapse in judgment, which I had yet to tell Rik about.

I was off the ground. With my weight on one jumar, I could reach down and slide the other one up the rope. I slogged upward, transferring my weight back and forth as if I were on some defective step machine at the gym. Not that I spent any time at a gym. My idea of training was ski touring, climbing or hiking, then drinking beer and doing finger pull-ups on door jambs, especially when I had a male audience.

"You're doing good, Jan!"

One hundred and fifty feet off the ground, I secured myself to the anchor, unclipped my jumars, and transferred them to the next rope above me.

"I'm off!" I yelled down to Rik.

While I hung there, resting against the wall, I watched Robbie farther along the base, starting a climb with a couple of students. He was pretty cute, but he had a girlfriend. He was on the Yosemite climbing rescue team with Rik. They got a free campsite and showers, and a small pittance for each idiot they rescued off a climb. Business was brisk.

I checked my jumars twice before I unclipped from the anchor and once again entrusted my fate to the two pumpkin-coloured pieces of metal. Slide, step, reach, slide, step, reach. My technique was getting smoother, and after a few minutes, I started to enjoy the motion.

"Can you speed it up a bit, Jan? It's getting late."

Rik was already near the top of the first rope. As I tried to go faster I lost my rhythm. Sweat trickled down my sides even though I was wearing only a tank top and shorts.

I transferred to the next rope as fast as I could and kept going.

"Rope!" He warned anyone who might be below as he dropped the first one. Then he glided effortlessly up the second toward me.

Rik was one of the top climbers in the valley. I wasn't drawn to him romantically, but I wished I could be. We could talk for hours, the way I talked to girlfriends—comparing our screwed-up childhoods, talking about what we wanted to do if we ever "grew up"—and he was always giving me things, like a gear sling that was too small for him or his favourite wool earflap hat. But I must have read too many Harlequin romances in high school, because I had an image fixed in my brain of a hairy-chested guy who'd scoop me into his arms and rip off my bodice or my harness or whatever, without stopping to ask my permission.

Someone like Gary, for instance—the mountain guide from

Alaska whose tent was right beside mine and Niccy's. He was the latest, totally unexpected, complication to my love life.

At the top of the third rope, I unclipped and transferred to the fourth. I let myself look down, and wondered how long would it take for my body to reach the ground. Five, ten seconds? A wave of dizziness forced my focus back to the rock in front of me.

"Rope!" The next rope slithered all the way down the face to the ground.

As I slid my jumars rhythmically up the rope, my thoughts strayed again to Gary—his big dome tent and thick foamy, how he'd tossed me around like a weightless rag doll. I had to stop to let a shudder travel through my body.

I hadn't even been attracted to him at first. He was loud and hyper—too much like me. And we looked funny together, my five foot one and a half inches to his six foot four. But that body . . . He was lean and dark, with hands the size of dinner plates, a thick mop of black hair, and a bushy moustache under the biggest nose I'd ever seen that wasn't plastic. He was so . . . swarthy. So Harlequin. He told me he'd had his eye on me since that humiliating day when I'd been on my way to a climb with Niccy. I was walking backwards, waving at him, and fell over a log. He said when I popped up laughing, he knew he had to have me. I gave him my usual line—*I'm not looking for a boyfriend*—the same line I'd given Rik, but he'd just laughed and said, "Bullshit."

I fended him off for a couple of days then gave in one night while Rik was climbing. We'd been sitting around the fire drinking real beer—Moosehead, not Budweiser—just a short crawl away from his tent. I could blame it on our quality Canadian breweries.

The fourth rope went more quickly, but the whole step/slide/reach routine was growing monotonous. The sun had dipped behind the mountains, and in spite of the cooling air, I was sweaty and hot and my mouth was drier than dust.

"Rope!" Rik dropped another rope.

"Rik, I need water!"

I expected him to say, "Just wait there, I'll bring it up," in his typical accommodating fashion, but instead he bellowed back, "Just hold on till we get to the top!"

There was something different about Rik, something in the tone of his voice. He was no longer fawning. His new impatience was a bit of a turn-on.

I started to jug up the next rope.

At the next anchor, I was surprised to find there was no rope above me. Between my rhythmic jumaring and pornographic fantasies of Gary, maybe I'd lost count. I clipped in and yelled, "I'm off!" then hung from the bolts to take the weight off my feet. When I looked down I saw boulders turned to pebbles, and massive ponderosa pine to shrubs. My bowels constricted.

When he was halfway up the last rope, Rik yelled, "What are you doing? Why'd you stop?"

"I'm at the end."

"You can't be. There are six ropes."

I looked back up at the blank rock. "There's no more rope! I'm at the top of the last one."

"Maybe you can't see it. The last one's black."

"Hey, Rik, I think if there was a rope above me I'd see it."

He ascended the last bit quickly, till he was hanging beside me. He looked up, his face streaming with sweat. "What the fuck?" I watched the colour drain away beneath his tatty red beard. "Where's the rope?" His voice was hoarse with panic. I'd never seen him unravel like this. He sagged against the rock. "Jesus fucking Christ."

"Rik, did you drop our last rope?" But I already knew. There was no rope trailing from his harness.

"Rik?"

Rik pounded the rock with his fists till I was sure he'd draw blood. He pounded and cursed while I cringed, suddenly transported back to Munster Hamlet where my father, fuelled by Scotch, and my brother by rum and Coke, had pushed each other around, screaming. Panic cut off my breathing and I needed to escape, but there was nowhere to go. We were hanging off the same bolts. I stared off into the valley and let myself detach, until I barely registered the rage spewing beside me. Tufts of smoke rose from barbecues by the Winnebagos. My stomach growled.

As I waited for Rik to calm down enough to figure out how to save us, the reality of the situation started to sink in. I was hanging, clipped by a locking carabiner and one-inch-thick nylon webbing to two bolts, 750 feet up a vertical wall of granite, with no way down. The bolts were drilled 150 feet apart, the length of a climbing rope, which meant that with two ropes we could descend. With one rope, we were screwed.

Eventually, Rik pushed wet hair off his face and looked around. "Jake must have taken the last rope down when he came up for his haul bag. Un-fucking-believable."

The sound of laughter wafted up from the base.

"Robbie's still down there with his students." I leaned out from the rock and screamed, "Robbie!" I couldn't see him, but I knew he was there.

Rik put his head in his hands and groaned, "This is fucking embarrassing."

"Embarrassing? Are you serious? How else are we going to get down?"

Rik hesitated, then his voice pummelled my eardrum. "Robbie!"

Eventually Robbie came into view and looked up. Waved both arms above his head.

After Rik was forced to broadcast our predicament to the whole valley, Robbie disappeared with his students. I waited for him to run down the hill through the trees and out to the road to get help, but he didn't reappear.

"Why isn't he going down?"

"He'll finish up with his clients first."

"You've got to be fucking kidding." I put my forehead on the cooling rock. "So now what?"

"Just let me think."

Refusing to look down, I stared at the wall and thought of Gary, how safe and protected I'd felt under his huge body. I wondered if he'd notice if I didn't show up that night, but I'd only done two climbs with the guy and spent one night in the sack. He was as much my boyfriend as Rory. A familiar longing jabbed at me, a craving for someone who would notice whether I was dead or alive at the end of the day. Someone who could keep track of me, tether me to the ground so I'd stop floating off on any little breeze that blew my way.

I closed my eyes and kissed the rock. *Please keep us safe.*

"The guys can't get to us in the middle of this wall." Rik sounded calmer. "We have to get to that crack system. It's the only way down." He pointed to a crack in a left-facing corner. It looked very far away.

"Maybe we should just wait for a rescue." I wanted to curl into a ball and hang from the bolts, like a pupa.

"No, we have to get as close to the ground as possible. I'll have to pendulum."

Rik set up the rope and lowered himself fifty feet. He ran across the rock away from the crack as far and high as he could go, let gravity swing him back, and sprinted toward the crack, straining for it, but it was too far away. He plunged in a long arc below me, ran back to the top of the pendulum, higher than before, then raced again across the rock. Again he missed. This went on and on, until finally his fingertips—conditioned from hundreds of vertical miles of climbing—clamped in the crack like vise-grips. They held his 180 pounds.

By the time Rik lowered me over to him the sun was going down. He grabbed my harness and pulled me toward him to clip me in. I let him. I didn't give a shit anymore whether he thought I was tough.

I just wanted to get down alive. Once I'd settled my feet on the small ledge, the blood rushed back into my legs.

We were both clipped into a single rusted piton poking out from the crack, and a carabiner that Rik had wedged in as a backup. We had no equipment with us to use as anchors to rappel from, so we had to rely on any gear previous parties had left behind.

"How old do you think that thing is?" I asked, rubbing goosebumps off my bare arms.

"I don't know. Old. Probably put in on the first ascent in the seventies. It's all I could find."

"So now what?" I forced my mind away from the elements the piton had been exposed to: sun, rain, ice, sleet, snow. . .

"I'll keep going down, see if I can find some bolts. You'll have to unclip in case the anchor doesn't hold."

Rik watched me closely to see if I had understood. I had, but I wished I hadn't. If the anchor failed while Rik descended and we were both clipped to it, his weight would pull me down and we'd both die. If I unclipped, just Rik would die, and I'd be clinging to a two-foot ledge in the dark, a few hundred feet up without an anchor.

"That's fucked."

"I know. Don't move till I tell you to. If it holds my weight, it'll probably hold yours. I'm really sorry. I don't know how I let this happen."

After I unclipped, Rik slowly lowered himself onto the rope. Neither of us took our eyes off the piton. Fear ate at the inside of my belly. I realized how badly I didn't want him to die.

"Maybe we should wait."

"We'll be okay. Just don't move." He forced a smile as he lowered himself below an overhang and out of sight.

On the valley floor, headlights moved toward the village, like a procession of fireflies. My legs cramped. I was thirsty and hungry and could take only tiny breaths because I was too scared to move.

"Rik!" No answer.

I wrapped my arms around myself but couldn't stop shivering. The rope was still tight from his weight, so he hadn't found an anchor yet. I pinched the piton lightly with my fingers for the false sense of security it gave me. One slip and I was gone.

If I had just paid attention before he dropped that last rope. As usual, I'd just bumbled along with my brain on pause. When I climbed with guys, even when I went first, I followed. No matter what I liked to tell myself. Just like a few days ago, at the Cookie Cliff. Rik and I had been scrambling across a sloping ledge between pitches. It was exposed, about three hundred feet straight to the ground, but it was easy so we hadn't roped up. I was looking at everything but my feet, the waterfalls spilling off the mountains, the spires of granite, the clouds in the sky. Rik got to the base of the next crack, looked back at me, and right then my foot slipped on some pebbles and I started to slide. His eyes went the size of boulders and he reached out his hand as if he could save me. In those few seconds—before I caught myself from going over the edge—I realized he couldn't. No one could. It felt like an epiphany. I was all on my own.

And now here I was again, having the very same epiphany.

"Rik!" I called again.

The rope went slack. He'd found another anchor. "Rap down slowly!" His voice was faint.

With the rope through my rappel device, I lowered my weight onto the piton. I started to descend into the night, cringing as the rope ran in quick jerks, putting more strain on the anchor. My jumars and etriers dangled from my harness, clanging against the rock, the only sound except for my breathing as I took short, quick sips of air.

"Be careful. I barely made it to the anchor." Rik appeared in the moonlight just below me and off to the right, still several feet away. Relieved to see him, I descended faster.

"Watch your brake hand! You're going to run out of rope! STOP! NOW!"

As the words ripped from his mouth, I felt the tape that marked the ends of the rope and instinctively squeezed before the last bit of nylon could slip through my rappel device. Three inches. That was all that stood between me and the paper bags of shit at the base that climbers jettisoned during their multi-day climbs. If Rik hadn't shouted at that moment, I would have rappelled right off the end of the rope.

I hung, over five hundred feet up the wall, paralyzed. I didn't weigh enough for the rope to stretch those extra few feet to the anchor.

"Rik, what do I do?" To keep from crying, I clenched my teeth.

"Just don't move. Don't let go. I'll get to you." I could hear him unclip from the anchor but didn't dare move my head. By the time he rigged up a sling and hauled me over to him, I was shaking like an epileptic.

"It's okay. We have a good anchor now." He clipped me into two bolts and I slid my back down the wall to sit on the ledge. My feet dangled into nothingness. Rik sat and put his arm around me but I couldn't calm my body, couldn't stop the tears.

"I'm so sorry. We'll get down. I promise." He unclipped his water bottle from his harness and passed it to me. I gulped it down. Terror had sucked up the last of my saliva. "The guys should be here soon, but I think we can get down another pitch."

"I don't think I can move."

"It's okay. We'll take our time."

We watched headlights creep along below us on the road. One of the cars was in dire need of a new muffler, just like my own, and out of the blue, homesickness exploded in my chest. I wanted to go home but I couldn't even narrow "home" down to an address. Home was Canada. Home was my car. The most stable thing in my life was a rusted-out Dodge Dart.

Rik eventually broke the silence. "Can I ask you something?" His voice was strained.

"What's the matter?"

"I just want to know something." He paused. "Why Gary?"

His dark eyes shone and his mouth twisted under his beard. Shame burned through me, like I'd been caught screwing around.

I cleared my throat. My mouth was so dry. "I don't know. It just happened."

It just happened. Like everything else in my life. Like hanging off El Cap without a rope, waiting to be rescued.

Rik removed his arm from around my shoulders. A shiver coursed through me as I lost his body heat. "I thought you didn't want a boyfriend."

"I didn't think I did."

"Gary is almost old enough to be your father."

"I know."

"He just separated from his wife."

"I know, I know."

Gary was seventeen years older than me but he seemed young for his age. Playful. Just the other day he'd said, "I bet I can bench-press you," and got me to put on my harness so he'd have something to grab on to when he lay on his back and hoisted me into the air like I was a barbell. Rik would have had no trouble doing the same thing— I'd watched him do endless pull-ups—but the thought wouldn't have even occurred to him.

"I don't get it," Rik said.

Had I been leading Rik on? My friends seemed to think so. After I crawled out of Gary's tent that first night, Janet, one of our Canadian contingent, said, "What about Rik?" and I said, "What *about* Rik? He knows we're just friends."

"You've been flirting with him."

"I do that with everyone. That's just my way," I joked.

"It's not a very good way."

Niccy hadn't said anything, but Doc, a friend I'd met at NOLS, had defended me in his North Carolina drawl, "She doesn't do that with me."

"You're not hardcore enough," Janet told him.

Was I really that shallow? But I couldn't go out with a guy just because he wanted me to, though it was probably as valid a reason as going out with a guy because he could bench-press me.

While I searched for the right words, Rik said, softly, "They're here," as though the zombies had found our hiding spot.

I leaned out and looked over the edge. The blackness below was punctuated by a procession of headlamps bobbing through the trees. I wanted to dance on the ledge and yodel, partly because I knew we'd survive the night, and partly because I wouldn't have to continue our conversation.

"Thank God. I could use a beer. Even gutless American beer."

"Don't get too excited. It'll take them a couple of hours to climb high enough to shoot us another rope. Hopefully they've brought the rope gun with them." Rik stood up. "I'll head down and find another anchor."

Suddenly a blast of white light pinned us to the rock. When my eyes adjusted, I saw two huge spotlights tilted up toward us from the ground; half a dozen bodies fluttered around them like moths.

"Hey, Rik! What the fuck you doing up there?" someone hollered.

"Rik, you moron! Is this whatcha gotta do to get a date with a chick?"

Rik turned his back to the taunts and set up to rappel while I yelled down, "You assholes sure took your time! We're freezing our nuts off up here!"

He leaned out from the rock and started to descend.

———

At two in the morning we walked through a quiet Camp 4. Neither of us spoke. Most of the tents were dark, but the occasional fire still crackled in a campsite, with climbers huddled around in pile jackets and down vests, passing joints and sipping beer. There was no sign of life in the sagging tent I shared with Niccy, nor in Gary's big yellow dome beside it. Rik and I said goodnight and he turned to leave, paused, then came back and gave me a hug.

"Sorry 'bout the fuck-up."

"Hey, don't worry about it." I punched his arm. "At least now I can say I've been rescued off El Cap."

"You did good up there."

"No, I didn't. I was scared."

"You were brave."

I waited till he faded into the night, then knelt in front of Gary's tent and unzipped the door.

4

SPEED RUTS

She was a fast machine . . .

Bellowing out AC/DC, I stepped hard on the copy of *Shōgun* I'd duct-taped to my gas pedal. Because I had to sit on a pillow to see over the dash, it was the only way I could reach it with my foot. This was my second Dodge Dart, a green '73 I'd bought for five hundred dollars after a bunch of kids took my first Dart for a joy ride in Calgary. They'd left it wrapped around a telephone pole and took off.

You shook me all night long . . .

The highway, a shimmering black line, led straight into the white-tipped Rocky Mountains, and beyond that, another ten hours from here, my tree-planting camp in the bush outside Hope. The lights of Calgary faded in my rear-view mirror. I was still jet-lagged from the flight from Indonesia, but it felt so good to drive after spending seven months in the passenger seat on the other side of the world.

A year and a half earlier, I'd parted ways with Gary in Yosemite, come back to Calgary, and started climbing frozen waterfalls with Jim, a Scottish climber. When he was offered a job as a geologist in Jakarta he invited me along. Accepting that invitation had not been my smartest move. We'd already failed the compatibility test during a road trip to Yosemite, where I discovered he was prone to fits of car-punching rage. But as usual, I was broke, homeless, in love, and looking for a new adventure. And who could turn down an all-expenses-paid trip to Asia?

Not once had I dared drive in Jakarta's traffic, which was left-sided and terrifyingly unpredictable with its spontaneous lane reversals. Either our driver, Siyarifudin, or Jim had done all the driving. Of all the expat women I met, Australian, British, American, German, not one drove a car: not to the Western-style supermarket, the high-end shopping mall, the tennis courts, the Hilton for lunch, or their kids' international school. We all had drivers.

The flat prairie gave way to the dips and rolls and curves of the foothills, and off to my right, the grey fin of Yamnuska pushed up from the earth: a crumbling mountain of limestone where I'd spent hours climbing in various states of exhilaration and terror. I was itching to get on the rock again, to move my body, find my muscles, bloody up my hands, get grubby, smelly and tired. To breathe fresh, clean, Canadian air instead of thick, mucus-coloured Indonesian smog.

I steered past Canmore, Banff and Lake Louise, past tree after tree, lake after lake, mountain after mountain, and had them almost exclusively to myself. This was what I missed the most. The wilderness, the space. Jakarta had been like a stirred-up anthill teeming with eight million bodies.

Down the long hill into the Yoho Valley, toward the Kicking Horse River and the tiny railway town of Field. Water seeped out of the mountains that soared on either side of the highway. Last winter, before Jakarta, Jim and I had ice-climbed routes here named after beer: Extra Light, Cool Spring, Massey's. That was in the first few months of our relationship, when we still got along.

The winding hairpin turns of Kicking Horse Canyon kept me edgy and alert, but by the time I hit the drab strip of gas stations and restaurants of Golden, drowsiness had set in. I was still hours away from Hope. It looked like I'd be trying to find our camp in the dark. I opened my window and breathed in the wood smoke, then pulled out my tin of Copenhagen and tucked a pinch into my lower lip. That perked me right up.

Seven months without chewing tobacco. I'd visited tobacco shops in England, Hong Kong, Thailand, Singapore and Jakarta asking for snuff. No one knew what I was talking about, and my charades-like explanation had them looking at me the way I looked at the lepers and limbless children squatting on the streets. Jim had finally begged me to stop. One of the first things I did when I got home was buy a tin.

Revelstoke, Salmon Arm, Kamloops. I tried to imagine what it would be like to live in each town I went through. I needed to settle somewhere, find a home and a real job. Jim had given me some money to get on my feet again, but I'd spent most of it on a tent, a rope and some climbing gear. Fortunately I had a job for the next two months with the tree-planting company I'd worked for last season, so I'd soon be making my own money again.

I reached Hope just before dark. The mountains here reminded me of Indonesia. Green, tropical bumps—soft compared to the Rockies. I found the turnoff to the logging road and followed a creek of raging white foam that spilled off the mountain like an upside-down geyser.

At a fork in the road, I stopped to dig out my map to the camp— pencil scrawls on the back of a paper bag. I'd been tipsy when my boss, Troy, gave me directions over the phone. Now I could barely read them, but there was definitely no mention of a fork in the road.

Eeny meeny miney moe. My finger landed on the road to the right.

Jakarta was, to date, the blackest period in my twenty-three years. Dumping me into a professional, wealthy, clean, middle-aged expat community was like plucking Tarzan from the jungle and dumping him in New York City. To fit in as a kept woman, I'd shaved my legs and armpits, then spent the next few months drinking gin and tonic, gaining fifteen pounds, and waiting for our sea freight with my climbing gear to be released so I could get the hell out of there. I often stayed in bed all day, making hysterical calls to Jim's office from our townhouse compound where Indonesian men ogled me through the barbed-wire fence whenever I hung out by the pool. As soon as I'd gotten my hands on my climbing gear and secured a job tree planting, I booked my flight back to Canada, hauling packs and duffles back with me on the plane.

It was completely dark when the car dropped into a ditch that sliced across the road. I could sense but not see the thick trees to my left, the steep ravine to the right. My Dart crawled out the other side, tires spinning. I drove on, bouncing through rut after rut, stopping a few times to stare at the map. There was supposed to be a turnoff.

When I plunged into the deepest rut yet, I heard a familiar metal-on-rock screech from under the car, then a roar worthy of a Harley. Churning up gravel and dirt, the car barely crawled out the other side.

"Shit!" With my headlamp and the work gloves I kept handy for this purpose, I slid under the car, lifted the muffler out of the dirt, slipped it back into the exhaust pipe, and tightened the wire that held it in place.

At the next rut the muffler dropped off again, so this time I pulled the hunk of rust from under the car, tossed it onto the back seat and carried on.

I stopped when I heard gushing water, got out and looked down at a stream raging across the road. This could not be the way. I took a closer look at the ruts, saw evidence of a backhoe, and it finally dawned on me: the ditches were here for a reason. To decommission the road.

The way behind me looked like a black hole, and backing up was not my forte. But turning around would be a bitch too. The road was only a single lane, with a ravine to the right, a stream in front of me, and trees forming a wall to the left.

My bones went soft and I slumped against the car. A yearning for Jim coursed through me. I wanted him and our driver to come rescue me in our Jeep. Siyarifudin would have been so shocked to see a white woman out in the bush alone like this. He'd shadowed me everywhere I went, up and down streets as I shopped, and especially when I took photos at the sprawling cardboard ghetto across from the Western-style supermarket. He'd said over and over, "Not safe for you on your own here, missus."

Not safe. But Jim had been able to go anywhere, any time. The crowds had parted for him like the Red Sea. Groups of school boys hadn't come up to him saying, "You wanna fucky fucky?" White men were gods in Jakarta; Indonesian men came next, then white married women. Unmarried fornicators like me placed somewhere with Indonesian women near the bottom. I'd like to have seen the expats' faces if they'd known my little trip to Singapore a couple of months after we arrived hadn't been a shopping trip.

Siyarifudin must have suspected. I'd thrown up in a bag all the way to the airport and he'd kept asking, "Why Mr. Jim not coming?" In the airport I passed out going through customs and woke up with a bunch of Indonesians arguing around me. Then I threw up the whole flight to Singapore. Jim arrived at the hospital the next day, just before they wheeled me away. In the middle of a huge operating room, as cold as a meat locker, I'd waited, my feet up in stirrups, alone except for a worker who mopped the floor around me. That's all I remembered. That's all I wanted to remember.

I pulled out my tin of Copenhagen and tucked some tobacco in my lip. My courage in a can. My handy-dandy man repellent. I spat out a long stream of tobacco. Clint Eastwood could hit a lizard from a couple of yards away. I was lucky to miss my feet.

"Fuck 'em if they can't take a joke." My voice sounded loud in the silent forest. One of my planting friends, Shelly, used to say, "Don't fuck 'em if they can't take a joke." I was going to take her advice. Maybe become a nun.

I climbed into the car, backed up to the widest section, cranked the wheel, inched toward the trees till I felt the car dip, reversed, then crept backwards again. I couldn't see through the rear window, couldn't see the edge of the ravine, so I only went a couple feet at a time. By the time I was turned around and pointing downhill, I'd done at least an eighteen-point turn.

Going downhill gave me momentum through the ruts, and I had more clearance without the muffler. I drove too fast, every once in a while pounding on my steering wheel yelling, *Stupid, stupid, stupid!* Normal people would have figured it out by the second rut, but no, not me.

When I finally got to the fork, I turned up the left-hand branch this time, onto a smooth, well-maintained but narrow gravel road. As I rounded a steep bend, the high beams of a pickup truck suddenly blasted me and I slammed on the brakes. We both sat there. It was a standoff. One of us was going to have to back up and it sure as hell was not going to be me.

The doors to the truck opened and two men stepped out. I froze for a moment, then slammed my lock down, slid across the seat to lock the passenger side door and back doors, then peered through the windshield at the men walking toward me.

I let out a yelp, unlocked my door and jumped out. "Brad! Troy! You guys scared the shit out of me!"

"We were starting to get worried about you. Thought you might need rescuing."

"Yeah right, do I look like I need rescuing?"

Troy smiled beneath his blond handlebar moustache. He was the owner of the outfit. Last year, he'd hit on a few women until one of the rookies moved into his trailer. She'd looked miserable for the rest of the season.

We hugged, but I kept it brief, so he'd know right away not to bother. He was over thirty, and I was done with old guys. The older they were the bossier they were. Jim had been only eight years older than me but due to his receding hairline, the Indonesians had thought he was my father. It had been an improvement over the seventeen years between me and my Alaskan guide, but if I ever looked at a man again, it would be one closer to my age.

Brad gave me a drawn-out hug and said, "Wow, you look great."

It was dark. He couldn't see the extra fifteen pounds. He'd figure it out tomorrow.

I hadn't gotten to know Brad too well the year before. He was cute, but in a friend's-little-brother kind of way. He was a serious kayaker, so whenever we had time off he'd be on a river somewhere and I'd be climbing. I did know he and Shelly were a tree-planting couple, and at the end of the season he would go back home to Fernie to his girlfriend, Becca. She'd visited once, unannounced, and everyone in the cook shack had watched them sit awkwardly together at one of the picnic tables, while Shelly ate at another. Brad had looked extremely sheepish, but it had made for good camp gossip.

Troy looked under the car. "Lose your muffler?" He must have heard me coming around the corner before he'd even seen my headlights.

"Nope. It's in the backseat."

"The road's not that bad. You should have had enough clearance."

"Guess not."

"I'll back up to the last pullout, then you can follow us back to camp."

"See you there," said Brad, and it seemed like we exchanged one of those unmistakable *looks*. Which surprised me, on account of Becca and Shelly, and the fact that I was never going near a man again.

5

LEARNING TO ROLL

My planting bags thumped against my legs and butt, the one on my back and the other two on either side, the weight trying to squish me into the ground. The rough needles of the tall pine seedlings scratched the soft undersides of my arms, even through my sleeves. I bent over for about the seven-hundredth time that day, screefed the thick duff with my caulk boots down to mineral soil, speared the ground with my shovel, grabbed a tree from my bag, tucked the long, spidery roots into the opening with the blade, kicked the hole closed with my heel and continued walking, without straightening up, pacing out my next tree and looking for the next spot at the same time. For a few trees, I could almost pretend I was one of the more productive planters, a highballer.

Cheryl, a UBC student from Vancouver, was a few paces off to my left. We'd been paired up because we were both lowballers. The block spread out before us, patched with snow and covered in so much slash, half-rotten logs and stumps that it looked like it had been logged that morning. The closer we moved toward the line of trees in the distance, the steeper the pitch.

Every muscle in my body felt like it had been put through a meat tenderizer. I had trench foot and my heels were rubbed raw. My hands were claws with blisters the size of bite-sized Ritz crackers, I was starting to get tendonitis in my wrist, and I had black fly bites on top of mosquito bites on top of no-see-um bites. Even worse, I'd finally remembered something I'd forgotten thousands of miles away in Jakarta: tree planting sucked.

I straightened and pushed my red bandana up my forehead with my pesticide-soaked glove. Cheryl stopped when she saw me stop. We were both always looking for the slightest excuse to take a break but we'd only just refilled our bags.

I leaned on my shovel, shaking my hair like a horse's tail to discourage the swarm of mosquitoes homing in on me. The sky was grey and thick as dishwater.

"Time for a smoke break?" Cheryl asked.

We dropped our planting bags. Minus the weight of the trees, I felt like I'd been set free, floating like a helium balloon. We plopped down on a wet log, pulled out bags of Drum tobacco and started rolling. If I was going to breathe in pesticides all day, I might as well throw a bit of arsenic, tar and nicotine into the mix. Besides, it warded off the bugs, gave me an excuse to take a break, and kept me from chewing tobacco.

I took a drag off my cigarette, blew the smoke into the swarm of black flies and mosquitoes. The sweet cigar aroma of tobacco blended with the half-bottle of bug dope I'd soaked into my clothes. DEET perfume.

"So, how's it going with Loverboy?" Cheryl asked, elbowing me.

I groaned. "Oh my God. He makes me so horny."

In my five sexually active years, no one had ever affected me like Brad. I fantasized about him all day long. I was so wound up my metabolism burned faster than a hummingbird's and I'd dropped all the weight I'd gained in Asia, and then some.

Two weeks earlier, we'd had our first date, kayaking on an "easy" section of the Chilliwack River after a day of planting. I'd paddled a kayak only twice in my life; once on a lake, and once the previous summer on the Similkameen River when I was an assistant instructor with Outward Bound. I'd dumped in the first thirty seconds and gone for a harrowing swim, pinned to the boat by the windbreaker I'd wrapped around my waist under my spray skirt.

The Chilliwack took me for a similar romp. I dumped in the first few seconds, got back in my boat, then dumped over and over again for the rest of the evening. By the time I flipped the final time, it was dark and I was so disoriented and hypothermic that I forgot how to get out of my boat. Instead of leaning forward, I arched back, scraping my face through the rocks on the bottom of the river before I finally remembered how to exit. I came up bleeding. After Brad hauled me out, he kissed me and said, "You're a tough one. I like that." The next day, I packed up my pup tent and blue, half-inch Ensolite pad, and moved into his eight-man canvas tent with the six-inch foamy.

"What about Becca and Shelly?" Cheryl asked.

"Over. Shelly's moved in with some guy in Canmore, and Becca moved out a while ago. To Revelstoke, I think."

"Just be careful. He likes the women."

I looked down at my boots. I wanted to stick my fingers in my ears and go *la-la-la-la-la-la* but I didn't want pesticides in any orifices.

Troy had told me the same thing but I'd chalked it up to jealousy. There were only eight women in camp this year and we'd all been snatched up during the annual tree-planting mating ritual.

"Brad's a free spirit. He just doesn't want anyone trying to control him." As an afterthought I said, "And so am I."

One last puff from my cigarette, then I squished it into the wet log. The ember went out with a hiss. I forced myself to my feet, strapped on my bags, grabbed my shovel. The weight of the wet trees dug into my shoulders, dragged down on my hips.

The calm water of the eddy rocked my kayak gently as I stared downstream at the logjam. Years of dead trees and branches—the length of five railway containers—were piled high like a massive complex of beaver condos. Sweepers. One of the most dreaded hazards on a river.

"That looks nasty," I said.

Brad bobbed in his kayak beside me, his blond curls stuck up through the holes in his helmet. This was my sixth time on the Chilliwack. We'd been paddling after planting but we finally had a day off so we were doing a longer stretch of the river.

"Just don't come out of your boat. Get aggro. And don't forget to lean downstream."

He powered through the eddy line, sliced across the current, and ferried into the middle of the river, still pointing upstream toward a surf wave. He caught it, started to carve back and forth, perfectly balanced, his kayak almost an extension of his body. Electricity jolted through my lower abdomen and almost winded me. He was so beautiful to watch.

A small tree flowed by in the rushing spring melt-off. It made a beeline for the logjam and got pinned there, blending in with the rest of the pile. I pulled my eyes away and studied the turbulent eddy line near my boat, visualized myself leaning downstream. *Downstream, downstream, downstream!* If I leaned the wrong way, the water would grab an edge and flip me.

After I'd set my boat on an angle, pointing upriver, I took three hard strokes with my paddle to cross the eddy line into the current. I did an upstream sweep to initiate the turn, but it shifted my weight in that same direction. Upstream, instead of downstream. The river flipped my kayak so fast I didn't have time to take a breath before I was over. The frigid water shocked out any air left in my lungs. I hung upside down in swirling blackness, plunged into a muffled roar. Leaning forward, I pulled the cord on my spray skirt and slid out of my kayak into the river.

When my head broke through the surface, I grabbed the end of my boat, but couldn't find my paddle. Brad was always telling me, *Never let go of your gear!* I twisted my body to look downstream, and there was the wall of logs. I was heading right for it. I let go of my boat, spun in the water, searching for Brad. He'd save me. He had always been right there, ready to pluck me out of the water. But he was paddling full-bore downstream, looking back over his shoulder at me, like a skier watching a partner disappear into an avalanche. I floated, like a piece of debris, at the mercy of the river.

My kayak got sucked under first. Disappeared. I took a deep breath before I, too, was pulled down, like an astronaut getting sucked out of her spaceship into the cosmos.

Everything went black. A churning, roaring black. My body tossed and scraped and sifted through branches. Water punched into my mouth, up my nose. I didn't know if my eyes were open or closed. Just before my lungs exploded, my head thrust through the surface and I gulped in air, then the sweepers swallowed me again, pulling me deeper under the branches. I popped up again, took a deep breath, and down I went, back into the abyss. Branches grabbed at my clothing, my spray skirt, my feet—like a sea of writhing, grasping arms. Up again for air. Slits of daylight, high above through the jumble of trees, teased me before I was sucked back down. Knocked back and forth like a pinball, my body squeezed its way though any opening large enough to allow it passage.

Suddenly, I jolted to a stop. The water tugged on my body, trying to pull me downstream, but I wasn't going anywhere. My helmet was jammed between two branches. I was stuck, totally submerged under a ton of dead trees. I wrenched my head back and forth, trying to twist free. I grabbed at my helmet, but my hands couldn't fight the onslaught of water. Terror gripped me, but I couldn't scream. Instinct took over and I snapped my neck back, like I was head-butting an attacker. My helmet wrenched free and I was moving again, sucked on through the churning blackness, till finally, my head thrust back through the surface. Air rushed into my lungs, screams rushed out.

"It's okay. You're safe. I've got you." Brad was there, beside me in his kayak, and I was bobbing away from the logjam. "Grab onto my boat."

My arms flopped against the fibreglass, useless, like prosthetics. I hooked one arm through the loop of rope in the stern and let it droop. A cut on my hand bled into the water.

Brad paddled for shore.

"You've got to learn to roll," Brad said as I stuffed a cream cheese and blueberry Danish into my mouth. You'd think *I'd* been the one to smoke a fatty that morning, not Brad.

We were sitting on the patio in the sun at my favourite bakery in the world, in one of my favourite rock climbing areas, Leavenworth, Washington. I'd been taking Brad climbing, and he'd been taking me out on the river.

A few days ago in Hope, we'd woken to snow—four inches of it on the lowest cut block. We couldn't plant until it melted, so we'd loaded Brad's orange Ford pickup with all the toys: kayaks, climbing gear, a unicycle, bike, juggling pins and a hacky sack, and headed south yelling, "Freedom from treedom!"

"As soon as you get your roll, you'll be able to look after yourself on the river."

I wasn't the only one rattled by the incident on the Chilliwack. Brad had readied himself to retrieve my body, just like a friend of his had had to do when his girlfriend accidentally went over a deadly waterfall near Whistler. I forced myself to paddle the next day because I knew if I didn't, I'd never paddle again. At first I was as stiff as a Barbie doll in my boat, but I loosened up eventually. Down here in Washington, I'd finally figured out upstream and downstream, which way to lean, how to ferry across the river, and yesterday I'd kayak-surfed my first wave.

"Don't you think it's pretty cold for rolling?" It was early May and there was still snow in the mountains.

The thought of intentionally flipping my kayak and hanging upside down in water wasn't too appealing. For three nights in a row after getting sucked under the sweepers, I'd woken up screaming from nightmares of being buried alive, sometimes in water, sometimes in snow. I'd discovered that one big difference between Brad and me was that I'd rather die falling off a mountain, and he'd rather drown.

"I can't keep rescuing you," he said.

Brad stood up to his waist in the lake in his wetsuit holding a paddle, while I sat in the kayak. The water felt like a melted glacier, which is exactly what it was, and I was supposed to tip upside down, reach around underwater and grab the paddle for leverage to flip myself back up.

"This is fucking freezing."

"Good incentive to learn quickly," Brad said.

He had such even, white teeth. With his wild, wiry blond curls and soft blue eyes, he was completely unlike Jim.

Tucking my head and body, I leaned forward and flipped my kayak. As soon as the water closed in around me I was back in the blackness, under the sweepers. I panicked, started thrashing around under water until Brad managed to hoist me back up. I spluttered and coughed as water poured off me.

"It's okay. Calm down. I'm right here."

My head pounded with an instant ice cream headache.

"Try again."

Staring into the water, I took a deep breath and flipped. I twisted my body, reached up, grabbed the paddle with both hands, and pulled. Brad still had to do most of the work.

"Try again. This time flick your hips more. Your head's the last thing out of the water."

I tipped myself over again, and instead of trying to escape the cold as quickly as possible, I hung upside down, my eyes wide open, focused on Brad's paddle, a wobbling line beyond the blue-green water. I reached up, grabbed the paddle and snapped my hips. My head came up last. Water streaming through my hair rushed into my huge grin.

"Fuckin' A!" I shouted.

"All right! You'll be rolling in no time." Brad thumped me on the back. "Let's try it a few more times, then I'll show you how to set up with the paddle."

Five submersions later Brad handed me the paddle, but I was shaking so hard I could barely hold onto it. To warm up, I paddled hard into the middle of the lake till I felt my muscles come back to life, turned and paddled back.

After Brad showed me how to set up—my paddle in the water, parallel to the boat—I leaned my body forward and tipped upside down. My hands punched through to air, and Brad guided my paddle in a skimming sweep across the surface of the water, from bow to stern. When my body was stretched out, almost lying back on my kayak, I flicked my hips and I was up.

"Oh my God! What an incredible feeling. Let's do it again!"

But after ten more tries, with Brad supporting my paddle less and less, I still couldn't roll on my own, and we were both in the early stages of hypothermia.

"Hot cocoa and peppermint schnapps." Brad's words quivered through blue lips.

"One more time. I know I can get it."

Plunging back in the water, I swept my paddle across the surface and I was up.

"I didn't touch your paddle that time," Brad said. I could hear the approval in his voice.

I was shuddering with cold, sporting a headache worse than any hangover I'd ever had, and the words *I love you* banged against the back of my chattering teeth. But I fought them off. Even I knew three weeks was too early for that.

I threw my arms around him instead.

6

BUGABOO

Scrambling along the knife-edge Northeast Ridge of Bugaboo Spire, I eyeballed the two thousand feet of air between me and the glacier. Oceans of white surrounded us, as though we were marooned on top of a pointy, barren island of granite. I felt a brief jolt of panic as I fought off a bizarre urge to jump, and forced myself to focus on where I wanted to go, not where I didn't want to go. It was what Brad kept telling me on the river.

Ronnie edged along carefully just ahead of me, the coiled rope over his shoulder. We'd finished the technical climbing, about twelve pitches of solid hand and finger cracks, and we were now scrambling, unroped, between the north and south summits.

Ronnie was Brad's best friend. I'd paddled with him a lot, but this was our first climbing trip together. Brad was scared of heights so he hadn't joined us. A few years earlier, he'd almost died climbing with Ronnie. Brad and a girl they were with had slid right off the edge of a mountain and Ronnie had managed to dig his axe into the ice and save them both. Brad had followed me up a few rock climbs over the summer, but he would never go into the alpine again. So he was back at his place in Fernie.

Fernie is a cute little mountain town in southern BC. When I finished tree planting in June, I'd gone straight there with Brad, and now I couldn't imagine living anywhere else. It had a ski hill, mountains and rivers. It was the dream home I'd fantasized about on my drive from Calgary to Hope.

Ronnie and I moved quickly along the ridge. Many parties got "benighted" up here, and we didn't want to be one of them. We'd left our campsite six hours earlier and still had the tricky descent down the Kain Route ahead of us, with some very airy downclimbing and several rappels before we would even reach the glacier. And then there was the bergschrund—a huge crevasse—to cross before we could do the snow descent back to our tent. But I was feeling strong. The climber in me was back. We'd swung leads on the roped section, and I'd led the crux pitch. Up here I didn't feel like a rookie floating behind an expert like I did on the river with Brad. Up here I was "one of the boys."

We stopped at the gendarme, a tooth of rock jutting out from the ridge.

"We start rappelling here," Ronnie said.

With my head stuck through a "V" slot, I looked down. The rock was overhanging. It would be a steep rappel. The blood in my temples pumped against my helmet. I could count the beats of my heart without even taking my pulse.

The guidebook had said that *bugaboo* meant "an object of obsession, usually exaggerated fear or anxiety," but this wasn't fear. Just excitement. It was the same rush I got when I could hear the roar of rapids around a corner on the river, but climbing didn't have the same bowel-releasing quality. It was pure, pleasurable adrenalin. Like a fix. This was what had been missing in my life. I'd spent the spring and summer paddling with Brad and my roll was now bomber, but I was always on the edge of my ability. I felt like a climber in a boat, not a real paddler. It was Brad's sport, not mine. I needed the mountains.

We took off our packs and hunkered down for a quick snack, munching in silence as we stared out at the Purcell Mountains. The massive granite pyramids of the Bugaboo range jutted up against blue hazy peaks that stretched all the way to the horizon. Turquoise lakes looked like puddles a few thousand feet below, as though we were staring down from an airplane. The Himalayas of British Columbia. It had been one of my dreams to come to the Bugaboos, ever since I'd started climbing. World-class rock climbing in an alpine setting.

"So, you and Brad seem to be doing well," Ronnie said as he passed me the water bottle.

Brad and I had been together now for three months. It was my longest relationship apart from my year with Jim, and none of the intensity had worn off.

"Yeah. I don't think I've ever felt this way before. It's like I've found my soulmate."

I washed my chocolate bar down with fluorescent-orange Tang. The sugar buzzed through my veins.

"Good," he said, and I hoped he meant it. But I knew he didn't think I was a good match for his friend, that I was too possessive.

Ronnie stood and started to uncoil the rope. His sleeves were pushed up to his elbows and his forearms bulged in the typical climber fashion. He was a talented guy. A pilot, avalanche forecaster, paddler, climber, skier, hang glider. The kind of guy I was normally drawn to: dark, remote, hairy-armed, older than me. The Heathcliff type. I

END OF THE ROPE ᴳ 75

took it as a good sign that I was finally attracted to someone like Brad—sensitive, able to talk about his feelings, an attentive lover. I felt safer around his blondness, his stature (under six feet), his age (only four years older than me). Finally, I'd chosen a man who was good for me.

"Brad thought we'd end up sleeping together on this trip," Ronnie said.

The saliva in my mouth dried up and I couldn't swallow the last of my chocolate. I grabbed the water bottle again, took a swig.

"You and me?"

Brad had actually given me his blessing to sleep with Ronnie before I left, but I'd thought he was joking. We were only out for two nights, and I was pretty sure we could all survive that long without sex.

"Don't worry. That's just Brad. He's a free spirit. I'm sure you know what you're getting into."

"Hey, I'm a free spirit too. The last thing I want is some guy telling me where I can go and what I can do. Been there, done that."

"Good," Ronnie said. "Just making sure."

Brad had told me he was into "unconditional love," by which he meant free love, but I knew he wasn't going to want to sleep with anyone else. He was in love with me. He'd already told me. I'd been paddling bigger and bigger water and once, as I'd surfed a big wave, I'd caught a glimpse of his grin of approval as he sat in the eddy, watching. But I did worry that we hadn't yet talked about what was going to happen at the end of the summer. My tree-planting money was drying up. I'd have to figure out my winter soon.

The sky, solid blue all day, now looked like a blue-grey sheet slowly being pulled over a skylight.

"Altostratus clouds. We shouldn't hang out too long. They mean bad weather."

We threw the ends of the ropes down the rock wall and I set myself up to rappel. Because I couldn't turn sideways with my pack on, I squeezed through the narrow slot face first, staring down through two thousand feet of air. Feeding rope through my rappel device, I swung out, hanging free a few feet from the overhanging wall. Never touching rock, I spun all the way down, a hundred and fifty dizzying feet to the first ledge.

The next afternoon, on our way back to Fernie, I noticed a familiar white van parked on the side of the road at the takeout for the Elk River, just west of town. Straps for kayaks hung from the empty roof rack. I steered my Dart slowly past. There seemed to be a mottled black-and-white cow pattern on the seat covers but I had to turn my eyes back on the road before I was sure. I watched the van in my rear-view mirror.

"Isn't that Shelly's van?" I said.

"I don't know. Could be." Ronnie stared out the window.

We continued east toward the Rocky Mountains and Fernie, and a few minutes later, I pulled up beside Brad's truck in front of the sun-faded brown house. He lived in the basement suite.

The place was empty, so I grabbed a couple of beers and Ronnie and I started sorting climbing gear on the front lawn. Soon the big white van rolled up—with kayaks on top, one of them Brad's—and parked right behind the truck. My breath sucked in sharply as Shelly and Brad stepped out.

"Jan!" Shelly said.

"Shelly!" I synchronized my expression to my friendly voice. "I haven't seen you in ages!"

I hadn't seen her since my first season of tree planting.

We hugged, my face squashed against her chest. She was like an Amazon, sturdy, the same height as Brad, with long, straight, almost white-blond hair. While she hugged Ronnie, Brad hugged me. I wanted to melt into his familiarity, but I couldn't. I stood rigidly, arms at my sides, then pulled away.

"So that *was* your van on the side of the highway. I thought I recognized the cow print seats."

"Just passing through on my way to Canmore. Thought I'd get in a quick paddle." On top of the van, her big plastic kayak looked like a monstrosity compared to Brad's high-performance fibreglass boat. She wasn't a serious paddler. She liked to float.

"I hear you moved in with a boyfriend." My smile was congealed on my face.

"Yes, yes. With Mark."

We stood there looking at each other, till Shelly finally said, "Well, I better get going. I've got to get home."

"I'll grab my boat," Brad said.

I turned to Ronnie, "I'll get a couple more beers," and escaped down the stairwell into the dim basement. I couldn't watch Brad say goodbye to her.

As I headed toward the kitchen, I noticed through the door of the bedroom that the waterbed was stripped, which was unusual. In my two months in Fernie, Brad had never changed the bed, never cleaned a toilet, never vacuumed. And I'd thought *I* was a slob.

The sheets were crumpled on the floor at the base of the bed. I nudged them with my sandal. I wanted to hold them up to the light, check them for stains like they used to check sheets for blood after the wedding night.

A few days earlier, I'd been wearing one of Brad's jackets and pulled a tiny piece of paper out of the pocket. On it, he'd written out a Van Morrison verse, about rocking a gypsy soul, and he'd written Shelly's name a few times below, but I'd thought the paper was old. Pre-me.

Brad came up behind me. "Hey." He wrapped his arms around my waist, pulled me against him, but I shook free, turned on him.

"Did you sleep with her?"

He only hesitated a moment. "Yes, I slept with her. You know Shelly and I have a special connection."

A groan slipped out before I could stop it, the sound of a wounded animal. I tried to step around him to get to the door. I wanted my car, something familiar and loyal. I wanted to curl up in the back seat and cry where no one could see me. "I'll start packing up my stuff."

He blocked my way. "It doesn't have to be like that. I love Shelly, but I love you. Don't you believe you can love two people at the same time?"

"I don't know." I wrapped my arms around my head. It was starting to hurt. "I don't know anything." When he'd told me he was into "unconditional love," I'd agreed in theory, but here it was in reality and it didn't feel like love at all.

"Come here. Talk to me." He pulled me into the living room onto his ratty orange couch.

"When we met, you said you'd never let anyone control you again," he said. "You said you wanted to be wild and free."

It was true. I remembered that conversation. Diatribe was more like it. How I'd never get sucked into a middle-class existence again, how it was a thinly disguised form of enslavement.

"You said you'd never shave your legs for a guy again. I liked that."

A tiny laugh slipped out as I looked down at my shaggy legs. But I'd noticed that Shelly's legs were smooth and hairless.

"We're the same kind of people, you and me. We're free spirits. That's why we're together."

My body loosened up and I leaned against him, remembering how, on my way to Hope that first week back in Canada, I'd stopped on the side of the Thompson River—a river I'd since paddled with Brad—and made a vow to never depend on a man again. Brad would not let that happen.

"I love you," Brad said. "I want you to stay. We can ski all winter, kayak all summer."

And then he was kissing me, and I was letting him. All I could think was, *I have a home!* My relief was like a flash flood in the desert, surging through me.

We moved back to the bedroom, peeling off our clothes, fell on the bed. The water swayed me, like I was in my kayak bobbing in an eddy. The bare plastic mattress was cold against my skin so I rolled on top of him, dissolved into his warmth.

7

WORLD'S TOUGHEST
MILKMAN

Yosemite National Park, 4 Miles. The green highway sign whizzed past. Geoff shifted down to second gear and the Volkswagen van heaved and whined up another steep hill. Beside him, Rory was fixated on the scenery, waiting for a glimpse of the massive walls of granite. It was his first trip to Yosemite, so we'd made sure he got the front seat.

This was my fourth trip to the valley, and Geoff probably couldn't count how many times he'd been. This time I was heading south to escape not only the early snows of Canada and the loose Rockies limestone, but also Brad.

"Christ, I can't believe it. We might actually make it." There was a hint of excitement in Geoff's voice, but none of us would relax until we actually pulled into the campsite.

"Never doubted it for a moment." Rory patted the dashboard and twisted around to look at me on the seat at the back of the van.

Geoff snorted like he was choking on a burrito. "Right."

This was our sixth day into a journey that should have taken twenty-four hours. We'd left Calgary in a blinding snowstorm, in Geoff's van with a classically inept VW heater, waving and smiling in kinship at other VW vans and their frozen, parka-clad occupants before breaking down three hours later in front of a gas station at Radium Hot Springs. With a new clutch, we headed south, only to break down in Reno. With new brakes, generator and flywheel, and our sense of humour drying up, we headed back out on the road, only to break down fifteen miles south at Carson City. Every time Geoff pulled out his charge card his already sharply angled face got more haggard.

I undid my seat belt and moved up to squat between the two front seats, supporting myself with the armrests. We passed through a tunnel of ponderosa pines, way bigger than our spindly little lodge-pole pines in the Rockies, then the road plunged steeply downhill.

"I sure hope the brake guy in Reno knew what he was doing," I said.

Rory looked at me with a gentle smile that moistened my eyes. Red tufts around his ears and the nape of his neck were all that was left of his hair, but what was lacking on his head he made up for with his bushy red beard. Our winter affair a few years back hadn't affected our friendship, though he hadn't been too popular with his girlfriend because of it. At the time I hadn't felt any responsibility for her reaction, since I'd only met the woman once. But now I knew better. Brad had taught me well.

Rory ran his hand lightly over my hair. "How's the heart?"

"The farther I get from the shithead, the better it feels."

My tough words wouldn't fool my friends. They'd seen me like this before. After saying goodbye to my Alaskan mountain guide. After the adventure with Jim in Indonesia. Whenever I came hobbling back to Alberta with a broken heart my friends were always there for me. Usually I bounced back quickly, but this time I was losing more than just a boyfriend. I was losing my home in Fernie, my paddling community, my ski hill job, and my best friend, Dede, who'd been my confidante through all of Brad's indiscretions until she became one of them herself.

The Merced River to our right gushed white through the gorge and I felt the familiar pull of the rapids. Before I left Fernie, I'd contemplated jumping up and down on my kayak, the one Brad had given me, leaving it smashed in the front yard to symbolize what he'd done to my heart. Instead, I left the words to a Bonnie Raitt song on the kitchen table: *That ain't no way to treat a lady. That ain't no way to treat a woman in love.* I strapped my kayak to my Dodge Dart and escaped back to Calgary, and I'd been couch surfing ever since.

The first person to take me in had been Laurel, who'd been a friend since our summer together as counsellors at Camp Chief Hector four years earlier. She'd just split up with her boyfriend, so we'd drunk cider and danced to hurtin' music, laughing and crying to "Your Cheatin' Heart" and "Love Don't Care Whose Heart It Breaks."

Next I crashed at the big heritage house down the road from Laurel that Geoff, Rory, Saul and Martha, all friends from their McGill University days, were renting. But I couldn't tolerate the city for long and headed back to the mountains to Canmore to room with Dave, my old NOLS buddy, and two Outward Bound instructors, in a condo we dubbed Heartbreak Hotel, because we'd all recently been dumped. But I couldn't keep sharing a king-sized bed with two guys I wasn't even having sex with, so I'd lined up another place with Sharon (the first accredited female mountain guide in Canada, whom I'd met a couple of years earlier) and soon I'd have a whole loft bedroom to myself.

Rory wound down his window and a flood of memories hit me with the dry scent of pine. I loved California. It felt right to be here, to put my focus back on climbing. For the past year and a half I'd latched onto Brad's life. It was time to be a climber again.

"There she is!" Geoff pointed, as the pale granite of El Capitan peeked through the trees and then disappeared.

El Cap kept teasing us with glimpses of her brilliance till all of a sudden we dropped into the valley and there she was. White granite walls swelled three thousand feet from the valley floor, towering over the hundred-foot forests. On my first trip to Yosemite, Geoff and Saul had made me cover my eyes until El Cap had come into view for the full impact.

Rory let out a long, sinking whistle. "Well, I'll be damned. . . ."

We followed the Merced River—now slow, wide and subdued, unrecognizable from the wild turbulence just miles behind. Cliffs lined both sides of the valley, waterfalls gushed white foam over the edges, six hundred feet to the valley floor. We passed El Cap Meadow, a quarter-mile stretch of grass where climbers and tourists hung out with coolers of beer and binoculars to watch big wall climbers crawl up El Cap's face. Most of the routes took several days to climb.

"Looks like a couple guys on the Shield," Geoff said, his neck out the window, eyes half on the road, half on the rock. Rory and I squinted to bring the tiny red and yellow splotches, like squished bugs, into focus, about 1,500 feet up the face—halfway.

Gary, my Alaskan mountain guide, had been part of the first ascent of the Shield in the early '70s, about the time I was in grade six in Whitehorse. I had no aspirations to do a big wall climb anymore. It didn't seem to be in the stars for me. Two years earlier I'd made two failed attempts on the South Face of Washington Column here in the Valley. The first time, with Karin, a Swedish friend, I got halfway up. We climbed the hardest part, the Kor Roof, then left our ropes up and rapped back down to Dinner Ledge to spend the night. The next morning a Parisian couple who were also doing the route woke early and snuck up their ropes ahead of us. They were so slow we had to bail before we ran out of water. I made a second attempt at the same route with Jim on our compatibility-testing trip, and we'd screamed at each other for a few pitches till we finally rapped off. Now I just wanted to be able to lead moderate routes without shitting myself.

While Geoff steered us toward the campgrounds, I settled into the back seat, plugged my earphones into my ears, cranked my Walkman. All the way from Canada, Rory and Geoff had been hassling me about my singing too loudly to my Walkman. It was like hanging out with two big brothers, except they'd never given me a nosebleed, or painted my face with model paints, or emptied an ashtray down the back of my jeans.

"How does it feel to be on your own," Bob Dylan whined in stereo. I tried not to sing along. I tried not to cry.

Smearing my rock shoe on a tiny edge, I locked my fingers into the crack. They sank past the second knuckle. I did three moves up before panic seized me and I reversed the process, three moves down, till my feet were back on the ground.

"This is fucking hard."

"It looks desperate." Rory eyeballed the crack that went for a hundred and thirty feet to a big ledge. This was one of the hardest leads I'd ever attempted. After three days in the valley, I was climbing better than I'd expected to after too much time in a kayak and not enough on the rock. I'd done some good leads and followed Geoff up a few really hard routes. I knew this climb was well within my physical ability. I just had to convince my brain of it.

"Jan. You can do this one. Just trust yourself," Geoff said.

Trust myself. Right. How the hell could I trust myself after Brad? Brad and Dede's betrayal of me wasn't nearly as bad as my own betrayal of me. I'd stayed, like a kicked puppy waiting for another kick, for a whole week, trying to convince him to pick me. When Brad finally decided he was in love with Dede, not me, I'd felt dismissed. Erased.

I turned back to the rock, unclipped a small stopper from my rack and put it between my teeth.

"Okay, I'll try again," I slurred through the metal cable.

With my fingers crammed into the crack, I moved up the same three moves, but this time I managed to slot the stopper far above my head. I reached below me and pulled up the rope, clipped it into the carabiner.

"Yeah!" Rory hooted. "All right! Keep going!"

I leaned out from the face, with three fingers of each hand sunk up to the knuckles in the rock, the rubber of my shoes smeared on pebble-sized nubbins, and studied the crack. The belay ledge looked very far away.

I knew I could power over these hard moves—it was a short section—but could I stay in control of my fear all the way to the anchor? I was a sprinter, psychologically speaking, not a long-distance type.

A familiar tremor in my legs. I started my retreat.

"No, no, don't come down!" Geoff said. He was getting tired of my waffling.

I stepped back onto the ground. Shook out my arms.

"You're going to fry your fingers if you keep doing that," Geoff said.

"No fucking kidding."

My hormones were either raging with PMS or Brad-withdrawal. Maybe the problem was sex. Or the lack of it. I'd gone seven whole weeks without Brad, and now he and Dede were probably humping like rabbits all day and all night, like we used to.

I felt myself curl up inside. Those two had knocked something out of me and I didn't know how to get it back.

"Jesus." Geoff put his head in his hands, rubbed his forehead. The exhausting process of urging me up my leads was hard on my belayers, but Geoff was a psychologist. He should have been used to people like me.

Rage burned through me, at Geoff, at Brad, but mostly at myself. I knew I had to lead this route. Since I was no longer the girlfriend of an extreme whitewater kayaker, if I couldn't climb, there was nothing setting me apart from any other waitress or tree planter or trail-crew worker. Climbing was all I had left.

"Fuck, fuck, fuck!" I pounded on the rock with my fist, then kicked it till pain shot through my foot and snapped me out of my funk. Breaking my foot on the rock was not the way to get to the top of this climb.

Geoff and Rory snuck a look at each other. Geoff's eyes rolled slightly.

"I saw that," I said.

"Jan, just go for it. You've been climbing great. I know you can do it." Rory's gentle voice calmed me.

Facing the rock, I filled my belly with air, let anger balloon in me till there was no room left for fear. The trick was to use my anger and angst to get up the climb, not to let it deflate me.

With my fingers crammed into the crack, I climbed past my piece of protection, placed another stopper a few feet above the first, paused. My protection was good; it had slotted perfectly into the crack, so I was protected from a ground fall. I felt strong from kayaking all summer, from another trip to the Bugaboos before the Brad-Dede debacle. I knew I could do this.

I reached high, locked my fingers and powered through the hard moves, then slapped in another stopper, climbed past that protection and kept climbing. The hesitation was gone, but this wasn't the Zen-like state of calm, control and quiet that other climbers seemed to achieve. I wasn't "at one" with the rock. I was in a rage. Images ricocheted around in my head: Brad taking Dede down the river in a two-man kayak, chatting away, while I paddled my one-man kayak. I should have known. I'd been warned. Dede hadn't been the first. She'd just been the first to replace me.

The crack widened to hand-sized, then wider, almost too big for my fists. It was not my favourite kind of climbing, but my momentum didn't falter, even when I ran out of bigger pieces of protection and had to downclimb a few feet, retrieve my last piece, place it above my new piece, leap-frogging them up the crack. My life depended on two large pieces of metal and I didn't give a shit. I didn't want to die, necessarily, but I wanted to live a bit less now than I had before.

The campfire crackled and spluttered and bits of flaming wood popped out at the climbers sitting in the dirt, circled around the warmth. They were talking climbing. Miming climbing, more like it. They bounced off their butts, their scabbed-up hands gripping imaginary holds above their heads, their faces contorted into exaggerated expressions of terror.

"Shit, that second pitch was fucking awesome."

"Did you see Ian cruise the crux of . . ."

"I had a manky finger lock and had to dyno for that jug . . ."

"And then I got a heel hook . . ."

One of the guys lifted a long leg, swathed in fluorescent green Lycra, to feign hooking his heel on a hold above his head.

Most of these guys were from Banff. The top rock climbers in Canada. I'd always hung out with the Calgary crowd, a more well-rounded bunch of climbers who wore cotton climbing pants, not Lycra. Who had professions and university degrees and long-term relationships. Some even owned houses. These Banff climbers didn't seem to work very often. They just climbed.

I didn't know where I fit in this world anymore. Maybe somewhere in limbo between the groups, because my life combined the least desirable qualities of both: I worked as little as possible, just long enough to qualify for unemployment insurance so I could climb or kayak; I wore red, disintegrating rugby pants, not Lycra; I had no profession, didn't have a degree, didn't have a home.

"Well, I think I'll crash." Geoff slapped his thighs and rose from his lawn chair.

Rory had retired to his tent ages ago to read. This was not his scene at all. He listened to classical music, wrote poetry, and spent his money on multivolume dictionaries. Geoff could fit in easily with these guys because he had a reputation as a hard climber. Rory was more an all-round mountain guy, a hiker and backcountry skier.

My can of beer was still half full, so I stayed at the picnic table. If I went to my tent too early, I'd be alone in the dark with my thoughts: of Dede strutting around my house in Brad's clothes, cooking in my kitchen, sleeping with him in our waterbed. She didn't even kayak or climb. But she was a lot of fun. Maybe that was the attraction. Someone who wouldn't wave books like *You and Your Pot Addiction* in his face.

"Night." A chorus went up around the fire as Geoff headed to his van.

With Geoff and Rory here I'd felt comfortable, but now I felt very single. I was too far away from the group around the fire, but I didn't want to move closer. I was just about to stand and head to my tent when one of the Banff climbers, a big guy with neatly cut, wiry blond hair and the typical climber's ape arms, got up and walked over to me. The black-and-white zebra stripes of his Lycra accentuated his massive quads. Skier's legs. Most serious rock climbers tried to keep their legs skinny as kindling so they'd have less weight to haul up. He looked more like an alpine climber.

"Hey, Jan, right?" He stood awkwardly beside the picnic table. "My name's Dan. Dan Guthrie."

"Yeah, I remember." He was one of the guys that had shown up at the cliff today to cheer me on.

"Mind if I sit? My butt's going numb on the ground."

Yes, I do mind, was what I wanted to say. I'd noticed him stealing glances this way and I was pretty sure he hadn't been looking at Geoff.

"Go ahead." I took out my pouch of Drum tobacco and rolling papers and started rolling a cigarette.

"Nasty habit."

"Yup." I ignored his attempt at humour. I didn't feel like being nice to him. I wondered what he'd think if I'd stuffed a wad of Copenhagen into my lip instead of rolling a cigarette.

Licking the edge of the paper, I glanced at him. He was a good-looking guy. Big features, but not unappealingly so. White-blond hair. Blue, squinty eyes. Squinty in a nice way, as though he were looking into the sun. He was probably my age or a little older, which was too young for my taste. But what type of man was to my taste? Mildly abusive? Either too controlling or out of control. A sex addict?

My last annual trip to Ottawa had shed some light on my string of doomed relationships. My mother had sent me to her counsellor, who had handed me a list of characteristics of an Adult Child of an Alcoholic. I'd ticked every single box, except for the one about being super responsible, but one really stood out for me: *ACOAs are extremely loyal, even in the face of evidence that the loyalty is undeserved.* Further proof that I had to stay away from men.

"Nice lead on Sherri's Crack today," Dan said.

"Thanks." I lit up my cigarette. A smidgen of pleasure crept in. I'd felt strong on that climb. Once I'd gotten off the ground. One of my hardest leads yet. Luckily, the Banff crowd hadn't shown up until I was most of the way up and thus missed my rock-kicking hissy fit.

When the smoke hit my lungs, I coughed. It had been almost two years since I'd last smoked, since tree planting. I wasn't sure why I was doing this to myself. Maybe it was the image. Tough. No one could hurt me. No one but myself.

"It's a hard route," Dan said.

I blew out a long stream of smoke. "Should I stick to the easier ones?"

"No, no, that's not what I meant. It's just . . . there's not a lot of girls . . . er, women. . . . It's just . . . you looked really good." I seemed to make him uncomfortable. I seemed to *want* to make him uncomfortable.

"So you just moved back to Canmore?" He probably already knew everything about me. There weren't too many female climbers, especially single ones, and word got around quickly.

"Yeah, my boyfriend's fucking my best friend so I didn't have much choice." I took a swig of beer and glared at him, like he was somehow responsible because he belonged to the wrong half of the human race. But the truth was, I fantasized more about strangling Dede than Brad.

"Gee, that's too bad." He looked at a loss for words. I felt a bit sorry for him.

"I'm crashing at a condo with Colin and Dave and Neil until I move in with Sharon." Sharon was about to become the first North American woman on Everest, if all went as planned, so all these guys knew who she was. "Rafael had a wee fling in base camp so she kicked him out," I added, choosing to ignore that fact that Colin, Dave and Neil had been betrayed too. By women.

"That's weird. Seems to be an epidemic. My girlfriend started screwing around on me too. With some tubby bald dude." He shook his head like he couldn't believe she'd pick someone like that over him. I found it hard to believe myself. He really was quite cute. Like a little boy trapped in a big man's body.

"I was just back from climbing in Squamish," he said. "Driving down Banff Avenue, and there they were, kissing on the side of the road. What are the odds of that?"

He looked so sad I almost reached out to put my hand on his arm, but I took a drag off my cigarette instead. Encouraging him would do no one any good. He was a nice, decent guy. I'd been with a couple of nice guys before, including Rory, and it hadn't worked out. But then again, it hadn't worked out with the not-nice guys either.

We sat quietly for a moment. I forced myself not to fill the silence with inane chatter like I normally did.

"So, looks like we're both single." He grinned, revealing a chipped front tooth, the same side as mine. His blue eyes arched into dark crescents under white-blond eyebrows, and a dimple appeared in his chin.

"Yeah, and planning to stay that way." I spat out a piece of tobacco. My cigarette seemed to be unravelling. "I'm taking a hiatus from men."

After today's climbing, I was starting to think the key for me was to stay single. The more angst-ridden I was, the better I seemed to climb.

"Can I give you a call when we're back in Alberta?"

This guy was just not getting it. He was like a friendly St. Bernard who thought everyone liked slobber. How could he be so optimistic and upbeat while his girlfriend was fucking around with some little bald-headed guy?

"Probably not a good idea."

"Well, where will you be working?"

"I might have a job waiting tables at the Rose and Crown." Why was I telling him this?

"Too bad they get their dairy from the competition. I'm the Alpha milkman. You know, like the World's Toughest Milkman." He flexed his biceps and I could see them push against the fleece of his jacket.

I laughed, in spite of myself. "I have no idea what you're talking about."

"Like the comic strip. You've never heard of the World's Toughest Milkman? I have a copy on the back of the toilet at my place."

There was a steep climb with a big roof in Squamish called the World's Toughest Milkman. When I'd led it a couple of years ago I'd hyperventilated with fear. Must have been named after the same comic.

"So you're a milkman? For real?"

"Yeah, it's a great job. Starts at five a.m., finishes by eleven. I climb the rest of the day and can still pay my mortgage."

He has his own house?

I took another swig of beer and burped. Just a medium-sized burp, not an offensive one.

"That's real ladylike."

"Do I look like a fucking lady?" The words popped out before I could stop them. A harshness that wasn't meant for him.

He watched me for a moment. "That guy sure did a number on you."

My throat constricted and I took another drag, then rubbed my cigarette out with the heel of my sandal. If I started crying I'd never get to sleep and we were planning to do some hard routes on the Cookie Cliff in the morning.

When I looked back up, our eyes met. For several seconds, neither of us could look away. When we finally did, I felt like we'd shared something profound, but I had no idea why. He wasn't even my type.

8

FRAGILE ICE

The snow had been trampled flat by dozens of ice climbers over the past couple of months, and my plastic mountain boots crunched with every step. Dan's steady *crunch crunch* ahead of me sounded out of sync with my quick *crunch-crunch-crunch-crunch*. If I moved my legs any faster I'd be jogging. The Bow River, partially locked in ice, flowed beside us, and Mount Rundle rose above the trees to our right, streaked with vertical lines of frozen ice. No time to stop and enjoy the scenery. We had slept in, snuggled up in Dan's bed, not wanting to go out into the crispy winter, so we were off to an "alpine start" at ten in the morning.

"Here we go!" Dan called back over his pack as he turned off the path and followed some footprints into the trees. The trail angled uphill here and soon we broke out into a gully, where we stood for a moment on snow-covered ice, water trickling deep below our feet. A hundred metres ahead we could see the first three tiers of the water-fall. The Professor Falls, named for the University of Calgary profes-sor who had kept falling on the first ascent. We trudged to the base of the rock and stood under the first tier. Forty metres of blue frozen water, as though a fairy had waved a magic wand and turned it to ice mid-splash. It was steep. But I knew it wasn't as steep as the pitch at the very top, the one we couldn't see from here.

I'd had only one real season of ice climbing, mostly with Jim, and that was almost three years ago.

"Looks pretty steep," I said.

"Ah, you'll cruise it," Dan said. "I solo this all the time. Best time was two hours and forty-five minutes from my door."

"Jesus!" I looked at my watch. We'd left over an hour and a half ago.

"That was on a mountain bike," Dan added.

We threw down our packs and pulled out the gear. I slipped into my harness and strapped my crampons to my boots. Dan clipped half a dozen ice screws to his harness and uncoiled the rope, then snapped on his foot fangs in half the time it took me to do up the leather straps on my metal crampons. Foot fangs were the new rage in the ice climbing community: metal points on a plastic base. They didn't adjust to the size of my boots, though, because the outdoor industry still hadn't twigged to the fact that women climbed mountains.

Dan had had a near-disaster with them the first time out. He'd come up here to solo Professor on early-season ice, "a web of icicles and air," as he'd described it, so thinly formed it barely held a person's weight. Partway up, one of his new foot fangs popped off and he'd struggled to get it back on without falling. He knew he should have gone down, but he wanted to just look at the last crux pitch, and on the way, his foot fang had fallen off a second time. Another little hint that maybe he should retreat. But no, he'd decided to do the crux after all. The foot fang stuck it out for that pitch but fell off a half dozen more times on the descent. "Good thing it didn't come off on the crux, though," he'd said.

That had been only three months ago. He'd let me read the pages in his climbing journal: "I was going to dance my own ice dance by myself, a reflection of my personal state: climbing alone and sleeping alone." His former girlfriend had moved in with that "tubby bald-headed dude," and at that point I was still turning down his offers of dinner, or an ice climb, or a ski together at Lake Louise.

I unhooked my ice axes from my pack, old tools I'd bought second-hand a few years ago.

"I have a present for you." Dan was vibrating with excitement, as though I'd just told him I had a present for *him*. He reached into his pack. "Your birthday present."

"My birthday's not till the end of the month."

"I know. I'll get you another one then."

He handed me a brand new Stubai ice axe. It was made for technical ice, a huge improvement over my two clunkers. It was much shorter, with a steep, serrated pick that could dig easily into the ice, and a bent handle so you wouldn't bash your knuckles. Big, ugly, bruised knuckles were the sign of an avid ice climber.

"I set the wrist loop up like mine," he said. He'd slid an extra rainbow-coloured sling over the wrist loop to keep it from biting into my skin.

"Oh my God! These are over a hundred dollars!" My last paycheque at the restaurant had been $175 for two weeks, and tips had barely doubled that. I grabbed the tool and swung it above my head. "It's beautiful!"

"I get a good discount." Dan had given up his milk route for a job as manager of an outdoor store in Banff. "Do I get a kiss from my girl?"

My girl. I still felt like Brad's girl, six months after leaving Fernie. But Dede was Brad's girl now. I stood on my front points with the hand holding my new ice axe wrapped around Dan's neck and gave him a noisy kiss on the lips, then shoved one of my old axes into my pack. It would be a good spare.

Dan had shown the same persistence courting me as he had climbing this waterfall with a faulty foot fang. He would come into the Rose and Crown while I was waitressing, and the cook would say, "Your milkman's here again," and there was Dan, sitting on a blue milk crate at the back of the kitchen, his Alpha Milk truck parked outside. I'd finally agreed to dinner at Georgio's in Banff, which led to too much wine, which led to my inability to drive home to Canmore, which led to spending the night, which led to us becoming an item. Jan and Dan. He was tickled pink. I was conflicted. Waffling. One foot in, one foot out. He'd said, "Come on. If you don't end up with me, you'll end up with some other guy anyway." Which was probably true.

As I slipped the rope through my belay device, Dan swung his tools above his head, sinking them with a dull thud into the ice. "It's in good shape," he said.

He stepped up the ice, pulled out his tool and swung again, first one, then the other, dancing his way up the waterfall. He climbed the way he skied. In complete control. Expending only as much energy as he needed to.

A vapour mushroom billowed from my mouth as I breathed out the glacial air. I pulled my neck tube over my face, breathed through the old saliva-smelling nylon. Stamped my feet to keep my toes alive. Fed out the rope. Belaying was the worst part of ice climbing. Standing in one spot, trying not to freeze to death. It was also hard on the back. I bent over sideways, trying to stretch it out.

Dan pulled over the lip at the top and disappeared onto the flat section between tiers, off to find the bolt anchor. He hadn't put in one ice screw as protection. He was only tied into the rope so he could bring me up.

"I'm off belay," he yelled, and started pulling up the slack. He'd used most of the 150 feet of rope. When it went tight on my harness, I started climbing.

Stretching high, I swung my new ice axe with a flick of my wrist. The dull *thunk* meant a secure placement. Then with my old ice axe I swung one, two, three times before I got a good placement. Kicking my front points into the ice, I stepped up, keeping my feet flat, trying to hang off straight arms to conserve energy. I'd learned some technique from a three-day ice climbing course with the Yamnuska Mountain School four years ago, back when I'd had big plans to become a badass female ice climber. It hadn't taken long to figure out climbing rock in the sunshine was a more pleasurable way to go.

Tap tap tap. Tap tap tap, tap tap. It took several tries to get each axe in this time. To me, the ice was brittle. To Dan, because it was more than a few inches thick, it was "primo." I scrabbled instead of danced my feet up, forgetting to drop my heels. The waterfall was so steep I could have stuck out my tongue and licked it. The higher I got, the more difficult the axe placements, and I sent off cascades of shards as I dug for a secure hold. My calves felt like they were being branded and my hands were numb from my death-grip on my tools. The only upper-body strength training I'd done since my fall trip to Yosemite had been holding a tray full of food over my shoulder, and that had exercised only my left arm.

"This is fucking steep!" I yelled up. No response. He either couldn't hear me, or he was choosing not to. He had a tendency to ignore me at times, which was irritating. I knew he couldn't figure me out. Hot and cold. One day, willing to fall in love, staying over at his place in Banff; the next, retreating to my loft bedroom in Canmore, curled up with my book, *The Cinderella Complex,* and yellow highlighter pen, half hoping he'd given up on me.

Finally, at the top, I pulled myself over the lip onto flat ice. Dan was at the base of the next tier, another steep bulge of ice, about the same height as this one. He was stamping his feet, trying to keep warm.

"There's my sweetie!"

He was grinning a full-face grin, hunched over slightly, probably trying to keep his core warm but it made him look like he was taking a little bow. He was so open about his feelings for me. On our first unofficial date I'd made him a breakfast omelette at my place halfway through his milk run. We'd kissed, just a little peck on the lips on the porch before he left, and he'd run all the way back to his milk truck, jumping and hooting.

My roommate Sharon had said, "He's a really sweet guy, you know. You should give him a chance. And he's beautiful too. You'd be nuts to pass that one up."

"He's almost too nice," I'd replied.

She knew what I meant. We both seemed drawn to guys with an edge. She still missed Rafael and I still missed Brad.

Dan was not a "free spirit" like Brad. He was a monogamist and had stayed with his previous girlfriend for four years. I'd only made it to a year and a half with Brad and about the same with Jim but, even so, I'd managed to completely throw myself into their orbits. If I ever spun around one man for four years, I was sure I'd whittle myself down to space dust.

Sometimes I felt like the only cure for whatever I had was to live in a cabin in the bush, alone with myself, where no one could influence my decisions, my lifestyle, what I ate, said, did, or felt. I was a chameleon; if I sat down beside a blue person I'd turn blue, beside a green person I'd turn green. I didn't have my own colour. The only thing that had seemed like my own was climbing, but compared to Dan and his group of hardcore Banff climbers, all my accomplishments seemed trivial. I'd been climbing molehills but mistaking them for mountains.

The other day at the Rose and Crown I'd served Sepp Renner, a famous Rockies guide, and I'd asked him if he had any advice for an aspiring guide. He'd said, "Go to university." I was starting to think he was right. My sister was finishing up her degree at Trent and my brother had quit drinking, completed his high-school education, and was now studying engineering at Carleton. My father had his master's, my mother was a nurse, and I was a waitress and climber. Maybe it was time to grow up. Get a real life. Maybe I should become a teacher.

When I reached Dan under the next pitch I said, "I can't believe you solo this shit!" and shook my arms out.

"Do I get a victory kiss?"

He leaned down and I let him kiss me. His lips were soft. Not as soft as Brad's but pretty soft for a guy with muscles growing on muscles.

The second pitch went more smoothly. It was all coming back to me. My muscles seemed to have stored the knowledge, even after so long. Halfway up, I started thinking this wasn't so bad after all. With a bit more time on the ice I could even start swinging leads with Dan. Be an equal partner.

At the base of the third pitch, after I'd bestowed the second victory kiss on Dan, I studied the ice. This section was shorter, not quite as steep. It was time for *me* to get a victory kiss instead of give one.

"I'll lead this," I said.

"You sure?" Dan's face scrunched up with concern. "What about your back?"

"It's holding up," I said, arching backward. I'd seriously wrenched my pelvis in an accident while working with the ski patrol a few weeks earlier, and Dan was getting sick of being my physio exercise slave. Every time I lay down on the counter and begged him to hold my leg while I pushed against his hand to put my pelvis back in place, he groaned.

"You don't have to, you know. I don't mind being your fearless leader."

"I don't need a goddamned leader!" I growled.

He held his hands up as though I'd grown fangs and claws. "Here, take the rack. It's all yours," he said, handing me the ice screws.

I clipped them to my harness while he put me on belay, then I turned to face the ice, to the left where it looked easiest. I glanced back at Dan. He smiled, and his blue eyes disappeared into those loveable crescents, the ones I'd been trying to resist. I wanted to ask him for a guarantee, maybe in writing and signed in the presence of a lawyer, that he'd always be there for me, that I would never, ever walk in on him in bed with some hot chick who could climb harder than I could and never whined. That he wouldn't ditch me when he really got to know me.

I crunched a few steps back to him, dragging the rope behind me, then stood on my front points and gave him a kiss.

"Sorry."

"I forgive you."

"Good."

I crunched back to the ice, swung one tool and got a satisfying *thwunk*! I sank the other tool and stepped my feet up. After a few more moves I looked down. This pitch was shorter, but still about 130 feet. I was at least thirty feet up.

I unclipped an ice screw and started twisting it into the waterfall. The sharp teeth caught right away and the hollow metal tube spat out a cylinder of ice as it slowly sank up to the hanger. I clipped the rope and let out a whoosh of air. It took more energy to protect the climb than to climb it. No wonder Dan didn't bother. I shook out my arms, each of my legs. My calves were cramping up.

I continued, close to the edge of the waterfall. Being near bare rock gave me a false sense of security. Rock I knew. Ice, not so much. Another thirty feet up I placed another screw. Dan was stomping his feet, slapping his arms, trying to stay warm, but he yelled, "You're doing good!"

Another thirty feet, another screw. Each screw took an interminably long time to place, but each reduced my fall to a maximum of sixty feet. Still too far by my standards, but better than hitting the deck. The irony was I could end up falling from the sheer effort of trying to minimize my fall.

"That's where my fucking foot fang fell off," Dan yelled as I was placing another screw. I couldn't imagine hanging here with only one crampon on barely formed ice.

"You are fucking crazy!"

By the time I got to the lip, my calves were totally seized up and my arms were pumped with lactic acid, but my back was holding up. I dragged myself over, turned and faced the valley and let out a yelp of triumph. My best lead on ice yet! I'd barely whined. I hadn't even come close to shitting myself.

I clumped over to the chains of the anchor and clipped into the bolts. By the time Dan had taken out my four screws and reached me, the sky felt close. It was getting late.

"Good lead! Takes a lot of strength to put in so many screws," Dan said with a grin.

"Ha ha," I punched him in the arm. "Victory kiss?"

"Coming right up," he said, and leaned in.

We moved together, still roped up, on two short tiers of ice and flat stretches of snow till the last pitch came into view. It was a whole waterfall in itself. A steep 150-foot column, with bulging overhangs at the top.

"Probably don't have time to do the last pitch," Dan said, "but we've got a good view of the Terminator. That's it, on the far left." He pointed at one of three thin lines of ice hundreds of feet above Professor's last pitch, on the upper part of the mountain. The Terminator was a long, thin drip that hung suspended, like an icicle hanging off a roof. Last year, Dan and his friend Joe had climbed its four pitches of grade seven, overhanging, fragile ice. It had only been done twice before, partly because there were so few climbers who could survive it (the grading system goes up to only seven), and partly because it rarely formed enough to touch down.

"The Terminator." Dan deepened his voice to an ominous growl. "We made it up in eight hours from our bivy."

From here, it looked stupidly impossible. The exposure would have been incredible, hanging by two tools on thin ice, thousands of feet over the valley, not knowing if the icicle would break off under their weight and come crashing down. It could easily have happened. They'd discovered two horizontal cracks in the ice, one of them four inches wide, almost completely severing the pillar. To date, it was one of Canada's hardest ice climbs.

"The fucking pick on my tool malfunctioned on the third pitch, then the pins broke in my third tool and the pick folded up like an accordion," Dan said. "Had to set up a hanging belay, three hundred feet up. It was so out there it was absurd."

He'd left out that little detail in his earlier rendition of the climb. That was way worse than malfunctioning foot fangs on Professor. My hour-long lead of 130 feet of less-than-vertical ice with four ice screws looked like an amble up a green run at the ski hill in comparison. I felt my badass, superhero female ice climber slink away, leaving a vertically challenged waitress with an expensive ice tool and a badass, superhero boyfriend.

I turned and looked out at the mountains. Cascade was glowing in the lowering sun, like a giant pink pyramid. "We'll end up spending the night if we don't head down soon," I said.

"Guess we'll have to get out of bed a few hours earlier next time so we can do the last pitch." Dan chuckled. He knew I wasn't a morning person.

We dragged the ropes over to the rappel chains and got busy setting up for the descent.

9

WE'RE GATHERED
HERE TODAY

"We're gathered here today to celebrate the life of Alan Deane." The minister's voice burst out of black speakers suspended in the corners of the room. The shuffling feet and muffled whispers ebbed away.

"Alan was a devoted father, husband and dentist, who was proud to be a member of the vibrant climbing community here in Canmore."

I smiled at the minister's words. From what I knew of Alan, he would have liked being described as a climber as well as a dentist. Unlike a lot of us, Alan had moved back and forth comfortably between two worlds. He'd had a grown-up life during the week, then snuck out to climb wild, frozen waterfalls on the weekends.

I looked down the row of folding metal chairs at the jeans and hiking boots, the scattering of dress pants. Niccy, Wendy; Barb and Joe; Dan's roommates, Grant and Ian. It was easy to pick out the climbers in the crowd. The farther back in the room, the scruffier the clothing. We hadn't even made it to the main part of the church. We were the overflow. The family was in the front pews in the main church, the women in sombre dresses and the men in suits and ties.

The minister's voice bounced off the sterile white walls and laminate flooring, taking on the tinny quality of a small-town AM radio station. I was always surprised when otherwise rational people held a ceremony in a place like this. This adjoining room reminded me of my year and a half of brainwashing in the Pentecostal church basement near Ottawa. Being told at thirteen that my parents and siblings and friends were all going to burn in hell unless I saved them had instilled in me a permanent terror of death—and religion. If I ever got around to making a will, if I ever owned enough to bother making a will, I'd put in bold capital letters *not* to have my funeral in a church. It had to be outside in the open air with not one mention of a god who was sadistic enough to take a healthy young man away from his wife and four-year-old daughter.

"Let us bow our heads and pray." Rows of heads bowed obediently, but I stared straight ahead and imagined Alan's wife, Cathy, with her daughter, Molly. How was she surviving this? I hoped Cathy was getting some comfort from this place—that it wasn't just their families who'd arranged this ritual.

I leaned my head against Dan's shoulder and stared at the fleece jacket in front of me. My snot and tears were flowing once again. Dan slipped his arm around me, pulled me against his side. He still hadn't cried. Not one tear, after spending so much time climbing with Alan. Yet I was losing it over a guy I barely knew. What was the matter with me? Maybe it was because Dan and most of my friends were climbers. Because *I* was a climber. I never wanted to put my family through this.

My friend Jeff, a.k.a. Dr. Risk, squirmed on the other side of me, making his chair creak. We'd worked together at a climbing store in Calgary and I'd bought my first harness from him. After that I'd climbed with him a few times in the Rockies and Yosemite. Of all the climbers in this room he was probably the most aware of his own mortality. He kept taking huge falls in the mountains. One of his biggest had resulted in his partner breaking both femurs. And he'd been there when Alan fell.

The minister droned like a mosquito trapped in a tent. I squinted, trying to bring the pictures of Alan, arranged on tables up front, into focus. He'd been such a good-looking guy. Dark hair, intense blue eyes, clean cut, professional. At twenty-six, he'd already completed seven years of university, established a dental practice, built a huge home, and started a family. He'd been only two years older than me. Dan's age.

The minister invited Alan's brother to come to the front and I tried to steady myself by holding on to my contempt of religion, but it was no use. Tears dribbled down my face faster than I could wipe them away with my sleeve. I hadn't brought any Kleenex. I glanced at Jeff. His eyes were dry, like Dan's, but he looked as if he was going to be sick. He stared at his boots even though the prayer was over. Was he wondering how many lives he had left? I reached over and squeezed his hand and he looked grateful for a moment, then turned back to his boots.

Alan was supposed to rope up with two of our friends, Clive and Choc, but he'd gotten to Slipstream, a serious waterfall, ahead of them, and for some reason had decided to solo without a rope. No one knew what had gone wrong, maybe a spindrift avalanche, maybe a cornice broke, maybe he tripped over his crampon strap, but he'd ended up falling from the top, about 1,300 feet. He fell right past Jeff, who'd been halfway up. Jeff told me he'd heard him breathing as he plummeted past.

"Cathy has given me something she'd like me to read." Alan's brother was not a climber. Cathy was not a climber. No one in this family but Alan had ever climbed. How did this poor guy address a church full of people who would be strapping on their crampons, maybe even the very next day, to head up a frozen waterfall like the one that had killed his brother? Maybe even the same one.

"Do not stand at my grave and weep; I am not there, I do not sleep. I am the thousand winds that blow; I am the diamond glints on snow. . . ."

I dug my face into Dan's sweater, trying to staunch the flow of tears. I had no right to them. I hadn't known Alan well enough and Cathy had been my friend for only a few months. What was wrong with me?

"Do not stand at my grave and cry, I am not there, I did not die."

When the poem finally, mercifully, ended, I sucked in a deep, shuddering breath. It sounded loud in the silence. Dan squeezed my fist and I noticed I was clenching a handful of his sleeve. Jeff passed me a Kleenex and in seconds I turned it into a wet clump.

Alan's brother told the crowd that Cathy and Alan had been high-school sweethearts. Cathy had told me she'd never been with anyone else. Alan had been her first and only. They'd built a mansion up on the hill with a full gym and granite countertops and multiple bedrooms. They had a beautiful daughter, and now Cathy and Molly would be all alone in that huge quiet house, while everyone else's lives went back to normal.

I pulled my fist from under Dan's hand, wrapped my arms around myself and squeezed. I could feel Cathy's grief as though I were in her skin. It could just as easily have been Dan. He'd climbed Slipstream more than once, and it was nothing compared to some of the crazy shit he was doing. Every day that he wasn't working, he was hanging off the side of a mountain, exposed to avalanches, rock and ice fall.

I rested my hand on his knee, on the smooth material of his cotton, pleated pants. Like Alan, Dan could blend in, in both worlds. He knew how to dress for a funeral. He had a steady job while most of our friends worked only enough to collect unemployment insurance and climb full-time. He owned his own place. My parents and sister had met him and loved him. And he wanted kids someday. With me. The bastard had finally gotten me to fall in love with him, even wanted me to move in with him, and he was going to go out and get himself killed. I knew it. I could feel it in every cell in my body.

People stood and started to mill around. Dan and Jeff hovered over me. It was time to go to the Canmore cemetery, to bury Alan's body almost within view of his house. I couldn't stand up. I was crying too hard. What was wrong with me? This was ridiculous.

"Jan, we've gotta go." Dan put his hand on my arm. He looked around, embarrassed. People were looking at us. He shrugged at Jeff.

"It's okay, Jan," Jeff said, patting my shoulder.

"What are we doing?" I could barely speak. "This is so stupid. *We're* so stupid!"

Dan and Jeff shifted from one foot to the other. Dan put his hands in his pockets.

"What if something happens to you?" I said, glaring at Dan.

"Don't say that," he said.

The look on his face told me I shouldn't have said that out loud.

"He'll be fine, Jan, I promise," Jeff said. "Nothing'll happen to him. He's too good."

I turned to Jeff. "If he dies, don't you dare say, 'He died doing what he loves.'"

"Jan, let's go." Dan pulled gently on my arm. I reached for his hand, entwined my fingers in his and we followed our friends out the side door.

Maybe Alan's death would slow him down.

10

ABERDEEN

As Niccy and I started up the trail from the Lake Louise parking lot, I shone my headlamp at my watch. Five-thirty. The guidebook said our objective, Mount Aberdeen, could take up to thirteen hours and we'd gotten off to a bit of a late start. My alarm had rung at 3:30 but I'd hit snooze until Dan finally rolled me off the bed onto the floor. Usually he was the one getting up in the dark for some long alpine climb, with me staying snuggled under the covers. It felt good not to be the one left behind this time.

Niccy, unlike me, had no trouble getting out of bed for a climb. For the past few years, while I'd had my romantic detours, she'd continued training to become an accredited mountain guide, and in the fall, she planned to take the guide's exam. And now I was back on track myself. In one week, Niccy and I would start work as climbing instructors at the Banff Army Cadet Camp for the summer.

I lifted my head and my light reflected off a large green sign:

BE ALERT. MAKE NOISE. CARRY BEAR SPRAY.
HIKE IN GROUPS OF FIVE.

A picture of a grizzly hunched behind the words.

"Hey, Nic. Are we supposed to fight or play dead with a grizzly? I always forget." I looked back over my shoulder and we squinted into the white light of each other's headlamps.

"I think you're supposed to play dead and let him chomp on you."

I'd only run into black bears over the years and that had been scary enough. I wasn't keen on staring into a grizzly's flat face and beady black eyes. We yipped like coyotes for a few seconds. As long as we didn't surprise one, we'd be okay. Maybe.

I tucked my thumbs into the shoulder straps of my pack and leaned into the switchbacks as we climbed. Our packs weren't heavy, nothing like the eighty-pound monster I'd carried at NOLS. Just two ropes, five ice screws, harnesses, our axes, crampons, clothes, first aid, food and water.

We slipped into an easy rhythm, taking switchback after switchback through the trees, hooting and yipping every once in a while. As the darkness turned to pale light, we turned off our headlamps and tucked them into our packs.

"How's it going living with Dan?" Niccy asked, after we'd been walking for a while. She didn't normally approve of my choice in men, but she loved Dan, who was close to our age and had listened to Meat Loaf and Supertramp in high school, not Elvis and Buddy Holly.

"Good," I said. "Except for the riff-raff eating all my peanut butter."

Our place was Banff climbers' central, and dinner seemed the most popular time for everyone to show up. From what I could gather from Dan, the climbing crowd had been one of the main reasons his old girlfriend had left him. I was starting to see her point.

"I like Dan. He's a good guy."

I liked Dan too. I thought maybe I could have his babies. But I didn't like *me* with him. The more we climbed together, the worse my head got for leading. He was so much better than me that whenever I got scared, I could just hand over the lead. And on our spring trip to Yosemite I'd moaned so much about my back on a few ten-pitch climbs that we'd almost split up. *No pain, no gain*, was one of Dan's mottoes. It was good to climb with Niccy again, to feel more like an equal.

The trees got smaller and scruffier the higher we went, reducing the likelihood of bumping unexpectedly into a bear, and after a two-thousand-foot gain of elevation we finally broke out onto the rocky, barren pass between Saddle Peak and Mount Fairview. Above tree line, it felt like we'd landed on the moon. There was Mount Aberdeen off in the distance, glowing in the early morning light, the snow on its col illuminated pink.

I took a deep breath. "Fuck," I breathed out. "It's gorgeous."

Niccy dumped her pack and pulled out a water bottle. Her face was wet with sweat and brown curls clung to her round cheeks. Her mustard-coloured earflap hat dangled down her back by the string.

"Don't think I'll need this," she said, pulling it off and stuffing it into her pack.

Niccy liked to be prepared, but sometimes she overdid it. I'd managed to convince her to leave her five-pound parka in the car. It was the end of June.

A marmot whistled its shrill warning to his buddies and I saw a brown hairy butt disappear into a hole in the rocks. The whistles followed us as we traversed through the scree on a faint goat trail skirting the lower slopes of Fairview Mountain. Eventually we started up the steep moraine toward the glacier. The thick ice disgorged from the mountain like a long, blue, swollen tongue, wide at the top, tapering at the bottom. Five hundred feet of forty-five-degree ice led toward a steep, heavily crevassed headwall. We could see the bergschrund from here. Once we got over that we'd be on the col between Aberdeen and Haddo. Then it'd be a long snow slog along the ridge to the peak.

When we reached the ice, we dropped our packs and stood together, studying the glacier. It was partially covered in snow, making the way through the crevasses trickier. Most people belayed each other for three rope-lengths from here. If a person slipped it'd be like jumping on a very fast, very long water slide, only they'd sail into boulders at the bottom instead of a pool of water.

Niccy looked up at the sun, already creeping higher in the sky. "Let's simul-climb till we get to the headwall," she said. Moving together on the rope instead of belaying would be faster, and the faster we got over the ice the better. The hot sun meant potential icefall from above, and it could also melt out our ice screws. If we took time to belay, we'd probably end up walking out in the dark.

"You want the lead?" Niccy asked.

"Yeah, okay," I said.

We sat on a couple of comfy rocks to strap on our crampons, then unhooked our ice axes from our packs. When we roped up, we both flipped coils of rope around our necks and tied them off to shorten the distance between us. I clipped the five ice screws Dan had lent me to my harness and headed off, sidestepping on all points of my crampons. The ice was perfect, like sinking into Styrofoam. After thirty feet or so, I felt the rope tug and looked down to see Niccy start climbing. I still hadn't put in an ice screw. It was feeling pretty casual.

As the ice became steeper my ankles were contorting like a Gumby, and I had to start an awkward mixture of front-pointing and side-stepping. I picked my way between the crevasses, trying to steer my mind away from the climber who'd fallen and gotten wedged headfirst into one. His partner couldn't save him, so he'd shouted down encouragement until there'd no longer been a response. I paused, thought of putting in an ice screw, then kept climbing. Dan had done the climb in eight hours. If we moved fast, maybe we could do it in ten.

Niccy and I kept up a steady rhythm, our crampons and axes digging solidly into the ice. As the sun rose higher, rivulets of melt water started to trickle in a Celtic-knot-like maze down the glacier. By the time I got to the bergschrund the sun was white hot, almost overhead. I peered into the gaping hole and couldn't see anything but black. The crevasse was possibly as deep as the glacier.

"Want me to belay you over the 'schrund?" Niccy yelled. I scanned the long crack and noticed a good snow bridge over to the left where I could cross. The slope above was steep, but it was snow, so we'd be able to kick steps.

"Naw, I should be good. You still comfortable?"

"Yeah, go for it! We're making really good progress!"

I traversed left on the spongy ice, following the edge of the bergschrund, avoiding the embedded rocks sitting in their melted-out holes, watching above for more where they'd come from. We hadn't heard any rock or ice fall yet, but we were in the heat of the day.

When I reached the steep snow bridge spanning the bergschrund, I paused. On both sides of it, the abyss.

"How's it look?"

"Pretty thick!"

I sank the shaft of my ice axe into the bridge. It felt solid. I kicked my feet as softly as I could, creating steps in the steep snow, hoping the bridge wouldn't collapse under my weight. With Niccy positioned lower on the slope like this, she would counterbalance my fall, but I had no desire to see how far into the hole I'd go before she caught me, and I refused to die upside down.

I kicked steps up the narrow band as fast as I could, then breathed out noisily when I was back on snow that was actually attached to the mountain. Niccy crossed and we picked through the heavily crevassed rolling glacier, following the edge of the bergschrund to stay in the snow, avoiding the more technical ice above. I kept looking into the gaping abyss a few feet below me, repeating in my head, *Please don't fall, please don't fall!* With us both above the bergschrund like this, we couldn't stop each other's slide. Niccy, in contrast, was the perfect picture of tranquility, looking out on the panorama spread around us.

Finally, we crested the slope that led to the summit. We dropped our packs, untied from the rope and removed our crampons. From here it was just a trek to the peak, as long as we didn't fall off the ridge. We dug out our food and water, got comfortable on our packs, and stared out at the mountains. The peaks spread out, one after another, glaciers spilling over the edges in super slow motion. Puddles of aqua spotted the valleys here and there.

"It's a good thing we didn't have to belay any of that. We'll be lucky to get back to the car by supper," Niccy said.

As I looked back down at the route, a sudden, exaggerated chill shook my upper body. My shirt was soaked from sweat. I pulled out my pile jacket and wool hat. "Good thing neither of us fell."

"Ah, I knew we'd be okay. It's not that steep," Niccy said.

I smiled. Dan would be proud of me. Somehow, I'd gotten through hours without my fear seizing me like a leghold trap. Once, on a climb, he had gotten so exasperated with my snivelling on lead that he'd said, "You were so tough when I met you. What happened?" With Niccy, I felt brave again. I felt like a climber. Maybe I was redeeming myself.

"We'd better get to the top. We're only halfway," Niccy said, standing up.

After the summit, we would still have the whole descent into Paradise Valley ahead of us. It looked like we could glissade for about

1,500 feet, but after that, it would take some careful route finding to downclimb several hundred feet of loose rock.

I started coiling the rope while Niccy stuffed gear into her pack.

It was 5:15 when we rolled into Banff. We stumbled into the kitchen and a table full of climbers swivelled around to greet us. Ian, Alain, Joe, Grant, Zac, Tim, Dan.

"They're alive!" Dan jumped up from the table and lifted me into the air. "My little hog!" While some guys used terms of endearment like *sweetheart* or *darling*, which sounded old and bugged the shit out of me, Dan's favourite was *hog*.

I pounded on his shoulders. "You moron, put me down! Of course we're alive."

"I was about to call out the cavalry."

"We weren't that slow. It took us twelve hours." Niccy threw her pack in the corner. "It would have taken forever if we'd belayed each other."

"Eleven hours and forty-five minutes, door to door," I corrected.

Dan put me back on the ground and I placed my hands on his cheeks, got up on tiptoes and planted a big kiss on his lips. "It was awesome! The conditions were so good we didn't use one ice screw."

I noticed an exchange of looks around the table. The guys must have been impressed. I grabbed a couple beers from the fridge, handed one to Niccy, then opened my jar of peanut butter. Someone had been whittling away at it. I felt a tingle of irritation, but I was too stoked to bother trying to smoke out the culprit. I slapped together a couple of peanut butter sandwiches, handed one to Niccy, and we squeezed in at the table.

Even though I was perched on Dan's lap, for the first time in a long time, I felt like one of the guys again, not their buddy's girlfriend.

After the house emptied out and Dan and I were alone in the kitchen, I discovered what the look the guys had given each other really meant.

"I gave you a bunch of ice screws. Why didn't you use them?" Dan asked.

"Because it was totally easy ice."

"Then you should have gotten rid of the rope. If one of you *had* fallen, you'd both be dead."

"We weren't going to fall."

"That's probably what that girl said in Peru before she tripped."

Two years earlier, my friend Kathy had been descending a peak in Peru with her partner, Wilma, someone I'd known vaguely from the Calgary Mountain Club. They'd decided to unrope on easy terrain, and Wilma had tripped on her crampon strap and fallen thousands of feet to her death. Some people had criticized Kathy for taking off the rope, and others thought she'd be dead too if they hadn't. Kathy moved back to Ottawa. She never wanted to climb again or see another mountain.

I stood up. Started to gather glasses off the table. The guys were all gone, but evidence of them was everywhere. "What happened in Peru was different. Aberdeen's just a long slog."

"Unless you fall."

"I told you I wasn't going to fall. I felt really strong." I started filling the sink to do the dishes. Dan was bursting my bubble.

"Jan, I can't figure you out. You're scared shitless when you shouldn't be scared, but you aren't scared when you should be scared. Some guy slid the whole way down from the headwall last year, dragging his partner with him, then busted up both femurs on the moraine when they hit rock. You can't stop a slide on blue ice."

Ignoring him, I squirted dish soap into the water. I wanted to hold on to my feelings of triumph. I started washing the beer glasses.

"You seem to be able to climb with everyone else. Why can't you get your shit together with me?"

I turned off the water, walked up behind him where he was still sitting at the table and put my arms around his neck.

"Because I love you," I said.

"That's stupid. It doesn't make any sense."

"I know." I kissed the top of his head, the wiry blond hair. "I don't get it either."

Just a week ago, I'd climbed with my friend Barry at Lake Louise and led with no problem. My head was clear and no fear crept in to pin me to the rock. I'd also been climbing with Niccy, Wendy, Julie and Barb. It seemed I could climb with other women, I could climb with guys I wasn't sleeping with, but I couldn't climb with the guy I was in love with.

11

SHOW NO FEAR

Stepping from posthole to posthole in the snow, I was almost doing the splits. Way up ahead on the glacier, the lead guide, Doug, strode along with his abnormally long legs, his three cadets strung out behind him, stumbling with their heads down. Following Doug was like following a sasquatch, but those boys would never complain. They were in the army.

My own four cadets bumbled along behind me, spaced out like preschool children along my rope. Spastic with puberty, they were like puppies that hadn't yet grown into their gigantic paws. Whatever signals their brains were trying to send to their arms and legs weren't getting through.

Our destination, Mount Saint Nicholas, emerged from the Wapta Icefield like a slightly tilted, narrow pyramid. It was just 256 feet shy of 10,000 feet. Two miles of crystalline white stretched like sparkling sand between us and the mountain. The new snow slowed us down and covered the crevasses, but with the heat of the summer sun, long, dark indentations crisscrossed the glacier, warning us of their locations.

A few days ago we'd driven from Banff in a convoy of green army trucks and school buses up the Icefields Parkway north of Lake Louise. From Bow Lake we'd hiked to Bow Hut in the rain with fifty-pound packs. The four-hour hike had taken eight hours. The boys had stewed in sweat under their army-issue waterproof ponchos while we, their Gore-Tex-clad guides, had stayed dry under the umbrellas we'd strapped to our packs. By the time we'd reached the hut, the rain had turned to snow and the boys had gotten their first taste of winter camping in the summer. They set up tents, started stoves, heated the foil pouches of food they barely had energy to eat, stuffed wet clothes and boots into sleeping bags to hopefully dry with body heat, then passed out, only to be dragged from bed at five in the morning to go climb a mountain. This was definitely not Outward Bound. None of the guides was doing much coddling, maybe because we'd all lived through our own character-building initiations into the mountain life.

With my next step, the rope pulled on my harness and stopped me short. My closest cadet, thirty feet away, was at a standstill. "Benoit, *qu'est-ce qui se passe?*" I yelled.

These fifteen-to seventeen-year-old boys were from rural Quebec and barely spoke a word of English. Apparently my nine months of French in Katimavik plus my two seasons of tree planting with French Canadians qualified me as a bilingual instructor. I'd been doing a lot of gesturing.

"*Je suis fatigué,*" said Benoit.

"Of course you're tired. You're in the army," I said.

He stared back at me blankly.

If I'd been working with English cadets I'd be saying, "What the fuck's going on? Why'd you stop?" The other guides said the kids liked us to be tough with them, but I couldn't remember the French swear words my dad had taught me after his government language training. I'd have to give him a call.

"*Ce n'est pas loin*," I added, which was exactly what my parents used to say as we drove the unpaved Alaska Highway, five of us squeezed into a Volkswagen station wagon, choking on my father's cigarette smoke with the windows closed tight against the dust. "Not much farther!" he'd say. He couldn't very well tell us, "Only a few hundred miles to go!" Just like I couldn't tell Benoit, "Only two thousand vertical feet to go!"

The other three cadets ambled along in a daze until the next one in line, Marcel, was only ten feet behind Benoit, leaving twenty feet of limp rope between them. We had to stay spread out for safety and keep the rope tight. There could be hidden crevasses. I'd pounded this into the cadets over and over when we were practising glacier travel and crevasse rescue.

"*Qu'est-ce que vous faites?*" I widened my arms to indicate *Spread out!* but I couldn't remember the words in French, so I used the closest I could come up with: "*Bougez, bougez!*" *Move!*

Yesterday, my friend Barb, one of the other female guides, had been crossing a glacier with her cadets when she fell into a crevasse up to her thighs. Instead of spreading out to hold her fall, all of her cadets, overwhelmed by curiosity, had kept walking toward her until they were bunched up on the same crevasse. It could have been disastrous.

Marcel backed up, tripping over the rope and landing on his side. Sylvain dropped his ice axe, bent to pick it up and got pulled onto his butt by Claude, who'd also started to back up. A Quebecois Laurel and Hardy show. Maybe I should have put Marcel directly behind me instead of Benoit. It had been a toss-up. The weakest link was nearest me, but this was the most bumbling group I'd had this summer, and I couldn't keep them *all* close.

Doug trucked along ahead, widening the gap between us. He weighed over two hundred pounds and had twenty-five years of experience in the mountains to my five, but had one less cadet. "Seniority," I'd been told. There was also a surplus of French cadets, and a dire shortage of guides who could say more than *merde!* in French.

We waited while Benoit removed his mitts and groped around in his pockets to find a baggie of trail mix.

"*Vite, vite! Criss de calice de tabarnac! On y va!*" The rest of the cadets urged him to get a move on when they saw our third party gaining on us—Niccy's three cadets with Karen, the camp photographer, bringing up the rear.

"*Okay, Benoit, on y va,*" I said.

Benoit lifted a big foot, let it drop heavily in the snow, lifted the other one. My '73 Dart started up more quickly after sitting through the whole winter than this kid. It seemed every time I gave a command my cadets took their sweet time, like they wanted to make it perfectly clear they found taking orders from a civilian distasteful, especially a female civilian. Out of thirty instructors, only five of us were women, and these poor sods just happened to have drawn a really short straw: me, the runt of the litter of instructors.

Niccy pulled up behind my boys, then wound her group around us. I shook my head and groaned as she looked back, her laughter jiggling her big mirror glacier goggles on her nose, white with zinc oxide. "Having some fun yet?" she said. Her party of five stretched from footstep to footstep, leaving us in last place. Karen brought her camera up to her face, pointed at us and clicked. My cadets groaned and swore at Benoit.

"*Ce n'est pas un . . .*" I hesitated. What the hell was the word for race? "*Race,*" I yelled with a French accent, so that it rhymed with "ass."

But it *was* a race. For me, anyway. I'd been hired on for my French and my gender, not for my glowing resumé—one summer as camp counsellor at Camp Chief Hector, another as an assistant Outward Bound instructor, Industrial First Aid, and five years of climbing. I knew I had to prove myself.

At the base of the mountain, Doug, Niccy, Karen and I stared straight up at the northeast face of Saint Nick. A long, steep snow slope led to the spectacularly pointy summit. There was a more obvious way to go, though. About a quarter-mile farther along we could access a gentler route up the mountain by walking up to the lowest point— the col—between Saint Nick and its immediate neighbour, Mount Olive. From there we could follow a low-angle ridge to the peak. If a cadet fell, he'd land on his butt in the snow, not tumble a few hundred feet to the glacier, dragging us all with him.

The camouflage-clad boys sat in the snow, munching on choco- late bars, their laughter interrupted by their universal language— imitations of machine gunfire and explosions.

"Hey, Benoit! *Ça va mieux?*" I wished I could communicate better with them. They were so young. Even if they were the cream of the crop, I was sure they were homesick and scared much of the time. Most of them had never climbed. Some had never even seen a real mountain. Few of them had slept on an inch-thick blue Ensolite pad in a tent in the snow and subsisted on foil pouches of army rations that could be mistaken for wet dog food.

Benoit looked over and grinned. "*Oui, oui, madame.* It is much good now. Much good."

"So, the northeast face or the col?" Doug asked. "The face looks in good shape."

I craned my head and looked up, way up, at Doug, like at the Jolly Green Giant. Had I heard him correctly? Why was he suggesting something that steep with this bunch?

"Let's do the face," Niccy said. "The col's just a slog."

My head swivelled to Niccy. I had to clench my hands to keep from wrapping them around her neck. Was she trying to prove something to Doug? He was a full guide and could be the examiner on her guide course this fall, so she probably felt her every move was being scrutinized. But she was bigger and stronger than I was, and she'd had more practice short-roping. She had a better chance of holding her cadets if one of them fell.

I looked at my boys, who were now spitting wads of chocolate bar wrapper at each other. At fourteen, Benoit was a foot taller than me, and the rest were not much smaller. On rock I'd stand a chance. I could zigzag through rock features, make sure there was something I could wrap the rope around, find spots to secure myself to belay them if I had to. On snow we would be fully exposed. If the cadet closest to me lost his balance, and if I noticed right away, I could pull on the rope to keep him upright. But if one of the other boys fell and I had to hold two bodies, or three, or four? Worst-case scenario would be if Claude at the back of the line fell and dragged Sylvain with him, who would drag Marcel, and all the way up the line.

"I'd prefer to do the col," I said. "I don't think these guys should be on the face."

"Well, majority rules," Doug said.

I stared at Doug, opened my mouth. I had to say something. That was not the way it worked in the mountains. You always went at the pace and comfort level of the weakest member. But saying that to him would mean admitting to being the weakest member. And if I told him how much I'd short-roped—a few hours with Dan in preparation for this job, and once up Mount Joffre with my Outward Bound students three years ago—he would have said, "What the fuck are you doing *here* then?"

I was also hoping to do my guide's training someday, like Niccy. Doug could easily be one of my examiners too.

So I clamped my mouth shut.

Doug started to prepare his ropes. I stared up at Saint Nick, a snowy, jagged tooth. The few hundred feet of steep snow leading to the summit was interrupted by a band of exposed rock about three quarters of the way up. Fear spread its tentacles through my belly, wrapped around my bowels.

Fake it till you make it. That's what Dan would have told me at that moment. But he was back in Banff, working at his safe indoor job, and he was a better faker than I was.

Niccy squeezed my arm and her smile was like a kid's in front of the biggest Christmas present under the tree. "It'll be great. The kids will love it."

"Let's get this show on the road!" Doug clapped his huge hands and the cadets leapt to their feet as if a grenade had rolled into their midst.

I huddled with my group and pointed out the route. When their excited cheers had died down, I looked each kid in the eye. "*Tu tombes, tu meurs.*" You fall, you die. They stared at me like I was a lunatic.

"Nic, you can lead us up," Doug said.

I started to prepare my rope, thinking, *He picked her, not me!* Years ago I used to lead her up routes she could barely climb. Now she was Doug's protégée.

Niccy started up the snow slope, her cadets and Karen following behind, the rope now set so they were only a few feet apart. Doug led his cadets up next, and when I followed with mine, it occurred to me that maybe Doug was doing with me what I was doing with Benoit, keeping the weakest link close.

We kicked our boots into the footsteps, sank our axes to the hilt and moved slowly up the slope. The snow was deep, to my thighs and to Doug's knees, but the slope was no steeper than a black diamond run at the Lake Louise ski hill. It wouldn't last long, though. After a short snow wallow, the angle would begin to tilt. Behind me, the boys laughed and blathered so quickly I only understood the occasional word. Every few seconds I barked orders over my shoulder: *"Attention! La corde! Ton hache!"* as I indicated sinking the shaft of their axe deep in the snow before taking a step, and keeping the rope tight. If they fell here, they could self-arrest. I'd made them practice the technique for hours over the past few days, sliding on their bellies, then sinking the pick of their axe deep in the snow, throwing all their weight on it to stop their slide. But we wouldn't be able to self-arrest farther up. If they slipped on the steep section, we wouldn't just slide. We'd fall. We'd be *fini*.

The wall of snow kept getting steeper. I twisted around to see Benoit ten feet below me with his axe only halfway in the snow, looking out at the view.

"Benoit!" He started and looked up. *"Ton hache!"* I pointed to my ice axe, then made the motion of slitting my throat. He sank his axe to the pick, his eyes as wide as Frisbees.

As the face got steeper, the cadets grew quiet. Each time I looked back, all four of them were methodically planting their axes, then step, step, with their mouths set in tight lines, their eyes looking straight ahead at the imprints in the snow, trying not to look down. I could hear Benoit breathing noisily, a combination of exertion and fear.

The higher we climbed, the longer the fall. Why couldn't I think, *The higher we climb, the closer to the top*? That's probably what Niccy was thinking: how cool it was to be hanging off the side of the mountain with a bunch of pubescent boys, while I was thinking how insane it was.

I stared at the army-green gaiters of Doug's last cadet twenty feet above. Approximately twenty minutes ago that kid had been joking about throwing himself down the slope to practise his self-arrest, but he was silent now, just like my cadets. No laughter. No whoops. No yelling back and forth. Just the repetitive *thud, thud* as we kicked our boots into the steps, the *shush* of the ice axes sinking into the snow as we followed the steep band of white toward the summit.

Off to our right, a sharp ridge delineated the northeast face from the southwest face, which was a two-thousand-foot rock wall. One by one my boys paused and looked over into the abyss as though they were at a viewing in a funeral parlour. I clamped my glove down on the rope between me and Benoit. Marcel whistled, the same long, eerie dropping sound that accompanied Wile E. Coyote when he fell off a cliff chasing the Road Runner. Whistle, whistle, whistle, splat.

Benoit looked up at me, his mouth drawn down. He probably wanted his mother, like I wanted Dan. We'd both risk death before admitting it.

Doug's last cadet stopped. Niccy had reached the rock band. We stood still as granite, in mid-step, right beside the two-thousand-foot drop, and waited. My legs quivered with fear and exhaustion. The cadets' legs must have been jelly.

It took over an hour for Niccy's team, then Doug's, to make it over the rock. They continued on, up out of sight, now on mellower ground on their way to the summit, while I shook the rigor mortis out of my legs and climbed on. At the base of the rock, I stopped again. Scrambling up was going to be challenging in stiff plastic mountaineering boots. My cadets stood, a few feet apart down the steep slope, looking up at me, waiting for the next instructions. I imagined the five of us sliding, tumbling, gaining speed, ice axes flailing, fifteen hundred feet to the glacier.

If anything happened to these boys, it wouldn't be Doug's fault. It would be mine. I should have spoken up.

I unclenched my teeth, forced my jaw to relax. I wanted off this fucking mountain. I slipped my ice axe into the side of my pack, stuffed my gloves down the front of my jacket, then dropped a few loops of rope, getting ready to climb by myself. I'd belay them from the top. The cadets leaned into the slope, exhausted, listening to my instructions. They probably wished they were on six-foot-four Doug's rope, already sitting on the summit eating gorp.

"*Touchez pas la fucking corde.*" If they accidentally pulled on the rope, or stepped on it, I'd get dragged off the climb. They all nodded like a row of bobbleheads on a dashboard.

I placed my foot on the rock, stepped up. The holds were big, but the angle was steep. I moved carefully, trying not to knock the loose rock off, trying to keep my thoughts fully focused on my task. If I could survive a few more hours, by suppertime tomorrow, I'd be snuggled up with Dan at home in Banff. Maybe I'd bake some banana bread.

I kept looking down at the boys to make sure they weren't moving, that their axes were deep in the snow, and that they weren't near my coils of rope. My neck-slicing gesture must have done its job. They stood still as plastic soldiers until I reached the comfort of the soft snow again. It had only been five or six moves. Easier than I'd expected, and if I hadn't been attached to four gangly, testosterone-flooded, *heavy* army cadets, it would have been fun.

The slope levelled off. I followed the footsteps up to the anchor, a mound of snow that Niccy and Doug had built to secure themselves to the mountain while their boys had climbed the rock. Niccy and Karen raised their arms in the air in triumph from the top, about thirty feet above me. Doug sat a few feet apart from his cadets. He lifted his hand in a wave, and grinned. I lifted my hand nonchalantly, then let it drop. I tucked my chin into the collar of my jacket to hide my huge grin. I turned and sat in the impression Niccy's and Doug's butts had made, sank my boots into their steps. With my rope wrapped around the snow anchor and clipped into my harness, the boys could no longer drag me off the mountain. I was secure. I put my head between my knees for a few seconds to savour my stay of execution.

I pulled up the slack in the rope, looped it around my waist. Mountains and glaciers stretched out as far as I could see in every direction. Bow Hut with our tents clumped around it looked like a tiny Monopoly house. Off to the north, three strings of cadets inched toward Mount Gordon, a long, safe hike up a snowfield. That's where we could have gone today, but we hadn't. We'd done the northeast face of Saint Nick. I couldn't wait to tell Dan.

I leaned over and yelled to my cadets, "Okay, Benoit! You can climb! *Grimpe!*"

Huddled together on my blue Ensolite pad in front of the tent, Ian and I passed a cup of cocoa back and forth. We were getting used to living together, out in the mountains and back home in Banff. His only real flaw as a roommate was that he ate too much of the banana chocolate chip loaf I baked.

"I can't believe he said 'majority rules.'" Ian slapped his knee and laughed.

"Shhh. Keep your voice down," I hissed. I'd described our day in a whisper, because Doug was only a few tents away.

I'd needed to do this little check-in with Ian to make sure I wasn't overreacting. It was as though my interpretation of reality wasn't valid unless someone else confirmed it. Maybe it had something to do with growing up in a crazy household that denied its craziness. Karen had also thought the day was insane, but she wasn't a climber. Niccy and Doug had had a grand old time.

"What if one of my cadets had fallen?" I grabbed the cocoa. Heat seeped through my gloves and sent shivers through me. Liquid chocolate, oozing down my throat, almost made up for the stress of trying to get my cadets over the rock band. None of them had fallen, but Benoit had started to cry halfway up. Maybe I'd done my throat-slitting gesture one time too many. While I'd coaxed from above, the other boys had screamed obscenities from below.

I knew what was really bugging me. It wasn't Doug. It was me. How come I couldn't stand up to him? If I'd pushed a bit harder for the easier route he probably would have agreed. But then he would have known I was a chickenshit. And how come Niccy and I looked at the same route and I saw blood and entrails and brain matter and she saw fun?

"Doug would never have let you take cadets up there if he thought you couldn't hold them. You've gotta have a little faith in yourself," Ian said.

Lots of people seemed to have faith in me, not just my mother, but it wasn't like I could stick them in my pocket and pull them out halfway up a climb when I started shitting myself.

"I don't think guiding is my forte. Maybe I should go back to school. Become a French teacher. I can't kill anyone in a classroom." I'd just received the catalogue for the University of Calgary in the mail and was highlighting all the courses I'd take if I could ever get my butt accepted there. Apparently, my high school marks were too low to get in (it was more fun to smoke up under the Jock River bridge than go to class), so I'd have to redo grade-twelve English first.

"Just mess up their impressionable little brains." Ian laughed and raised his arms, defending against my punch.

"Seriously. Don't you ever get scared in the mountains?" I asked.

"You kidding? I'm scared shitless half the time. Sometimes I can feel death following me up a climb."

But Ian's threshold for fear, like Dan's, was leagues higher than mine.

In the fading light, Grant, the last guide back, trucked toward camp with his cadets stumbling behind him. He stopped by our tent, pulled out a cigarette.

"We did three peaks," Grant bragged as he lit up. Five cadets sagged on the rope, their eyes glazed with exhaustion. They reminded me of horses run to death in cowboy movies.

Grant grinned, his teeth flashing white against his leathery tanned skin. He looked like the Marlboro Man. He used to be Dan and Ian's roommate. Now he was renting a room in a basement in downtown Banff, but still hung out with the mob in our living room.

"Grant, you're a slave driver." Ian shook his head.

"Hey, man, this is the army." He pulled on the rope and the six of them slogged toward the cadets' tents. They still had to make dinner, the poor slobs. They'd probably just eat their army rations right out of the foil pouch, cold.

"I'd hate to be on his rope," I said when they were out of earshot. But there was something magnetic about Grant. He was one of those bodice-ripping types. He was quiet about his accomplishments, but he was one of the hardest climbers in the Rockies, with his name in several guidebooks for the new routes he'd put up.

"He's the fastest guy I've ever climbed with on mixed rock and ice," Ian said. "I'd do any route with him."

Dan, Ian and Grant had been doing big alpine routes and extreme ice climbs all winter together. Some of the scariest stuff in the Rockies. From one day to the next I never knew if Dan was going to come home.

I rinsed out the cup with snow and we gathered our gear, stuffed everything into the tent. As we crawled into our sleeping bags, I pictured Grant's eyes, spots of brilliant blue leaping from his face, like a sepia photograph with painted-on colour. Almost too blue.

"I'm glad you and Danny are together. It's fun having you at the house," Ian said.

Shaking off the image of Grant, I joked, "A little feminine touch?" I felt about as feminine as the guys who lounged around our living room every night.

"Yeah, you *do* add a feminine touch. What's wrong with that?"

"Get serious." I studied his face to see if he was mocking me, but he wasn't. He couldn't hide anything. His face was too revealing: smooth and narrow and boyish. Unpretentious. He seemed young, but he was twenty-three, just a year and a half younger than me.

"I'm really falling for the bugger. It scares the shit out of me," I said.

"Well, you couldn't fall for a better man. I could see you two getting married someday."

A warm little soft spot sat at the base of my belly as I snuggled deeper into my bag. Tomorrow at this time I'd be curled up with Danny in my own bed, in my own bedroom, in my own home.

12

CLIMBING GIRLFRIEND

"Jesus, Jan, you just put in a piece. You couldn't fall if you tried to!"

Dan looked up from the ground where he was belaying me, rubbed his arm and stamped his feet, trying to warm up. From the top of his head to the bottom of my rock shoes, a height of about twenty feet, I could count four pieces of protection. And here I was, pulling another friend off my rack to place a fifth. The whole ordeal had taken over half an hour. His neck must have been killing him, he might have been almost hypothermic, and I had fifty feet to go.

"Fuck off." I pulled back the triggers of the friend and crammed it into the crack, let go and it expanded against the rock. I pulled up the rope, clipped it through the carabiner, studied the next move.

"It's only 5.9," he said, referring to the not easy but not desperate climbing grade, one that I was more than capable of leading.

"It's fucking hard for a 5.9. It's not Yosemite 5.9, it's Rockies 5.9."

The quartzite here at Lake Louise was steep and blocky, more intimidating than Yosemite granite, but I knew these routes, had even guided the cadets up the easier ones all summer. And Dan and I had just gotten back from a week in Squamish, so I should have been climbing well. But even on coastal granite, I hadn't felt any braver. In fact, that trip had obliterated any leftover scraps of my shaky climbing ego. I had led what I thought were some good pitches, but they hadn't been enough to impress Dan. He wanted a girlfriend he could swing leads with. He wanted me to be that ballsy girl he'd watched climb in Yosemite over a year ago, when we first met. I wanted to be her, too.

"Come on, Jan. It looks like it's going to rain."

I studied the crack above while Dan stared up at me, impatient.

Dan wanted so badly for me to climb well, but my heart didn't seem to be in it these days. I didn't know if my lack of motivation affected my climbing, or my chickenshit climbing affected my motivation. I did know I didn't seem to be climbing for *me* anymore.

I shook my feet out, one after another. They were cramping up in my climbing shoes. This was such a good rest spot, a nice ledge that fit almost a whole foot, and the problem with good rest spots was I wanted to stay on them forever. But if I could just make myself climb, I'd be at the bolted anchor in a few minutes and it would all be over. But if all I wanted was for it to be over, why was I climbing? And what was the point in my even leading this stupid route if Dan could just whip up it in a quarter of the time, with a quarter of the protection?

Shut up in there! I screamed at the gerbil that kept running around and around in my brain. Why did everyone else slip into "the zone" when they climbed, like a bunch of Buddhist monks, and I slipped into gerbil brain?

I made a few more moves, then with my last piece at my knees, stopped to take another friend off my harness. Dan sighed so loudly that even fifty feet up I could hear him.

"How come you shit your pants on an easy lead, then cruise up the harder routes I lead with no problem?" he yelled up.

Because of you! I wanted to yell back, but I knew it wasn't his fault. I was the perfect poster girl for the "Cinderella complex." The absolute worst feminist walking the earth. When I climbed with Dan, for some reason I felt like he should look out for me. The same thing had happened on the river with Brad. I'd been all alone in my very own boat and somehow I still thought he could save me from anything.

A few more moves, another piece. My stopper fit perfectly in the crack. Dan fed out the rope and I clipped in. Safe again for another few feet. I looked down.

"So. Remind me again. Why am I doing this?" I was only half joking.

"Okay. This is stupid. Why don't you just come down?"

"No, no. I want to do it."

"No, you don't. I'll lower you. I can finish the route."

"No! I'm doing it!"

When he wanted me to go up, I wanted to come down, and when he wanted me to come down, I wanted to go up. I stepped off my little ledge and moved up the rock. I had spent the whole summer dragging cadets up these climbs without killing a single one. I was going to get to that goddamned anchor or die trying.

I climbed on, anger fuelling me, finally made it to the big ledge at the top, pulled up some rope and clipped into the bolts.

"I'm secure!" I yelled, then let out my victory whoop. A post-lead, orgasmic euphoria washed over me. I loved this feeling! So why couldn't I skip all the drama in between and just climb? I always reached the anchor in the end anyway, in spite of myself.

I leaned over the edge, hanging off the bolt. "That wasn't so hard!"

Dan grinned up at me, happy now that my glacial lead was over. "How about you just rappel? I don't need to climb it. There's a guy in lederhosen yodelling in front of the Chateau. We can't miss that."

He looked beautiful standing there, like Hercules. His hair glowed, bleached almost white from a summer of sunshine, his eyes looked so blue against the navy collar of his jacket, even from here. It almost hurt to look at him.

The rain started as we merged onto the highway into the dribble of traffic heading for Banff. Tourist season was obviously over.

"Shit!" Dan cursed as he turned on the windshield wipers. "That could be the end of the rock season."

I watched a cloud of black descend on Mount Temple and felt something close to elation.

Winter coming meant I didn't have to climb for a while. It meant I could bake, make jam, knit Dan's sweater, and work on my distance grade-twelve English course before my ski patrol job started. I wanted to paint the house, rip out the floor in the bathroom and put in tiles, repot the plants. Anything but climb. But I couldn't tell Dan that. I could barely admit it to myself. Climbing wasn't enough anymore.

"You still love me?" I asked as I slipped my hand into the crook of his elbow.

"Of course I love you. You're my girl." He turned for a moment to smile at me.

We said *I love you* every day, sometimes several times a day. It had bugged me at first, like he was trying too hard. But maybe it was an indication of a healthy relationship. I couldn't remember ever hearing my parents say that to each other, and they'd only said it to me when I planted myself in front of them and refused to budge unless they said those three stupid little words.

"Even if I snivel up my leads?"

"Yup."

"Even if I go to university?"

"You won't go to university. You're a climber."

Dan kept his eyes on the road. He didn't want me to move to Calgary, even if I was home every weekend.

The rain turned to sleet and slapped against the windshield. Some days I wanted to marry him and have ten babies, and some days I knew I had to be alone, to finally make my own way in the world. So, I'd made a decision. I was going to university to get my degree in education. I'd move to Calgary and come home to Banff on the weekends. I'd be my own person during the week, and Dan's girl on the weekend. Until I could figure out how to be both at the same time. I just had to figure out how to tell him.

13

THE FINAL LAST STRAW

I leaned my forehead against the bar of the chairlift, watched Bill in his red ski-patrol jacket digging his edges into the steep icy run, then closed my eyes against the glare of sunlight bouncing off the snow. My head pounded. Dan and Ian were up on the Grand Central Couloir on Mount Kitchener, a serious route of ice, snow and rock—essentially a funnel for avalanches and rockfall. Before he left, Dan had been sorting gear on the kitchen floor, humming with energy, and I'd taken a snapshot of him in my mind, like it was going to be the last glimpse of him I'd ever get. The feeling was so strong I was sure it was a premonition. I'd slept in Dan's T-shirt and sobbed for hours, then finally took Gravol. Now I had a Gravol hangover.

The radio on my chest started to crackle. A 10-10 at the intersection of Upper Homestead and Eye Opener. I groaned. I was so close to this accident I was almost on top of it. I had to take it. I pushed the button on my radio. "Dispatch, this is Jan. I'm just getting off the Silver Chair. I'm in position to respond."

"Dispatch, this is Andrew. I'm at the top of Gold. I can take this one."

It was tempting to press the transmit button and say, "Yo, dickwad, I said I've got it!" but that would not be proper radio protocol. Now I wanted to take this call, just because I knew Andrew didn't think I could do it.

"Copy that, Andrew, but Jan's got this one," Dave, the dispatch said.

I found myself saying *fuck* every second word on this job to overcompensate for being the only female patroller. Bill said I swore more than the guys he'd fought with in Vietnam. Though I loved them all like big brothers, I was still thankful another woman would be joining us soon. We needed a bit more estrogen on the team.

When the chairlift deposited me at the top, I skied over to the warming hut where the rescue toboggan was leaning against the wall, ditched my poles, cinched the harness of the toboggan around my waist and headed downhill. As I skied, I could feel my heart pound against my radio. The guys all fought for 10-10s, while I got full-on anxiety attacks every time the radio crackled. I hated not knowing what I'd find. The Nakiska runs were steep and icy, so we got a lot of sliders. Most didn't stop until they hit a tree.

Ahead of me were two skiers sitting in the snow; one looked like a child. When I pulled up beside them, a little girl lifted her head off her father's lap, her blue eyes rimmed red. Her chubby, freckled cheeks and eyelashes were wet. I unstrapped the harness of the toboggan and stepped out of my skis.

"Hey, kiddo," I said, kneeling beside her. My voice automatically went up an octave. "My name's Jan. I'm a ski patroller. Did you hurt yourself?"

She nodded. Her lower lip jiggled, but she didn't cry.

Maternal juices injected into my blood stream like a morphine pump on an IV. I wanted to scoop her into my arms and hold her, sing the teddy bears' picnic song my mom used to sing when I was about this age, up in Fort Smith.

"And what's *your* name?" I felt a bit like an idiot, like I was talking to a puppy. When had I last spent any real time with kids? Only one of my friends, Jeannette, was a mom, and she lived in Field, so I rarely saw her.

"Leetha," she said in a tiny voice.

The man looked down at his daughter, tucked a lock of red hair under her tuque. It was the gesture of a good dad, who would protect his little girl from anything. I thought of Dan, holding his newborn niece in Calgary a few weeks ago. He'd handled her like an egg, terrified of dropping her, and I'd felt like flushing my birth control pills down the toilet.

"How old are you, Lisa?" I said as I pulled gear from my pack.

"Thixth."

We chatted while I removed her skis, did an initial examination, then stepped away to radio in a fractured tib/fib and a request for an ambulance.

"Do you need backup?" Dave asked.

I looked over at the father, who was standing there with his arms hanging uselessly at his sides, waiting for my next instructions. He trusted me completely with his daughter. Without one of the guys breathing down my neck making "suggestions," I actually felt competent.

"No. Everything's under control. I'll be down in thirty."

After I'd splinted Lisa's leg, the father and I loaded her into the toboggan together, but I could have done it myself. She weighed as much as a small sack of potatoes, nothing like the three-hundred-pound suspected heart attack (who had turned out to be an epileptic)

I'd had as my first accident. It had taken five of us to lift him. I'd let Andrew take the toboggan down that time.

Lisa's round face peeked out from the grey blanket like a papoose, and her tiny body spanned only half the length of the toboggan. She hadn't cried the whole time.

I harnessed myself into the toboggan and pointed my skis downhill.

At the end of the day, I grabbed a seat by myself on the Nakiska van for the ride back to Banff. I was glad it wasn't my turn to drive. My worry over Dan and Ian on their climb was back full force. A chinook was rolling in and warm winds did not mix well with winter climbing. I watched the mountains reel by as we headed toward the main highway, then propped my knees against the back of the seat in front of me and closed my eyes for a nap. Maybe I should just move to Saskatchewan where my biggest fear would be falling into a bailer.

Lisa had been so brave. I wanted a little girl like her. I wanted something permanent in my life. On the drive home from Calgary after seeing Dan's niece, we'd talked about having kids together one day, but I'd snapped out of my maternal buzz when he'd started packing his climbing gear for this next death route. After he left, I went to the post office and mailed my application to the University of Calgary. No more dicking around. Being a widowed mother making $5.50 an hour as a ski patroller did not appeal to me. I needed to get my degree.

I woke up when the van stopped in front of our house. Cars everywhere, as usual. I grabbed my pack and slid the van door open, and there, double-parked behind the rusted-out green Subaru I'd just bought to replace my Dart, was Dan's almost-new tan Subaru. The boys had survived another mountain.

"It was too warm. There was crap crashing down the couloir. Way too dangerous."

The guys described their brief outing while I perched on Dan's knee on the couch, still wearing my red ski-patrol jacket. The living room was once again full of climbers, but I didn't care. Dan was alive.

"You guys are amazingly cheerful," I said. "You just drove for hours and didn't even get a route in. I thought you'd be bummed."

"Well, get this. On the drive back, we got to talking and we decided to go for it. A big mountain. This May." Dan rubbed his hands together.

Zac, one of our roommates, turned down the volume on the TV and sat back into the plush brown sofa. He, Tim, Joe, Grant and Mark looked at Dan and Ian, avoiding eye contact with me.

Dan and Ian looked at me, then exchanged looks with each other.

"What are you two up to?" I asked.

"Alaska!" They said in unison.

I stiffened and removed my arm from around Dan's neck. My stomach suddenly felt like I'd done too many sit-ups. Dan put his arm around my waist so I couldn't stand up.

"Don't freak out, Jan. We're just thinking of doing the regular route on McKinley."

"Fuck McKinley," Grant said from the swinging wicker chair in the corner. "Go big or go home. This community is too fucking apathetic if you ask me." He took a swig of beer, oblivious to the warning daggers I was hurling at him with my eyes. *Shut up and go back to your grungy little basement.*

"So what should we do?" Ian asked.

"The Infinite Spur. On Foraker." Grant's answer was immediate, as though he wished he were going there himself, but he was about to go logging. His unemployment insurance had dried up.

I felt betrayed. Grant was the only guy who bothered to venture upstairs to see why I was always holed up in my room. He'd seemed impressed when I showed him the four-inch binder of coursework for English 12. He'd said sometimes he regretted dropping out of

McGill to be a ski bum in Whistler. Now he seemed to have conveniently forgotten that Dan staying alive was an important part of my big plan. Four years to get my teaching degree, then a job, then married, then babies.

"It's committing. It'd take about eight days, and after the first day, there's no backing off," Grant warned.

Dan sat up straighter, looked at Ian. "We could do it. We're climbing some of the hardest shit in the Rockies."

As the conversation got more and more animated and more beer caps popped off, Dan loosened his grip on me. I climbed the stairs to our room and sat at the desk, staring at my next assigned reading: *Wuthering Heights*. A burst of laughter wafted up from the living room, seeped under the door. I picked up a pen, put it down, closed my book.

May. Only two months away.

When Dan came upstairs, I was sitting on the edge of the bed in my pajamas. Our bed was just a hand-me-down mattress with no frame. He took off his clothes, sat down beside me in his boxers.

"Hey. Don't be mad."

I didn't answer.

"Remember the rules. Never go to sleep pissed off at each other."

"Fuck off."

He laughed and rolled on top of me, squishing me into the bed. I was pinned. It was as if a tank had landed on me.

"Get off me, you jerk."

"Thought you were tough."

"Get off!"

He finally rolled off and I punched him in the chest. "Asshole."

"PMS again? I thought that was only supposed to be once a month."

I elbowed him in the gut.

We lay on our backs, side by side, the soles of our feet flat on the floor.

"Don't go to Alaska."

"Hey, we'll be fine. I promise."

"I have a really bad feeling about this."

"You always say that."

"Don't go. Please. Or do something else up there. You can't back off the Spur, even if you get altitude sickness."

"Come on. You freak me out talking like this all the time."

He sat up and grabbed a book off the desk, handed it to me. "Look what Joe lent me."

Surviving Denali. On the cover, two climbers scaled the knife-edge ridge of McKinley, high above blue-white crevasse-riddled glaciers that flowed like massive rivers around the bases of massive mountains. Everything massive. An alpine climber's paradise.

I handed the book back without opening it. "I mailed my university application yesterday," I said, staring up at the ceiling.

When he didn't say anything I rolled over and leaned on my elbow so I could look down at him.

"I'll be home on weekends."

"You'll fall in love with some professor with a bunch of degrees."

So that was what he was worried about.

"No, I won't. I love *you.*" I rolled on top of him, my head on his smooth chest. He had almost no chest hair. He draped his arm across my back, pressing me into him. His strong heartbeat thumped against my cheek.

14

THE MEMO

Dan and Ian stood side by side against the lush, green Washington backdrop while I focused my camera. They grinned, blue eyes squinting into the sun as I pressed the shutter.

As they moved toward Scottie's VW van I got a sudden premonition—me, standing at a counter at the photo shop in Banff, staring at these last pictures, wishing I'd taken more. The image almost winded me.

"Wait! One more!"

"Come on. We've got to get to the airport." Ian crawled into the van to join Julie, who was already crammed in the back seat behind the mound of packs and duffle bags. She and I had been climbing together for three weeks in Oregon and Washington, then two days ago we'd met up with Dan and Ian in Squamish. We were about to drop them off at the Seattle airport and head to Burns Lake to tree plant, where I planned to work myself into the ground to keep my mind off the boys on the Infinite Spur.

Scottie, an old Ontario high-school friend of Dan's, started up the van. Last night he'd given us the "Presidential Suite"—his one bedroom—and joined the others in sleeping bags on the living-room floor just outside our door. Dan had bounced up and down rhythmically on the bed, making the springs squeak, laughing at my mortification, then he'd lain awake, too nervous to snuggle, too nervous to sleep.

I raised my camera to my eye. "Please, Dan. Just one more." I could hear the hysteria in my voice. Dan must have too. He turned toward me and posed in front of the van. His pale blond hair lit up in the sun as he stared into the viewfinder with a tolerant smile.

At the airport, I sat on Dan's lap with my arms around him while he tried to have a conversation with our friends, killing time before he could board the plane. He strained to look at his watch but couldn't see it with me cramming my face into his chest. Being near him wasn't enough—I needed to be on top of him. I would have wormed my way right inside him if I could.

"Flight 207 for Anchorage is now boarding."

I put my hands over my ears. Dan stood and I slid off his disappearing lap. I was sobbing now, and people stared as they milled past. Dan grabbed his bag and he and Ian hugged Scottie and Julie. When Ian hugged me, he whispered, "Don't worry, I'll take good care of him."

Dan let me cling longer than he wanted to, his muscles wound up tight, then peeled me off like a second skin. "I'll be fine. I promise. I love you."

"Me too. I love you too." *I love you so much. I need you. Don't die on me.*

As we walked away, Scottie put his arm around my shaking shoulders and said, "He'll be fine. I promise you he'll come home."

Like Lot's wife, I peered around Scottie to get another glimpse of the boys, wishing I hadn't, knowing it was bad luck. Dan was showing the flight attendant his boarding pass. He was too far away for me to see his face but I could see the energy ripple through his body as he shifted from foot to foot, clutching his paper bag, his version of carry-on. He was probably telling the attendant they were off to climb a big mountain.

They disappeared through the gate without looking back.

The boys are falling, their two bodies twisting around each other, ice axes flailing, legs and arms groping at nothing. Just thousands of feet of air. I'm clutching at the air myself, like it's me who's falling. I can taste their terror. I'm inside their bodies. Then I'm on my hands and knees on our kitchen floor in Banff, cleaning up a big pool of blood. I scrub and scrub, but the blood won't go away. I keep scrubbing and crying. No one tells me but I know someone has just removed their bodies.

I woke up sobbing and choking, twisted up in my sleeping bag in a dark room, not knowing where I was. Then I heard Julie breathing in the bed next to mine, and I was back in my cabin at Burns Lake. I wanted to wake her but I knew she was tiring of telling me Dan was going to be fine, so I lay there, the certainty smothering me like a ton of wet snow, muffling my sobs in my pillow until dawn crept through the windows and it was time to get up and plant another couple thousand trees.

The cut block was mercifully flat, but covered in waist-high bright purple fireweed that gobbled up each tiny spruce plug I put into the ground.

Pesticide-drenched water trickled down my pant leg from the hole in my planting bags, right through my duct tape patches. Plodding along, exhausted, my head in a fog, I counted out my steps, scraped the ground with my boot, speared it with my shovel, dropped in a tree, kicked the hole closed with my heel. Julie trudged along off to my left, her bright blond ponytail stuck through the back of her baseball cap.

The image of the boys falling clung to me but I plodded on. I had to make money. I'd been accepted by the University of Calgary pending the completion of my English course. Just the poetry unit was left to do, but it was hard to focus on iambic pentameter while Dan and Ian were hanging off Mount Foraker in Alaska.

Dan. Fear cinched my ribs, cut off my breathing. I stopped, leaned against my shovel. Julie had said the dream meant nothing, like I knew she would. I pulled my bandana over my face to wipe up the sweat, watched as Julie pulled ahead of me on her line. It'd be hard to space my trees properly from hers in this fireweed if we got too far apart. I counted out my steps, scraped down to good soil, speared the ground with my shovel. Planting was supposed to shut down my brain, but it seemed to be doing the opposite.

Julie, Wendy and I were squeezed into our cabin's tiny kitchen, chopping vegetables. Wendy was staying at camp but we'd invited her for supper. It was good to have her around. She had a calming effect on me. After our early days of climbing, she'd gone on to be a park warden, ski patroller and paramedic, so she knew the mountains well. When she said the boys would be fine, I almost believed her.

There was a light tap on the door. A woman's wide face blurred behind the screen—Betty, who owned the cabin we were renting.

"Message for Jan."

My knife clattered to the counter. Wendy looked at me strangely, nudged me toward the door. I didn't want to move. I didn't want to know. I wanted my life to stay like this for a while longer. Normal.

Betty pulled on the screen door handle and the mosquitoes floated in through the opening. She extended a small square of white paper.

"Shannon called." Shannon was an eighteen-year-old lift operator who'd worked at Nakiska when I ski-patrolled. She was looking after the house till we all got back.

Betty shook the paper at me till I walked over and took it.

Big block letters, WHILE YOU WERE OUT. A list of possible messages with a little check mark in the box beside *Telephoned*. Not beside *Rush*. Our phone number in Banff was written in the message section.

"She didn't leave a message, or say it was urgent?"

"No, just that you should phone her tonight."

Some of the tension eased out of my shoulders. If it was about the boys, if anything had happened, the box for *Urgent* or *Rush* would have been ticked. Betty turned and headed back up the hill to her trailer while I put the memo in my pocket. Back at the counter I picked up my knife and a carrot.

"Don't you think you should call her?" Julie asked.

"Shannon's just a kid. She probably can't figure out if she's supposed to water the plants once or twice a week."

"Just call her and see what she wants. We'll get supper ready." Wendy took the knife out of my hand.

At the trailer, Betty gave me a quick lesson on how to use the radio phone, then I dialled the familiar number to my house. After five rings, Shannon answered. She sounded breathless.

I pushed the button and talked into the receiver.

"I got a message to call you. Is everything okay?" I let go of the button to let Shannon talk.

". . . to call them right away." I just caught the tail end. It was obvious she didn't know this was a radio phone.

I pushed the button. "Shannon, this is a radio phone. You have to wait till I'm finished. Call who?"

But again, she was talking. ". . . phone the wardens in Alaska right away and . . ."

Wardens. Alaska.

I wanted to go back to my cabin. Crawl into bed. Put the pillow over my head. I pushed down the button, started talking. Now I must have been talking right over her voice.

"Shannon! What are you talking about?" I released the button.

I caught one word.

Avalanche.

A loud roar filled my ears as blood pumped through the veins in my temples.

I pounded the button down and yelled, "What the fuck are you talking about? What avalanche?" But again, only a few garbled words came back to me. I turned toward the doorway. "Someone, help me!" *Was that me screaming?* I'd meant to say, "Could you help me with the radio, please," but I kept screaming, "Someone, help me!" over and over.

Footsteps rumbled down the narrow hall toward me.

"My boyfriend. Something's happened." I couldn't talk properly. My mouth felt as though it were no longer attached to my face. Like it was full of cotton balls.

Betty looked at her husband. "I'll go get her friends." Larry sat beside me, pried the receiver out of my fist.

"This is Larry. This is a radio phone and we can only talk one at a time. Could you please repeat the message?"

With my head between my knees, I willed her not to say it.

"A warden called from Alaska and left a number and you have to phone him right away." She stopped talking, waiting for Larry to speak. I still didn't know what was happening.

"What the fuck is she talking about?" I was crying now.

Larry didn't say anything, just waited until Shannon figured out she should keep going.

"There was an avalanche on Mount Foraker. They need Jan to tell them what kind of equipment the guys were carrying."

"Why?" I ran my hands through my hair, pulled till the roots threatened to pop out of my scalp. It didn't make any sense. Why would they need to know that?

Larry asked for more details.

"There was a yellow climbing suit in the avalanche debris."

I stopped rocking back and forth on the stool. Ian's climbing suit was bright yellow.

Shannon didn't know anything else but gave Larry the number for the warden's office and said they'd be there all night. They were doing a search.

Wendy and Julie rushed in while I was pacing around the little room. Wendy would know what to do. She had handled countless disasters in the mountains. "It might not even be them," she said.

She dialled the warden's office in Talkeetna. Introduced herself.

"Is the girlfriend in the room?" the warden asked.

"Yes, she's right beside me."

Silence. After several seconds the warden spoke again. "There's been an avalanche on the SE Ridge of Mount Foraker." The route they'd been planning to climb before their attempt on the Infinite Spur. A warm-up climb. To adjust to the altitude.

I hopped off the stool, relief flooding through me. "Tell him it can't be them then. Tell him they're on the Spur. They did the SE Ridge when they first got up there." Wendy knew this. Repeated it into the phone.

Another long pause.

"We think the avalanche occurred on May 5," the warden said.

Two weeks ago! Four days after we dropped them off at the airport. Right when they were supposed to be on the SE Ridge.

The boys falling, twisting around each other.

I looked at Julie, then Wendy. Julie tried to put a glass of water in my hand, tried to get me to sit back down but I couldn't move.

"We're pretty sure it was them, plus two Americans from Anchorage. The tracks lead into the avalanche starting zone, and they don't come out. We got a report from other climbers going up the route, and we did a flyover, saw the avalanche site but we can't get in there on foot. It's too dangerous."

"How do they know they're dead? What if they're still alive? Are they just abandoning them?"

The warden had heard me. "I'm sorry. They fell three thousand feet."

I sank back onto the stool. I wanted to scream but a scream would have made this real. *Three thousand feet. Was that like falling off the top of El Capitan? How long did it take to fall three thousand feet?* I didn't want to be in my body anymore. I started to float. The voice of the warden sounded like it was coming through a tunnel.

"We'll have to wait about ten days, till they're overdue, before we confirm that they are . . . you know . . . That it was them. There's always a chance they're on another route."

Wendy wiped away a tear, but I jolted up. "Did you hear that? He said there's a good chance it's not them!"

Larry smiled sadly at me and nodded. Betty blew her nose noisily into a tissue. I couldn't figure out why they hadn't heard what the warden had said. *They must have been on another route!*

Wendy and Julie led me out and down the road to our cabin. They were both crying. I tried to feel something.

I paced the small floor, ten steps to the wall, turned, ten steps to my bed, sat on the edge of the mattress, my knee bouncing up and down like it did when I was scared out of my mind on a climb. Got up, paced again. Energy roared through me like I'd injected myself with twenty cups of espresso. Wendy and Julie watched me. I stopped. Turned to them.

"What am I supposed to do?"

"It's all arranged. Barb will pick you up at the airport, take you to Dan's brother's."

"But now. What do I do now? That's tomorrow." It was only eight o'clock, still light out. Too early to sleep. And how would I sleep anyway?

"Betty's going to try to find some Valium."

I started riffling through my backpack, looking for something, but I'd already forgotten what. My brain wasn't working. My hand closed around something flat and round. I pulled it out. Birth control pills. *You've got to be fucking kidding me.* Anger clawed, like some wild beast trying to rip out of me. I threw them against the wall. The plastic shattered and pink pills sprinkled across the floor like confetti.

15

IN THE ARMS OF
A MOUNTAIN

Grant was behind me on the trail, letting me set the pace. Up the switchbacks, through the trees, I tried to grind myself into the ground hard enough to beat down the panic that was balled up in the back of my throat. But my whole body felt mired in gravity thick as quicksand and I started to slow. At the next switchback I leaned over with my hands on my knees, suddenly dizzy.

"You okay?" Grant stopped beside me. He'd been hanging around the house for ten days now with the rest of our friends, taking me out hiking or climbing or mountain biking to exhaust me enough to sleep. The wardens in Alaska wouldn't declare Dan and Ian dead until they were officially overdue at the end of May. Tomorrow. But I seemed to be the only one who couldn't say out loud what everyone else knew. They were dead. They'd been dead for almost a month.

"Yeah, just give me a sec."

"Did you eat anything this morning?"

"No, I couldn't." I'd barely eaten since the phone call.

"Last night?" He was taking off his pack.

Last night. Had I eaten last night? I'd been in such a fog from the Valium. The half bottle of red wine I'd washed it down with hadn't helped either.

"I don't think so."

Grant pulled an energy bar from the flap of his pack, peeled off the wrapper and handed it to me. It was one of the expired army-issue bars we'd all filled our packs with after cadet camp last year. Free, and for good reason. It had the taste and consistency of cardboard, but I chewed on it and felt some energy seep back into my limbs.

"You want to keep going?"

"Yeah. I don't want to go home."

Home. Dan's house, which now belonged to Dan's parents.

I cinched the hip strap on my pack. I'd lost so much weight the buckles touched.

Grant threw his pack easily on his back and we continued on. After a few minutes, the quartzite spire came into view, the Tower of Babel, leaning toward Moraine Lake. We stopped and Grant pointed out our line, six pitches up the north side. Moderate climbing. Nothing difficult.

We headed off the path onto the scree slope, along the faint trail to the base where we dropped our packs. While I started stacking the rope into a pile in the scree, Grant pulled out his rack.

"You want to lead the first pitch? Good way to get your head back into it for the cadet camp."

My job at the cadet camp started in four weeks. We hadn't even had the memorial service yet. How was I ever going to feel normal enough to guide a bunch of teenagers around the mountains? But I needed the money for tuition. I was going to school in the fall as planned. My parents couldn't help financially with my dad's retirement looming, but they'd been urging me on, hoping school would eventually lead to a job that didn't involve climbing.

I knew the first pitch was easy. Grant was being careful with me. Everyone was. All tiptoeing around, trying not to say anything that would set me off. A few nights ago, at the King Eddy Pub, when everyone was talking about Dan and Ian in past tense, I'd yelled, "You all think they're dead. You're abandoning them!" People at the other tables had turned and stared at me like I was a freak. When I ran out into the street, Grant followed and walked me home. It seemed every time I fell apart, I turned around and there he was. Not exactly what I had expected from a guy with a reputation for being an asshole.

I looked up the route. Blocks of rusty-yellow quartzite covered in lichen were stacked for 1,500 feet of moderate climbing. The rock was broken up, lots of little ledges and huge holds, and it looked easy to protect.

"So, you want the first lead?"

Pulling on my climbing shoes, I nodded. I hadn't done a lead since my trip to Oregon with Julie, before dropping the boys off at the Seattle airport. It would be hard to work as a climbing guide if I couldn't climb. Over the last ten days I'd at least followed Grant up a few routes. If it hadn't been for him, I wouldn't have bothered getting out of bed. Every morning he was there like clockwork, ready to drag me into the mountains, indulging me in my fantasy that the boys were coming home.

That fantasy had come to an abrupt end the night before, with a phone call from Toronto. Dan's mother's voice. "He's gone, Jan. You have to let him go."

Dan's father and brother had just gotten back from Alaska where they had flown over Mount Foraker with the pilot, the last living person to have spoken with the guys. They took dozens of photos of the snow slope and the avalanche debris at the bottom. They were getting copies made for me. Ian's family had done the trip a few days before.

"It's a beautiful mountain, Jan," Dan's mom said. "It looks like she's cradling the boys in her arms, the way the rock wraps around their snow slope."

Dan's parents had booked flights to Alberta; they'd be in Banff the next day to plan the memorial service in the United Church. They seemed to think Dan believed in God.

I hung up and kicked in the stereo speaker. Grant and Wendy rushed to my side with a bottle of Valium. Then I phoned my mother. She would arrive from Ottawa in two days.

Grant passed me the end of the rope and I tied in. Once he had me on belay, I started the climb. It was easy. The rock was solid quartzite, quality climbing for the Rockies. I grabbed a huge handhold, stepped up on a small ledge, reached for the next hold. When my feet were above Grant's head, it occurred to me: *It would be so easy to die.* All I had to do was lose my concentration for a split second and slip, or be standing in the exact wrong place when a single rock dislodged above me. It didn't matter that this wasn't a hard climb. Dan and Ian had been on an easy slog, going up their descent route to acclimatize for the real climb. They just happened to have crossed the slope at the precise moment the mountain decided to shed a layer. If one of them had stopped to take a pee or to eat a chocolate bar, maybe they'd be home now.

But they weren't coming home. "They're gone, Jan. You have to stop waiting." His mother's words slammed into me like rock fall.

"I can't move!" My hands were glued to their holds.

Grant dropped his cigarette and looked up. He paused, like he was about to try to talk me into continuing. Then he thought better of it. He guided my feet with words, talking slowly and calmly like someone coaxing a child out of a tree, till I'd reversed the moves and was sitting slumped against the wall. My chest started to heave with big, messy sobs. I'd never cried on a climb. What was he going to think of me?

Grant took the rack from my shoulder and I started to undo my knot to give him the sharp end of the rope. I couldn't read his face. It was like a blank slab, no anger, no impatience, no pity, no sadness. Immutable as a mountain. He seemed to exert the same steely grip on his sadness that he exerted over his fear in order to climb death routes. I didn't know where he got that kind of control, but I wanted some of it.

He started up the climb while I belayed, and continued to cry, as quietly as I could. When the rope went tight, I cleaned the anchor, strapped on my pack, and followed.

On the summit, we sat on large blocks of lichen-covered quartzite that had been placed in a circle by previous climbers. Grant pulled two cans of beer from his pack, passed one to me. I popped the tab and took a long, warm guzzle as he lit up a cigarette.

During the whole climb, I hadn't led one pitch. Even following, I'd been consumed with images of falling through the air.

We were surrounded by summit cairns, rocks piled on rocks in all shapes and sizes. Reaching into a hole in the biggest one, which was almost as tall as I was, I pulled out a waterproof metal cylinder, the summit register. Dan and Ian had probably both done this route. They would have recorded their names. I pulled out the booklet and ran down the list. I couldn't find them.

"They aren't here."

"I don't always sign those either," Grant said.

"No. Dan would have signed it."

I started from the first page again, passing names of people I knew. Geoff, Niccy, Wendy, Barb, Joe, Peter, Saul, Zac, Guy, Ken, Julie, Mark. I was on the verge of tears again. Dan's name should have been there. He collected climbs like notches on a belt. In his climbing journal, he recorded every route in great detail: the gear he used, the weather, the ratings and a description of each pitch, the approach, the descent. The time it took from car to car. Leaving his signature in all the registers on all the mountains he climbed would have been important to him.

"Maybe they bring a new booklet up when the old one's full. He could be in an old one."

Grant sounded impatient, so I brushed away my tears and scratched down our names and the date—June 5, 1987. Seeing our names together like that, on the same line, sent a bolt of shame through me, like I was committing adultery. I wanted to erase Grant's name, put it a line or two down, but the pencil had no eraser. After I'd crammed the pages back in, I tucked the cylinder back into the hole.

Trying not to cry, I leaned back against the rocks, closed my eyes and let the sun soak into my skin. "I wish I could go up to Alaska. I think it'd help."

"You don't have to go to Alaska. Dan and Ian are here, in the Rockies, not up there." He sounded angry.

I rested my head on my knees. I was so sleepy. I didn't feel Dan's presence. I just felt his absence. "Aren't you ever scared of dying?"

"Yeah, of course, but I'm more terrified of the alternative. Coming home from a nine-to-five job and staring at a wall. Sinking into mediocrity." He stubbed out his cigarette, dug a little hole and buried the butt.

"Living in a blue split-level house with vinyl siding." I pictured my father mowing the lawn of our house in Munster wearing his plaid shorts and no shirt, his chest covered in curly dark hair, a middle-age roll starting to form around his waist.

"Yeah. Two-point-five babies and all that."

Babies. When was it that Dan and I had been talking about babies? Two months ago? Three?

"My father was an Air Canada pilot but he called himself a bus driver," Grant said. "He was bored out of his mind. I'll never end up like that."

Grant had been thirteen when his father's plane had crashed over Ottawa. He'd been instructing two new pilots. Grant had worshipped him. Maybe that was why he was hauling me around the mountains. He knew what I was going through.

We stared off at the glaciated peaks in the distance and sipped our beers. When he spoke again, he sounded beaten down and exhausted, like me.

"They wouldn't have been on that route if it wasn't for me." He crumpled his empty beer can in his fist. His face looked like it was about to crumple too and I wanted to go over to his rock, put my arms around him and let him cry, but he fought for composure and won. "I pushed them to go to Foraker instead of McKinley."

Any anger I'd felt toward Grant for his part in Dan's decision had disappeared near the beginning of the waiting. We'd been at the kitchen table, anticipating an update from the wardens, and Grant had let one tear slip out. He'd wiped it away quickly, thinking no one had seen. But I had.

"It's not your fault. Dan and Ian made their own choice."

Is that why he felt such a strong compulsion to look after the widow? Because he felt responsible? A pinch of disappointment, then burning shame spread slowly up my neck to my face. I wanted Grant to be hanging out with me because he wanted to be with me, not from some sense of loyalty toward Dan. How could I even be thinking that?

"I want to do the Infinite Spur in their honour," Grant said.

Panic closed my throat and I couldn't speak. I barely knew this guy, but I couldn't seem to get through the day without him.

A distant crash, like thunder, broke the silence between us. To the south, Mount Faye unloaded tons of ice and snow. We sat and listened until the rumble slipped back to silence.

16

THE UNDERWEAR DRAWER

My first night alone. I sat on the edge of the bed with the overhead light still on, not wanting to commit to getting under the covers, to trying to fall asleep before the Valium kicked in. Nights were the worst. So far, I'd been sleeping in the living room, tucked between sleeping bags full of climbers here for the memorial service. But everyone had cleared out except for Zac, fast asleep in his own room down the hall, and Laurie, our neighbour, who was staying in Ian's room off the kitchen. His wife had kicked him out again, and Dan had always taken him in, so that's what we'd done. My mother had left for Ottawa that morning, Dan's parents and two sisters had flown back to Toronto, and his brother was back in Calgary. Before they left, they'd sold the townhouse. I had to be out by the end of the summer.

I reached toward the desk, pulled open the top drawer. This was a ritual I'd been doing for two weeks, as though one of these times I'd find something personal, like a love letter to open in the event of his death. Maybe in a secret compartment. The drawer was empty, as I knew it would be. His family had gone through the whole house, including these drawers, trying to find anything with his mark on it, just as I was doing, as though they could whisk tiny pieces of him back to Toronto and reassemble him there. They had taken his climbing journal and the few climbing stories he'd written. I knew they would photocopy them for me, but it wasn't the same. I wanted to be able to touch the paper and know it was the same paper his hands had touched.

I *did* have his account of our trip to Yosemite tucked into my journal, though. I wasn't willing to share that with his family. *The definition of total frustration may be trying to climb with your girlfriend . . .* He'd also written of his drive to the coast to pick me up for our climbing trip to Squamish: *By Hope I knew I'd be in my sweetie's arms by four o'clock, but then a fucking road crew held me up for twenty minutes.* He'd written the date, May 5. He'd had exactly one year left to live.

The next drawer held his ledger of expenses. Tiny numbers and words, neatly written and calculated in pencil. He'd even written down each coffee he'd bought downtown on his breaks. He could never fathom how I would sometimes be overdrawn on my account, why I didn't know from one minute to the next exactly how much money I had.

The rest of the desk drawers were empty. He'd thrown out piles of other papers before he'd left, stuff he hadn't wanted anyone to read, as though he knew on some level he was never coming home.

In our dresser, one drawer was untouched. His underwear drawer. I'd given his sweaters and T-shirts to his climbing buddies—knowing if Dan suddenly showed up they would gladly give them back. I'd kept his blue down vest and navy pile jacket for myself. The rest had gone to the Salvation Army. But the Sally Ann didn't take used underwear, and I couldn't make myself throw them in the garbage.

I closed the drawer, crawled into bed, curled around my pillow. Maybe if I squeezed hard enough I could get rid of the ache in my belly—too much Valium, Gravol and alcohol, not enough food. I tucked my nose into Dan's T-shirt, the one our friend Jean had hand-painted for him in Vancouver. She'd told him to take it to Alaska for good luck but he'd forgotten it in the Subaru in Seattle. One sign after another.

A groan slipped out and I stifled it in my pillow so Zac and Laurie wouldn't hear. I had to get a grip. I wasn't the only woman curled around a pillow or riffling through a dead climber's underwear drawer. Dan and Ian had died with two Alaskans who'd left behind wives, and days after their avalanche, a popular Calgary climber, Dave Cheesmond, had disappeared on Mount Logan with his American climbing partner, Catherine. Again, no bodies. Dave had left his wife Gillian alone to raise their four-year-old daughter. At least she had a reason to get out of bed.

I wasn't planning to go to Dave's service. I'd had my fill of climbers' memorials. The only one that had been remotely fitting had been Ian's. His parents had held it outside on the property he'd grown up on near Fruitvale and had invited all his climbing friends. Afterward, as we played hacky sack, Ian's mother had said it made things a bit easier to see us laugh.

During Dan's memorial service, the minister had done his God spiel, and Dan's brother and sisters had spoken, but no one had talked about what a brilliant climber he was, or even acknowledged he was a climber. No one had mentioned the climbing community, though the church was a sea of Gore-Tex, pile and hiking shoes. And no one had mentioned me, even though I'd been assigned the whole front pew with my mother, opposite the family. It was as though Dan hadn't had a girlfriend, even though his family had met me several times. I'd even visited them with Dan in Toronto.

Afterward, I'd sat in the stairwell of the church, trying to wring out some tears. I couldn't. My soul had been given a big shot of anaesthetic. I reminded myself that his parents liked me, they just hadn't approved of Dan living with me. Dan had mentioned that once. They hadn't approved of the old girlfriend either. I reminded myself that his parents had lost their child, whom they'd had for twenty-seven years. My year and a half seemed paltry.

The silence of the house pressed down on me, nudged me closer to the edge of somewhere I didn't want to go. I reached for the small bottle of Valium on the bedside table, popped another pill and washed it down with a glass of stale water. If I could just get to morning. The days were a bit better than the nights.

I closed my eyes and tried to take deep, calming breaths, but it felt like a sandbag had landed on my chest. My breathing got shallower and I started to panic. Two nights ago, the night of the memorial, Wendy and Mom had sat on the edge of my bed, promising they wouldn't leave until I'd fallen asleep. Then it had hit. Dan was dead. He wasn't coming home. His house, my home, sold out from under me. Soon I was crying so hard my lungs had become a vacuum, deflated, turned inside out. I tried to suck in air, panicked. My sobs became strange barking sounds, but still no air. Wendy pounded on my back while my mother yelled, "For chrissake, Jan, breathe!" and the fear in her voice compounded my fear. She couldn't protect me. She couldn't make this go away. When the air finally whooshed into my lungs, I saw the relief on her face. But my fear stayed. I felt so completely alone.

Is that how Dan and Ian had died? Struggling for air? How long had they been alive during the fall? Had they suffered? When would the moment of death have come? At five hundred feet? Three thousand feet?

My breathing got more and more shallow, till I was taking tiny gasps of air. It was trying to pull me under again. A blackness. I needed something. Pills weren't working. Alcohol wasn't working. I needed someone in the room.

With my sleeping bag under my arm, I descended the stairs till I was outside Ian's room. Now Laurie's room. If I could just lie on the floor beside his bed, maybe I could sleep. A few nights ago, Grant had slept on the floor beside my bed, and for the first time since the phone call in Burns Lake, I'd gotten a decent sleep.

The door was closed. I knocked lightly. No answer, so I pushed it. It opened with a creak. A dim shaft of light fell on the bed from the hallway. A big shape convulsed for a moment, then my eyes adjusted and Wendy turned toward me, Laurie looking up from under her. She fell onto his chest, laughing. They were both laughing. I mumbled an apology, backed out of the room, shut the door.

Death is an aphrodisiac, someone had said in the bar a few nights earlier when we were discussing some other climbers who'd jumped into bed with each other. It seemed death was erasing everyone's brain cells, replacing them with sex hormones. But Wendy and Laurie? Wendy was my age. Laurie was a sweet, middle-aged, unemployed, newly separated alcoholic. Not even a climber.

Their voices followed me as I grabbed my keys off the counter, slipped bare feet into runners, and rushed to my car with my sleeping bag.

Banff Avenue was deserted. Too early for the summer tourist invasion. My car seemed to know where I needed to go; it barely paused before turning onto Wolf Street. Grant's house was pitch black when I pulled up in the alley beside Ian's beloved blue Honda Civic. His parents had given it to Grant. They had wanted one of his friends to have it.

I pushed on the back door. It was open. The stairwell leading to the basement smelled of cat urine, old sweat and spices. One bare bulb flickered at the bottom. I tiptoed down, past the common area, which was made up of a plywood counter above the concrete floor, with a hot plate and mini-fridge. Grant shared these cooking arrangements and one tiny bathroom with four Korean restaurant workers who rented the other rooms.

I'd been here only once, a few days earlier, to pick up some gear Grant had forgotten for a climb. I couldn't believe he lived like this. He seemed to like to suffer. He'd told me he liked the price.

There was no light under Grant's door. My arms tightened around my sleeping bag. What was I doing here? I knew I should go home and try to sleep alone. I'd have to get used to it eventually.

I tapped softly on the door.

"Yeah? Who's there?" His voice was gruff, like he was waking from a deep sleep.

"It's me. Jan."

Silence. What was going through his head? Was a voice screaming at him not to let me in?

"It's not locked," he said.

I pushed open the door. Grant clicked on the bedside light.

Words spilled with tears as I clutched my sleeping bag to my chest. "I'm sorry. I can't sleep. I just need to be near someone." A half lie. It was him I needed to be near. Someone who was missing Dan and Ian as much as I was.

He pushed himself up on his elbow and smiled a groggy smile. His shaggy blond hair shot off in all directions, uncontrolled. He wasn't pissed off.

"Don't apologize."

"I'll just sleep on the floor. You can go right back to sleep."

He watched me spread my sleeping bag on the thin rug. "Don't be crazy. You can't sleep on the floor. It's disgusting down there. There's room up here."

I barely hesitated before crawling into bed with him. With my sleeping bag over me but unzipped, I curled into a ball, facing the wall.

I lay there, barely breathing, his body so close I could almost feel his heat, and then his hand crept into my hair. Every nerve in my body was triggered, sensitized, alert. Blood beat against my veins, threatening to break through. I couldn't move.

Once Dan had been heading out for a climb and I'd said, "If you die, I'll just go out and get another boyfriend." He'd looked so hurt. I hadn't meant it. I'd been trying to threaten him into staying alive.

Grant's hand crept lower, rested on my hip for a moment, slipped around to my tummy. His thumb grazed my breast. I didn't stop him.

17

TEETERING ON THE EDGE

My English professor peered at me from behind round wire glasses, then looked back down at my essay. Red ink flashed as he flipped another page. Red ink was not a good sign. Red ink meant mistakes. Mistakes meant failure. Halfway through my first semester of university and I was a failure.

My hands clamped down on the arms of my chair. I'd only written one essay since high school, in my grade-twelve English course, and this first draft, combined with the final draft, was worth 30 percent of our mark.

This was our second one-on-one meeting. In September we'd met to come up with a topic for my paper. Climbing kept cropping up, how I'd built my identity, my community, my life around it, and he'd encouraged me to write about it. Then I'd told him about Dan. When he got that typical sympathetic look on his face and spewed out the requisite condolences, I suddenly felt like I'd taken off all my clothes and given him a private pole dance. *Why did I tell him that? Why can't I keep something about my life private?* Maybe I'd needed him to know I was different from the rest of the students in our class. I was special. I had a dead boyfriend. Of course, after a revelation like that, when I decided to defend rock climbers in my paper, prove that we had a life wish, not a death wish, he'd said, "Good luck with that."

So, with my boyfriend dead less than five months and my new boyfriend up on Mount Alberta, I'd written a paper about the climbers' "life wish."

And now my professor slapped my essay on the desk, leaned back in his chair and studied me. He looked like John Denver. His neatly cut hair was blond, not a trace of grey, unlike most of my professors. He couldn't have been more than a few years older than me, maybe thirty. At twenty-six, I was closer in age to him than to the students in our class. Most of them were straight out of high school.

I looked down at my runners, at my baby toe poking out of a hole in the side. I knew he was going to suggest—politely, even gently, no doubt, because he seemed like a decent guy—that I should give up my dream of university. That I just didn't have the aptitude. That I was stupid. And then what would I do? I had nothing to go back to in Banff. I'd moved out of Dan's place as soon as I'd finished my summer at the cadet camp. I could waitress, but I wanted to be a professional. A professional what, I hadn't decided, but when people asked, "So what do you do?" I wanted to be able to say: *geologist*, or *cartographer* maybe, or *French teacher*. Not *waitress*.

"This is a good first draft. In fact, an excellent first draft."

My death grip on the chair loosened.

"I initially had my doubts about your argument, but I must admit, you've convinced me. Not quite to the point where I'd try climbing myself, mind you."

I pulled the paper toward me. It was covered in red, but there was a huge, circled "A" right at the top.

"You're one of the best writers in this class."

I sat up straighter. He was telling me I was a good writer, and at the beginning of the year I couldn't even spell *a lot*. I'd thought it was one word.

My prof was smiling at me. *Does he just want to sleep with me? Is that why he gave me an A?* But no, when I stood up to leave, he didn't ask if he could buy me a drink. He shook my hand politely, not squeezing too much or for too long.

As I speed-walked down the hall to my French class, it was all I could do to keep my feet on the linoleum. I wanted to leap into the air and click my heels together. I had a brain! It was the first moment of joy I'd felt in months.

Shifting my butt carefully so I didn't dent the hood, I leaned back against the windshield of Ian's Honda and took a sip of the cold beer Grant had just pulled from the river. After a full day of sunshine, the sun was low in the sky and the cool air was a reminder that this was just a trick, an Indian summer. It could snow tomorrow as easily as be another cloudless day.

Castle Rock filled the horizon, a fortress-shaped mountain over nine thousand feet high. A few hours ago we'd stood on top of the middle buttress, staring down at the Bow River snaking its way beside the Trans-Canada Highway.

"Hey, I forgot to tell you! I got an A on my English paper!" I hadn't really forgotten. I'd just been looking for the right time. For some reason, Grant didn't like talking about my schooling. Wouldn't even read my essays.

"Good for you," Grant said from his perch on a boulder. He pulled out his pack of cigarettes. He no longer rolled his own now that he had a job logging in BC. He would work long enough to qualify for unemployment insurance, get laid off, then climb the rest of the year.

"I climbed not bad for an A student today, didn't I?"

My back was stiff, my butt and calf muscles already seizing up from the 4,600-foot elevation gain, but it had been worth it. Thirteen pitches, most of it really steep and exposed, and I'd swung leads the whole way. I didn't think it possible after my disastrous summer at the cadet camp, bumbling through the mountains in a fog of Valium. I'd made so many bad decisions I hadn't been invited back for the following year. But today I'd redeemed myself.

Grant grinned at me through cigarette smoke, which was nice to see. Ever since he'd started working in the bush I found it harder to reach him. He was broody and silent when I visited him at the house he'd moved into with a bunch of climbers in Canmore, and even more so after he drove the hour east to Calgary to visit me. I spent weekends seesawing up and down with his moods, wondering what I'd done wrong. Maybe we just needed to be in the mountains to get along with each other.

"It only took us six hours, car to car. And I never once felt like shitting my pants on my leads." A little voice in my head added, *Dan would be proud of me*, but I didn't say it out loud.

From Dan's climbing journal, I knew that Dan and Ian had soloed this same route in mountain boots. Without a rope, one little slip and they would have plummeted a few thousand feet. Going through that journal made me wonder how he'd lasted as long as he had. It must have been hard for his parents to read. His father had photocopied the whole thing and put it in a binder for me with a picture of Dan and the poem that started *Do not stand at my grave and weep.*

Sipping my beer, I gazed at the mountain. It rose up from the valley, a fortress with turrets. It had felt so good to be moving confidently on rock again. Maybe Grant was right. Maybe I shouldn't be going to that grief counsellor. I should be getting into the mountains. Exercising. Beating the grief out of me.

"So." Grant paused. "Barry invited me on his expedition to the Himalayas."

Barry. In my early twenties we'd climbed and danced and partied together, even made a half-hearted attempt at romance. He was an Aries like me, which led me to believe two such impulsive, temperamental personalities weren't meant to be together. And here I was with Grant, another Aries.

Dipping my head to let my hair cover my face, I took another sip, tried to wash away my panic while Grant talked excitedly about Nanga Parbat in Pakistan in May, then Everest at the end of August, up a route that had never been climbed. I clenched my teeth and willed myself not to cry. Grant thought there was something wrong with me because I cried so much. It had been six whole months since the avalanche. Time to move on.

"Barry's working on sponsors. We won't go if we don't get the sponsors."

Barry would have no trouble squeezing money out of companies for an expedition. He was one of the best-known climbers in Canada.

Another long swig of beer. I knew the statistics. One in ten climbers died over there. I closed my eyes tight against the tears, but they squeezed out anyway. I tried to wipe them away with my sleeve but they kept flowing.

Grant slumped on his rock. "Jesus."

Two months earlier, just before school, I'd tried to split up with Grant. I told him I couldn't deal with his climbing. But even as I said the words, I knew I'd never go through with it. For some reason, I was drawn to him as much as he was drawn to the mountains.

"I'm sorry," I said.

We sat quietly, staring up at Castle, down toward the river, into the trees. Anywhere but at each other.

———

"Do you ever come to one of these things and look around and count how many people you've slept with?" Geoff said.

We were leaning against the wall, watching couples sway to a James Taylor song in the dim light of the dance hall. My heart was still pounding from the last Rolling Stones tune. It felt good to dance, grind all the academic angst out of me, but any time a slow song came on, all of a sudden it was high school all over again. Anyone without a partner headed to the walls. I was at the Calgary Mountain Club Christmas party on my own because, as usual, Grant was hanging off a mountain with Barry, this time up the Icefields Parkway.

"Yup. All the time," I said. "We're such an incestuous bunch." In our climbing community it seemed like everyone had checked each other out over the years before settling down, most often with an outsider.

"I don't," Geoff said.

"Asshole." I backhanded him in the chest and he doubled over in mock pain.

I watched Saul and Judy sway to the music, holding each other as close as her nine-month bulge would allow. Saul had met Judy in Victoria at the tail end of her disastrous marriage and wouldn't even tell us her name for months. And now they looked like they had cupid's arrows twanging in their backs.

Saul stepped back from Judy and gave her a spin, gently, as though scared she'd break. When *we* danced together, Saul flipped me upside down and over his shoulder and dragged me through his legs. Once I slammed into a wall.

"They're so fucking in love." I took a swig of my beer. Happy couples were everywhere these days. My roommate Mike had recently had a croquet party with Christo and Babs, who was nine months pregnant. A few days later, out popped a little boy.

"Yup. They are that," Geoff said.

"It's so fucking unfair." I could hear the slurring self-pity in my voice. Trying to drink Dan away never worked. Instead it amplified

172   JAN REDFORD

everything. Tears began to burn their familiar path over my cheek-bones. Homesickness for Banff and the mountains and Dan gnawed at my gut, day in and day out. We would have been like Saul and Judy and Babs and Christo if he hadn't gone to Foraker.

Geoff looked down at me with an uh-oh look that was becoming as familiar as my meltdowns.

"I think you may have had enough of this." He pried the beer out of my hand. "I'll introduce you to Jim Bridwell."

"I met him already."

"Come on." Geoff pulled me toward Jim as I stumbled, trying to wipe my face with my sleeve.

Jim Bridwell, one of the world's leading climbers, had done a slide show the night before at the university and I'd gone up after-ward and reminded him that we'd played hacky sack together in Yosemite. He hadn't remembered me, but he did say, "You look just like a black-haired Lynn Hill." Lynn Hill, the world's leading female climber. I'd once played hacky sack with *her* in Joshua Tree. I couldn't think of a bigger compliment. I'd said, "Too bad I can't climb like her," and he'd laughed.

"Ah, it's the dark-haired Lynn Hill," Jim said as we approached. Jim was the first to climb El Capitan in a day, and now he climbed big mountains all over the world—the Himalayas, Alaska, Patagonia— in light alpine style, the way Grant and Barry were planning to climb Nanga Parbat in the spring. No porters, no camps to retreat to, no fixed ropes, no oxygen, and just a small team. Fast and dangerous.

Jim and Geoff launched into a discussion about some mountain and I tuned them out and stared at my feet. They were now bare. I'd danced my stockings to shreds, and what remained of the nylon flut-tered below my knees in long runs. My shoes were under one of the tables somewhere and my feet were starting to freeze on the hard wood. Winter had finally come to Calgary.

Climbing chatter was to be expected at a Mountain Club party, but I didn't need to be reminded that while Grant was off to Nanga in the spring, Geoff would be on a neighbouring mountain, Ama Dablam. Yet another potential dead friend in my future.

"So what does your wife think of your climbing?" I said.

I looked up into Jim's craggy face, my anger burning through me like acid. His handlebar moustache went still as he stared back.

At his slideshow, Jim had included a photo of his home in California, a trailer he shared with his wife and young son. They'd gotten married when she found out she was pregnant.

"She hates it," he said evenly.

"So how can you do that? How can you just leave her like that, with a kid, in a trailer while you go off and try to kill yourself on some fucking mountain?" The tears were flowing again and my voice was loud in the lull between songs. A whole table of Mountain Club members looked up from their conversations and watched me.

"What gives you the right to go off and die?" I sobbed.

Jim crossed his arms and looked at Geoff like he wanted to say, *Where'd you dig up this lunatic?*

The DJ put on a Buddy Holly song, interrupting my tirade, and then Saul was hauling me back to the dance floor. I stood there crying till he grabbed my hands, pulled me toward him then pushed me away, twirling me, forcing my feet to move to the music.

"Don't worry about it until we have to." Grant didn't look up from his climbing magazine.

I sat hunched in a ball with my arms wrapped around my knees, rocking back and forth, as close to the small portable heater as I could get without burning myself. Footsteps passed overhead. Mike, my roommate. He had the two bedrooms upstairs, the heated ones, and I had the two downstairs. I had to move the heater between my office and bedroom. The living situation wasn't ideal, but we were close to the university, the rent was cheap, and except for the dirty dishes he left in the sink, Mike was a good roommate.

A happy couple on the box of a pregnancy test smiled up at us from the floor. A pregnancy stick lay on a piece of Saran Wrap beside it. It had a blue tinge to it, but the picture in the instructions showed a definite blue. A person couldn't be a little pregnant. I looked at my watch. Seven more minutes.

To get As in my classes I'd been living on coffee, very little food, and four hours of sleep. I'd lost so much weight my clothes hung off me. I vibrated with stress. How could any sperm in its right mind fertilize an egg in this environment? But my period was a week late, and my boobs were so sore I was wearing two sports bras.

Grant, who had refused to discuss the possibility of my being pregnant until we had solid proof, flipped through his magazine, completely calm, just like I imagined he'd be thousands of feet up a mountain, hanging off his tools on thin ice. I wanted to be like him but my emotions were all over the place. My mind, my emotions and now even my body were betraying me.

"Could you at least talk to me?"

"I'm trying to read."

I looked at my watch. Five more minutes.

It would be karma if I were pregnant. Punishment for being with Grant. *A blasphemy to Dan's spirit,* was what one of our friends had called our relationship. When Grant had tried to explain that Dan would have wanted him to look after me, that friend had replied, "Look after her, maybe, not fuck her."

Four minutes.

There was a dream I'd been having over and over. Dan had survived the avalanche, made his way home and found out I was already with someone else. His climbing partner. The look on his face woke me every time.

What if he came back after six months to a pregnant girlfriend?

The second hand ticked by. I'd been working so hard in school. I'd gotten As in geography, English and sociology, and a B in French. I'd decided to go into geography and be a cartographer, travel around up north. Back to the Yukon and Northwest Territories. Back to my roots. Live alone in a cabin somewhere. I couldn't do that with a baby. And I couldn't stand the thought of the alternative.

Two minutes.

What would I tell my poor mother? She kept accepting collect calls from California, Indonesia, Fernie, Banff. She'd been so relieved when I started school. None of her training as a psychiatric nurse would have prepared her for this next bit of news.

I watched Grant, engrossed in his magazine. I wanted to crawl onto his lap and force him to pay attention to me. The more he distanced himself, the more I wanted him. The less he talked, the more I talked. The more stoic he was, the more emotional I was. If I had a baby with him, he'd have this control over me forever.

A few weeks ago at a pub in Canmore I was crying into my beer over Dan, yet again, and Grant said what I needed was to be alone, no boyfriend, until it hurt. It sounded like we were breaking up and I panicked, but he never mentioned it again. I knew he was right. This need for Grant felt like an addiction. I was going to suffer one loss after another if I couldn't learn to survive on my own. If I could glean anything positive from Dan's death it would be self-reliance. That was why I was in school. That was why I had to stay in school. That was why I could not be pregnant.

When the last seconds had ticked by, I stopped rocking and picked up the wand, compared it to the example of a positive test in the instructions.

Grant finally lowered his magazine.

The wand was a brilliant, unmistakable blue. A perfect match.

18

PINK WEDDING DRESS

At seven o'clock, the sun started to poke around the towel pinned over the window. I still hadn't slept and in six hours we were meeting Sarah, the marriage commissioner, on the banks of the Bow River. The front door slammed. I sat up. It was Grant. I could hear his body ricochet off the walls down the hallway toward our room.

"Shut the fuck up!" Jerry yelled from the bedroom next to ours.

I wouldn't miss our roommates when we moved out at the end of the month. Yesterday, I'd pulled my Häagen-Dazs ice cream out of the freezer and discovered someone had eaten it all and put the empty container back. None of the guys would own up but I knew it had to be Jerry. I was so pissed off I threw the carton against the wall. But it wouldn't be long before we had our own place. After the wedding, we were moving into Sharon's basement suite. It would be all ours. I was planning to buy a crib, make curtains, knit miniature sweaters.

Grant stumbled into our room. I lay still on our foamy, under the covers while he crouched in a corner with his head in his hands and started to groan. I regulated my breathing, tried to still the movement of my eyeballs under their lids, then realized he probably didn't even know I was three feet away from him.

Grant's three brothers had flown in the night before, and even though Grant had already had his stag, they'd decided to throw him another one. I'd met them only once, at Christmas, four months earlier in Montreal, and that one supper together had been enough to make me realize they were the absolute last people my future husband should hang out with the night before our wedding.

In a few minutes he lay quietly, his unshaven cheek flattened into the carpet. His muscles convulsed a couple of times as he slipped into sleep. I relaxed and drifted off.

At least he was safe.

Three hours before the wedding the alarm hauled me out of sleep. I propped myself up on the foamy, feeling hung over even though I hadn't touched alcohol in months, then noticed Grant, curled in a ball, fast asleep on the floor.

"Oh, shit," I said, and crawled over to him. "Grant, wake up." I shook his shoulder.

He groaned.

"Grant. Wake up. We have to go to brunch." The wedding wasn't until late afternoon, but we had a brunch planned with his family. My parents had bowed out. My father was experimenting with sobriety. He'd already lost over ten pounds.

He grabbed my arm, hard. "Don't ever leave me. I love you," he said, then curled back into a ball.

A little flicker of pleasure broke through my irritation. This was the first time he'd told me he loved me. Maybe alcohol brought his real feelings to the surface. But I didn't have time to savour it; we had to meet his family at the restaurant in ten minutes.

I shook him harder. "Grant, everyone will be waiting for us."

"Oh, fuck, I'm sick." He stumbled to his feet and ran to the bathroom.

Grant was a lightweight compared to his brothers. My own brother, before he'd quit drinking, could polish off a dozen beers and a mickey of rum in a night. And who knew how much Scotch my father could drink. I was relieved Grant didn't have the same insatiable appetite for alcohol.

As I dressed, I tried to ignore the sounds coming from the bathroom. I pulled my black wool tights over my beige, above-the-belly-button, control-top underwear—one of my future mother-in-law's contributions to my pregnancy. I'd bought the tights half price. There'd only been one pair left, size large, so they bunched at the ankle and puffed at the knees. I buttoned up my pink embroidered blouse from the church thrift shop. I hated pink but it seemed to be a common colour in second-hand clothing.

The shirt hung to mid-thigh, my attempt to hide my burgeoning belly. I was too short to pull off this pregnancy gracefully. At five months, I'd gained twenty pounds—and only one pound was attributable to the baby. I lay awake at night imagining my final metamorphosis.

I checked my teeth in a hand mirror, smeared some Chapstick on my dry, peeling lips. That was it for makeup. I tried to smooth down my thick, black hair, but it sprang back up, coarse like a horse's mane. I gave up and left to face my future in-laws. Alone.

The Sherwood House was a rustic log building in the middle of town where I had just finished working as a waitress. Grant and I had figured that his family, being from downtown Montreal, would enjoy the laid-back atmosphere of a climber, skier-type hangout. I pushed open the door and saw right away that the place was hopping. Cameron rushed by, balancing a tray of drinks, pausing long enough to roll his eyes behind his large wire glasses.

"You're lucky you quit. I've got a table full of morons drinking double Caesars for breakfast." He headed up the stairs.

A voice bawled from above. "*Garçon!*" The French was abysmal, the "r" anglicized and the "n" distinctly pronounced. No nasalization to speak of. Following the command came peals of laughter. I recognized Grant's younger brother's voice, Nate. I followed Cameron up to the loft, telling myself they probably hadn't slept yet, so technically they weren't really drinking in the morning. They were extending the night.

Grant's family found my soon-to-be-husband's absence amusing. His mother, Dorothy, laughed and said, "Boys will be boys!"

Grant was eight years older than me; he had just turned thirty-five.

Dorothy sat at the head of the table, nearest Nate, her favourite, and farthest from the eldest, Garth, her least favourite. Grant and these two brothers could have been their long-dead father's clones— blond, tall and slim with square jaws and dazzling blue eyes. Perfect pools of ice.

Greg, the second oldest and second favourite, was the polar opposite of his brothers—short with dark hair and a moustache. He was strategically placed on his mother's other side, beside a woman with very stiff blond hair. "*Bonjour! Comment ça va?* You haven't met Angie, my fiancée." Greg must have remembered I was studying French. He was the only one who was bilingual. The rest of them got by in downtown Montreal with no more vocabulary than "*Bonjour*" and "*le ketchup.*"

Angie smiled and extended a small, manicured hand. I tried not to squeeze too hard. Her lips were glazed a brilliant red, her skin concealed under a thick layer of beige foundation. Her soft green cashmere sweater looked very expensive.

I sat at the end of the table, facing my future mother-in-law, flanked by Garth and Angie.

The seating arrangement took me right back to Munster. My father at the head, my mother at the other end, and us kids spaced as strategically as Grant's family, my brother alone in his own little world of misery on one side, my sister close to my mother for protection from the males, and me, closest to my father, my job being to appease him with my charm.

"Let's get her a drink! *Garçon!*" Garth waved his hand in the air. I wanted to say, *His name is Cameron*, but I kept my mouth shut.

"Garth, she's pregnant!" Angie shot him a scathing look.

Dorothy said, "You must be excited." She was tastefully dressed in a silk pantsuit of varying shades of beige. My harshly contrasting pink nylon against black wool seemed garish.

"Yes, I am," I said, though she didn't look very excited herself, and I wasn't sure if she meant about the wedding or the baby.

Angie scooped up my hand. "You must be Irish with that dark hair and blue eyes. This baby is going to be just lovely with that yummy husband of yours."

Yummy. Weird choice of words, but it was true. Once, we'd passed by a bum in Calgary who asked Grant for a cigarette, then said, "Hey, you look just like Robert Redford." Grant got that all the time. His climbing friends sometimes called him Robert to bug him but I thought he secretly liked it.

"So Grant tells me you're a climber too." Garth leaned toward me, over Grant's empty seat. He looked good for a guy in his mid-forties. I could imagine him in his pilot's uniform with the flight attendants hanging off his arm. Seemed like aging well ran in this family.

Before I could answer he added, "Guess you won't be doing much of that anymore." Garth had barely said two words to me at Christmas, probably assuming he'd never see me again. Now I wished he'd put the muzzle back on.

I stared at him coldly. "I should be back on the rock by next summer, I figure."

Garth smiled like he knew something I didn't, took a swig of his Caesar. His first marriage had also been shotgun, but if that was what this family thought I was up to, I could give them an earful. If I'd gotten pregnant to snare a man, I sure as hell wouldn't have targeted a destitute climber who would most likely be on Everest when I was popping out his baby.

My future mother-in-law homed in on me. "I told Grant at Christmas, a baby is a big responsibility."

At Christmas, she had also approved wholeheartedly of our original plan: an abortion. Grant had no interest in becoming a father, and I didn't think I could raise a baby on my own. Dorothy must have wondered why I had suddenly changed my mind, but all along I knew I couldn't do it. I couldn't go through that again. I'd shown Grant pictures of the growing fetus so I wouldn't be the only one to suffer, and as the day of the procedure loomed, we'd discovered the baby had fingernails and could even be sucking its thumb. When the operation was postponed for a day, then cancelled due to a nurses' strike, I was too far along to try to reschedule in another province. After the shock wore off, I was ecstatic. I knew this baby had to be born. I think Grant, secretly, had also been relieved. We'd just needed the decision to be made for us.

"What about Everest? He has to go to Everest." Dorothy had photos on her walls in Montreal of Grant climbing.

"We've told everyone back in Montreal." Angie clapped her hands excitedly—Everest had that effect on people—then her smile disappeared and she dropped her climbing groupie persona, grabbed my hand again.

"I'm sure he'll be just fine . . ." She gave me that look I'd become so familiar with since Dan's death. Pity mixed with fear and relief. Fear that death was contagious, relief that she was not me. "He's lasted this long, hasn't he, love?" She patted my hand. Her South African accent was soothing.

I forced my lips into a smile. I'd spent many hours trying to change Grant's mind—pouting, cajoling, threatening, begging. But mostly blubbering. Just like I'd done with Dan before Alaska. I should have understood, since I was a climber too, but all I knew was that the old saying about lightning not striking twice did not apply to the climbing community. I couldn't go through it again, not with a baby.

Cameron appeared at the top of the stairs with a tray laden with steaming plates of grease: burgers, fish and chips, onion rings. My stomach turned.

"Ah, here it is. It's about time." Garth held up his empty glass and Cameron nodded, set up the stand, passed out the food, then headed back downstairs for more drinks.

"You must be so excited! Tell me about your dress!" Angie brought my attention back to the wedding.

My dress. Oh, Christ. I'd checked every second-hand store in Calgary and couldn't find anything that hid my body without turning me into a circus tent, so my mother had given me a dress I vaguely remembered her wearing twenty years ago in Whitehorse. Fuchsia-pink silk. Not the elegant raw silk of Dorothy's pantsuit, but the shiny, fluttery kind. Its only redeeming feature was that it was 1920s style, tight at the hips with billows of material to conceal my rolls of baby. To hide the dress, I'd accepted the loan of a jacket from my friend Barb.

Angie hadn't noticed my hesitation and just barrelled on, barely touching her salad. I could tell she was way more into this bride shit than I was.

This whole wedding had blown up in our faces. We'd originally planned to get married with one witness each, then quietly slink back home—no fanfare, no fuss and especially no family. Our union wasn't exactly the result of some magical alignment of the stars. But when Grant's brothers heard the news they invited themselves, which meant everyone had to be invited. My parents paid full fare from Ottawa, while Grant's family had flown first class with their airline passes. It had been too short notice for my brother and sister to come from Ontario. I couldn't believe I was getting married without Susan.

"You'll be just gorgeous. We'll just touch you up with a wee bit of makeup, fix up your hair . . ."

When I heard the word *gorgeous* in relation to me, I almost started to cry. Even though I had a beautiful baby to look forward to, I still disintegrated just about anywhere, anytime. I just needed to keep the tears plugged up long enough to get through the ceremony. Maybe a bit of makeup *would* help. Grant kept telling me I looked fine but he hadn't touched me in weeks.

"So, Grant tells me you'll be moving to Golden soon." Nate stuffed an onion ring into his mouth.

I almost choked on my toast. *Where the hell did he get that idea?* Golden was a small town a couple of hours away, just over the border in BC, where Grant was logging. I used to kayak there with Brad— the Kicking Horse River—and we'd drink afterward in a pub with dead animal heads on the walls and crack jokes about how the town was straight out of the movie *Deliverance*.

I took a sip of water and the toast finally scraped down my throat. "Actually, I'm going back to university in a year so we have to stay close to Calgary. We'll both be commuting."

I had quit school partway into the second semester. I'd finally reached my limit. Only six months had passed between the phone call from Alaska to the pregnancy test and in that time I'd gone to Dan and Ian's memorial services, picked up a new boyfriend, guided cadets while popping Valium, moved to Calgary, started university, and then gone to another memorial, this time for Steve Devine, the guide who'd taken me under his wing at cadet camp, knowing I needed to be guided more than the cadets did. Now I was getting married a month before the first anniversary of Dan's death.

"Who's going to look after the baby?" Dorothy and I eyed each other from our own ends of the table. "It's a full-time job, you know. I looked after my husband and children without complaining. That's just how we did things in those days. Then after Bill died, I raised four boys by myself."

"Mum, they'll figure it out. Don't get worked up," Greg said. "It's a good idea to have a degree." Greg was the only one in the family who'd gone to university.

"Who's going to look after Grant? A man needs hot meals," Dorothy muttered angrily.

"He'll be in camp, Mum. He'll have lots of hot meals." Nate was a bush pilot, so he was fully aware of the life Grant led while logging.

I pushed the eggs around on my plate, my appetite gone. *Golden. He'd need a straitjacket to get me to that little redneck hole.* I couldn't breathe with the cloud of perfume and cologne hanging over my new family. The blond brothers lit up cigarettes and I imagined my baby mutating inside me, screaming for oxygen.

I stood up too quickly, swayed a bit and grabbed the edge of the table. Greg and Angie jumped up from their chairs. Angie put her hand on my arm to steady me.

"I'm okay," I reassured them, then cracked a joke about having to drag Grant out of bed. They laughed politely.

I escaped down the stairs and had almost reached the door when Cameron cut me off. He leaned down and hissed into my ear, "If you marry into this family you're out of your fucking mind."

"Right, like I'm going to cancel two hours before the wedding." I forced a laugh as I pushed by him and out the door. I crammed my fingers into my worn-out tear ducts to postpone the flood, stumbled down the street. Yesterday, after the Häagen-Dazs debacle, I'd gone to my parents' hotel and told them I couldn't marry Grant. My father had said, "Jesus Christ. Now's a fine time to figure that out."

He was right. There was no way I could send everyone back to Quebec and Ontario with their wedding gifts. The hall was booked for a huge potluck tomorrow night. My dad had told me he loved me, had even shed a tear when he gave us a wedding cheque that would get us through the next couple of months. Even Dan's parents had sent us a cheque, and their blessing. My mom had shown up with a whole suitcase of gifts and a wedding cake, and she'd bought my bouquet; it was irreversible. Besides, Grant was nothing like his family.

I took the long way home along the Bow River. The frozen ground crunched under my hiking boots and the wind blew right through my knitted tights. The hairs on my legs stood up, a reminder that I'd better shave before putting on white nylons.

I stopped at the mound of gravel by the bridge where we would have the ceremony in two hours, found a bench and leaned back to dry my face in the sun. My hand instinctively crept to my tummy. I was going to rub it raw if I wasn't careful. I sometimes wondered if this baby was Dan's soul trying to come back. My dreams about him were still so vivid that when I woke up I could feel him in the room with me.

A reflection of the peaks of the Three Sisters wavered in the water and the cool breeze purged me of the perfume and second-hand smoke. The April air was cool and crisp, but it was the first sun we'd had in weeks. It had to be a sign of something.

Back at the house, Grant was still comatose. He looked vulnerable lying there, like our little fetus. I wanted to protect him, make up for all the hurt he'd suffered when he'd lost his dad. I knew he was damaged. I was going to be the first person to stand by him through anything. Through thick or thin. Our families would go back to where they came from, we'd move into our new home, he'd come back from Nepal and start work and look after me and the baby, and everything would be fine.

I lay down beside him, curling into his back and passing my hand over the veins in his forearms. Two months ago, when the abortion had been cancelled, he'd said, *I guess we'll have to get married*, and I'd felt such a surge of love and relief my legs had almost buckled. We'd gone ice climbing up Grotto Canyon that day and I couldn't stop smiling the whole time. I knew what most of our friends thought, but my romantic side wanted to believe that no ordinary lust could be so intense. There had to be a deeper reason why we were together. Even if it was just so this baby could be born.

"Hey, you want to get married?" I poked him, tried to tease him awake. Sometimes if I acted perky and optimistic, I eventually felt it. *Fake it till you make it.*

He let out a long moan and shook me off. "Not today. Tomorrow."

I sat up, pushed harder on his back, no longer playful.

"Sarah can't marry us tomorrow! You've got to get up!"

"Someone clean the goddamned bathroom! I've gotta take a dump!" a voice roared from the living room.

"Didn't you clean the bathroom?" He pushed himself up on his arms and looked at me, the sky blue of his eyes peeking through narrow slits.

"Are you serious? I'm not cleaning your fucking puke." I pulled away from him. He was joking. He had to be joking. But he wasn't smiling.

"Great. That's real supportive. Nice way to start a marriage."

I gathered up my trousseau: the startling pink dress, the jacket, the silver ring I'd bought downtown for thirty bucks, the white, polka-dotted nylons, the worn-out beige sandals I'd bought years ago in Indonesia—the only footwear I owned that wasn't designed for hiking, biking, climbing or skiing.

"You can have the shower. I'll get ready at Mom and Dad's hotel. Angie's going to try a bit of makeup on me."

"No. No makeup. You don't need it. You look good natural."

Standing in the doorway, I smiled. I liked that he liked me the way I was. I decided to take a risk. "I love you," I said casually, as though it were an afterthought. I'd never told him that before. I missed how Dan and I had said it every day.

I couldn't tell if Grant had heard me, so I said, "Do you love me?" My voice sounded high-pitched, babyish, and I told myself, *This is stupid. I should just go get ready. He's already said it, even if he doesn't remember.*

"Well, it's not that simple," he started. "We don't even know each other yet. We've only lived together three months."

I could tell he thought I was going to disintegrate again, because he quickly added, "People grow to love each other over the years."

The wedding was in less than an hour, so that would have to be good enough for now. I'd soften him up. And if I couldn't, a baby would. I shrugged. "See you in a bit." I headed out to shave my legs and don my fuchsia-pink wedding dress.

19

THE WAITING

Heading through Calgary from the airport, I aimed for the Rocky Mountains, still patched with white in late May. Concrete became suburbs, then flat brown fields, then rolling foothills. While I drove west, Grant was up in the sky somewhere, on his way to Pakistan to climb the biggest mountain face in the world, the Rupal Face of Nanga Parbat. Gone for two whole months, possibly three. Then after a two-week rest at home he would be off to Everest. The baby was due in early August. I had a two-week window between Nanga Parbat and Everest to give birth.

At the airport, while we were saying goodbye, Barry had given me a big bear hug and said, "Don't you worry about him. That man's a machine." And Grant had said for the umpteenth time, "Don't worry, I'm coming home," but as Grant, Barry, Kevin and Marc went through the gate, I was back with Dan and Ian all over again in Seattle, one year ago, watching them race to the plane, not knowing they had only five days left to live. The Himalayas were more serious than Alaska. And Nanga Parbat was nicknamed "Killer Mountain" because it had claimed fifty climbers.

By the time I turned off the highway and drove through the almost deserted main street of Canmore, it was dark and I was dehydrated. I pulled up in front of our new home, turned off the engine. Sharon looked out the brightly lit upstairs window, waved. My former roommate was now our landlord. Her speaking engagements about her Everest expedition had proven lucrative. The first North American woman to the summit. When her basement suite had become available we'd jumped at it. It was small and dark, but it was all ours. No more climbing roommates. We'd moved in three weeks ago. Three weeks before that was the wedding. I'd been a married woman for six weeks.

I heaved myself over the stick shift and skootched across the seat to crawl out the passenger door of Ian's old blue Honda Civic. Someone had bashed in the driver's side door and at six and a half months pregnant, I could no longer slip through the window.

I fumbled through the side door, down the stairs, through the laundry room, pushed open the door to our suite and stared into darkness, listening. Nothing but Sharon and her partner Chris's muffled voices, the squeak of floorboards above. I flicked the switch and light spilled into the long, narrow room.

Keeping all the lights and TV on, I slid into bed wearing one of Grant's unwashed T-shirts. Buried my nose in his smell, just like I used to wrap Dan's navy pile jacket around me, the one that still had his blond hairs woven through the fabric of the collar. A hollow ache burrowed into me, an ache that marriage, changing my name, and growing a little person was supposed to have erased.

———

Dan sits beside me on the edge of the bed. He is so beautiful. He smiles, revealing the tooth he chipped in hockey. His blue eyes crinkle, as though he were squinting into the sun. He's wearing his navy fleece jacket with the collar turned up. I say, "I miss you so much," and he says, "I miss you too," and he holds me. My yearning is a physical pain that reaches into every part of my body. He isn't acting angry or betrayed. I'm simply the girl he was going to marry, not the pregnant wife of one of his climbing partners.

My pillow was drenched when I woke up. I curled around my baby, heaving. Dan was still right beside me. I could feel him. My dreams were always of Dan, never Grant. Maybe that meant Grant would be safe.

It was day one of a minimum sixty-day wait.

The first letter arrived after only three days. I ripped it open in the post office, scanned the heading—*May 22 – Over Manitoba.* He'd started writing the same day he left. His words were big, loopy, as if he couldn't keep his excitement off the page. He was so happy. He was finally headed for the biggest mountains in the world. He felt alive. He really wanted this. His joy rubbed off on me and I started to perk up, until I got to the part about how he hoped I could be happy for him, how he had an obligation to his climbing. As I read, the baby kicked hard, right into my bladder as if to say, *What am I? Chopped liver?* I quashed my irritation, squeezed my thighs together to keep from peeing. I suspected the obligation he felt was more to Dan and Ian than to his own climbing. He had to keep climbing hard to honour their memory.

I kept reading till I got to the last paragraph where he admitted in ink what he hadn't yet said out loud—that he badly wanted to raise a family, that it was miraculous our child was alive inside me, and that he didn't want to miss any of it.

Caressing the hard bump of my belly, I whispered, "You hear that, baby? He wants us!" If I could have bent in half, I'd have kissed it.

Five days later, Grant called from Pakistan. They should have been in base camp by then but they were still in Rawalpindi. There were permit problems and the roads were closed due to heavy fighting between the Sunnis and Shiites.

"There's about a thousand dead. We won't get out of here for at least ten days."

He sounded so far away. He *was* so far away. I couldn't keep the panic out of my voice. "But my due date's the middle of August." Two and a half months away. "You said there was lots of time." What was wrong with me? Worried about my due date while terrorists were massacring people.

"Don't worry, I'll be back before the baby."

He described the city, the women covered from head to toe in black, people and animals everywhere. So much noise. The smell. Sewage running down the ditches. He just wanted to get going. He was homesick. He missed me and loved me.

He loved me! I couldn't savour his words after he'd hung up because I was late for my night shift at work. I pulled off my jeans with the big stretchy belly panel and pulled on the first skirt I'd owned since my blue tie-dyed wrap-around from my hippie days. My boss, Candace, was a tall, slim Mrs. Cleaver type who wanted me to be "presentable," even though the Parks radio I manned was in a little back room and none of the rangers cared what I wore. She endured my Birkenstocks.

Anxiety niggled away at me as I headed outside into the fading light. The guys could end up surviving the biggest mountain face in the world only to be shot dead by a bunch of rebels. And even if they did survive the mountain and the rebels, he'd likely miss our baby's birth.

I crawled into the car, turned the key. The *click, click, click* of an impotent battery was the only response. "Shit!"

I tried again, got the same clicking. Then again. And again. Pounding the dashboard I screamed, "You bastard!" and I knew I wasn't talking to the car.

The next letter didn't arrive for two weeks. With the music from my soap, *Days of Our Lives*, blaring out of the TV, I eased myself down on the couch, onto my pillow arrangement. Five pillows. That's how many it took now to ease the tension in my back. I was getting so big so quickly the doctor thought I might be farther along than we'd thought. I unfolded the crinkly airmail paper, started reading greedily, inhaling his words. The letter was from Rawalpindi, dated June 5. He'd gone jogging at four that morning in the smog, then for a bike ride to a shanty town on the poor side of town. He was dying in the over 100-degree heat.

He was dying? At least he could jog and mountain-bike. He should try gluing a medicine ball to his gut and waddling through an Alberta heat wave, see how that felt. Seven and a half months pregnant and I'd gained twenty-five pounds. At this rate, I was going to be the size of Nanga Parbat by the time Grant got home.

The more I read the crankier I got. There was another road closure until June 7 because the Sunnis and Shiites were still fighting each other in Gilgit. He was "heavily bummed" because it seemed to be an expedition just getting to the mountain.

So when he wrote this letter they hadn't even left for base camp. The expedition was now at least two weeks behind schedule, which put it that much closer to monsoon season, and that much closer to my due date.

The baby shifted, ramming a body part under my ribs so I flipped up my shirt to let my big white belly emerge, smooth and hard. Beautiful.

I am not going to cry.

Some of the women in my Lamaze class played classical music to soothe their little fetus. I just cried all day. What was that doing to my baby?

"Hey, little one. Your daddy will be home soon."

Maybe if I said it often enough and with conviction, I'd make it happen. That's what it said in the book I was reading about the power of positive thinking. But my thoughts were normally so demented that if the book was right, if my brain really was that powerful, everyone around me would be dropping dead like the Sunnis and Shiites.

A loud knock on the door made both the baby and me jump. I pulled my shirt down just as Niccy popped her head around the corner from the laundry room. Her round face was flushed and beaded with sweat.

"Hey, thought you could use some of this. Pretty hot out there." She held up a jar of pickles and a bucket of Häagen-Dazs ice cream. She'd shown up with the same offering when I was three months pregnant, just after my news had leaked out. It seemed her way of saying she didn't judge me.

I winched myself off the couch. I could live without the pickles, but Häagen-Dazs ice cream was my staple, which could explain the weight gain.

"We thought you might be lonely down here." Barb stepped into the kitchen behind Niccy.

The girls were obviously heading out to climb. Niccy was wearing rugby pants and a cotton T-shirt. A green bandana pulled her damp hair off her face. She and I had the same type of climbing wardrobe. Threadbare, baggy, like we were trying to hide our bodies. Barb was wearing black Lycra shorts and a sports bra that looked painted on her lean body. Her bare abs were naturally flat, not intentionally sucked in, and her arms hung slightly out from her body in that distinctive ape-like stance climbers get from training. We'd met on my third trip to Yosemite and then worked two seasons together at the cadet camp. For a few years we were equally matched, but recently she'd set the record for the hardest route climbed by a Canadian woman, while I was unable to picture myself doing a single pull-up ever again.

"Nice and cool down here," Barb said, wiping her forehead.

"Yeah, of course we'd have a damned heat wave at the height of my pregnancy."

"Are you watching soaps?" Niccy stared at the TV screen. "You are! You're watching soaps!"

"Fuck off!" I tried to push her out of the way.

I slammed the power button and the room went quiet. Barb came to my rescue. "Have you heard from the guys?"

"Just got a letter. They haven't even gotten to base camp yet. Permit problems. And then road closures. But it took that letter ten days to get here, so they've got to be at base camp by now. I hope."

Barb and Niccy looked down at my tummy.

"Don't worry. He'll get here in time," Barb said.

I changed the subject. "Where are you heading?"

"Up Grotto Canyon. Probably do Farewell to Arms."

One of my favourite climbs—overhanging, strenuous, but with huge holds and permanent bolts for protection. If you fell, there wasn't much chance of getting hurt. So far I'd only followed it, but Barb had been trying to get me to do it on lead. She said I needed to push my limits. Learn to fall.

Learn to fall. Exactly what Dan used to tell me.

"Shit. I couldn't waddle up the approach right now." I glanced at Barb's abs again.

"Don't worry. You'll be flying up it again next summer." Barb took the pickles and ice cream from Niccy, headed toward the fridge.

"Come see the crib." I pulled Niccy toward the bedroom to show off my second-hand crib with the pastel green bumper pads and sheets with the little yellow duck pattern. Barb followed.

"Listen to this. It's perfect for a little climbing baby." I wound up the mobile and the upside-down clowns started to spin to "The Bear Went Over the Mountain." I'd gone on a shopping spree for the baby in Calgary with my Mastercard. We stood there till it played out.

"Cool," Niccy said.

She and Barb glanced at each other. "We should get going."

After they'd gone, the emptiness of the suite settled on everything like dust. I grabbed a spoon and the tub of half-melted ice cream, turned on the TV. The music for *Days of Our Lives* filled my little space. I'd missed the ending.

Another letter arrived. The boys had finally reached base camp, at 11,000 feet. It had taken seventeen days. I pictured Grant sitting on a boulder, surrounded by the world's biggest mountains. Writing to me. Thinking about the baby and me. Missing me. He'd received my three letters and the Father's Day card. They'd also had to change their flights. They were now coming home August 7. My due date was August 10. Less than one and a half months away.

"I hope your due date is accurate," he wrote.

I laid the letter on my belly. Closed my eyes. Panic squeezed my lungs and it was hard to breathe. *I can't do this alone.*

There was a light knock on the door and the hinges squeaked as it opened. I sat up and saw Rory's bushy red beard poking around the corner. I smiled and my shoulders relaxed. He had come to show me his latest writing. He was one of the few climbers I knew who wrote poetry.

"Ready for the poem? You're in it."

Oh, shit. He didn't tell me he'd written about *us*. We'd happened seven years ago. My face still burned when I remembered his girl-friend looking at me with the same knowing in her eyes that I'd had when I'd looked at Dede and Brad, who were, miraculously, still together after three years.

I put Grant's letter on the carpet, got up to turn down the volume so I could still see the actors of my soap opera. Rory sat on the edge of the couch squinting at the TV.

"Don't tell me you're watching soaps." He looked at me like he'd never seen me before.

"Just shut up and read."

I pulled my feet under me, turned toward him, waiting.

He pulled a single sheet of paper from his pocket, unfolded it and cleared his throat. "'Meet Some of My Friends.'" He stopped, looked up. "It's not polished yet, I'm still . . ."

"Just read. It'll be great."

He cleared his throat again and read verses for several of our climbing friends: Geoff: *caustic and aloof, poised on the thinnest of holds . . .* Saul: *whose parents are scarred by the concentration camps . . .* Choc: *an enormous Irishman; he climbed hard with his best friend and now he loves the widow. . . .*

Choc's best friend, Dave Cheesmond, was the one who'd disappeared on Mount Logan just after Dan and Ian died. When Choc and Gillian, Dave's widow, got together, I'd felt exonerated somewhat.

Jan: Whose moods belay her ability on rock. At last found a man she could love like a river.

I thought of Grant. It was true. I really did love him.

When the mountainside in Alaska collapsed on top of him
eternity shattered
and the stain from her heart
smeared the entire range red.
Inconsolable, with fingers grasping,
she sifts the debris one more time,
one more time.

Hot tears erupted. I thought he'd meant Grant. Now I didn't know if it was Dan I loved like a river and I wished it were Grant, or if it was Grant I loved and it should be Dan. Maybe I was crying because

I was afraid I couldn't have loved Dan in the first place, given I'd jumped into bed with Grant two days after the memorial, and gotten pregnant with his baby.

But Rory knew I loved Dan. I'd howled for hours on his wood floor in Calgary while he held me. And here we were again. I put my head on his shoulder and he apologized over and over while I cried.

Grant comes home from Pakistan. He's smiling and happy and I'm so excited to see him. We go to a spa and I think we're going to make love, but there I am, sitting in my own tub, alone with my big belly, while Grant is in another, fucking a huge woman with tits like mountains.

My eyes popped open. I heaved myself up in bed, stared at the faint light coming through the slit of a window. Finally a dream about Grant and this was what I got? If I weren't pregnant, I'd take a Valium. If I weren't pregnant, maybe I wouldn't need a Valium. I'd be getting ready for my second year of university. I'd be skinny and strong and tanned after climbing all summer. I'd have a big, fat student loan in the bank and I wouldn't have to worry about having enough money for groceries.

How would I survive two expeditions? In one of his letters Grant had said he was now sure he wanted to go to Everest. I knew Everest would be the biggest thing he'd ever done, and that climbing was what made him feel alive and free, and even though I didn't want to squelch that, this baby was the biggest thing I'd ever done. If the boys came back with the second ascent of the Rupal Face, and on top of that, Everest, they'd be heroes. I'd just be another woman who'd popped out a baby.

I wanted to tell him if he went to Everest and left me with a newborn, I would leave him. But I knew I wouldn't.

———

Back at the post office. Maybe I should move a bed into the corner, set up a hot plate and porta-potty. I checked my box every day, sometimes twice a day. I hadn't received a letter in more than two weeks.

I opened the mailbox and there it was, a long, blue envelope with foreign stamps and *Air Mail* marked in red. The baby did a flip in my tummy and I whispered, "Yes, it's your daddy. He's alive!" Or he was when he wrote the letter.

I crawled back into my basement, my only reprieve from the sweltering heat. Temperatures had reached a record high. Parts of my flesh that never used to make contact glommed together, with sweat as the glue. I opened Grant's letter, dated June 30 in base camp. He'd gone barefoot under his neoprene socks while acclimatizing on a neighbouring mountain, and trench foot had turned his feet to raw hamburger. Now while the other guys climbed big peaks, he was acclimatizing by himself, hiking as high as he could go in his runners. He'd never be ready for Nanga at this rate. On top of that, the monsoons were on their way.

My stomach felt uneasy. Was there such a thing as third trimester morning sickness? Grant's words from an earlier letter rushed back: *I'm afraid of something happening to me.* Had that been a premonition? Like my dreams of Dan and Ian?

After I'd devoured the letter, I cranked the volume on the TV to fill the silence, listened to the angry voices of Roman and Marlena from *Days of Our Lives* while I started a new row on my blue baby sweater. I had to keep my hands, eyes, ears and brain busy.

The plan was to head up Nanga Parbat on July 10. Four days ago. That meant Grant could call any day. Or that he could be dying that very moment, buried under an avalanche, or falling thousands of feet while I sat watching soaps. Or maybe he was already dead and someone was about to pick up the phone.

———

The baby had the hiccups for the first time. It was a strange feeling, like a twitch that wouldn't go away in your calf muscle after a long climb on slabs. I was on the couch, as usual, stitching the little yellow bear buttons onto the blue sweater and watching *Days of Our Lives*, but the soap opera barely registered. I was trying not to think of Grant. I was trying not to think of Dan. I wanted to focus on the baby. The baby that would save me. The baby that would save us.

Grant should have been off the mountain. He should have called by now, but I knew he was dead. It was the same feeling I'd had with Dan—the dreams, the inexplicable crying, the heavy dread. What had I been doing at the precise moment Dan had fallen? He'd died four days after I dropped him off in Seattle, barely enough time to enjoy the view of the Alaskan mountains. Had I still been in Vancouver? I'd met my dad there for lunch when he was on a business trip, and when we said goodbye I couldn't stop sobbing, as though I'd never see him again.

Or maybe Dan had died while Julie and I were driving to Burns Lake on our way to plant trees. Or maybe while I was planting. He must have been dead when I sent him a long letter. The one they sent back to me with his personal effects, unopened. While writing it I'd had a strong premonition that he would never read it. Then came the dream of Dan and Ian falling. It had been so intense I'd almost thrown up. I hadn't slept the rest of the night.

"Roman! No! How . . . You're alive!"

This episode of *Days of Our Lives* wasn't getting my mind on the right track. Roman Brady had come home after being missing and presumed dead for years—after Stefano had kept him prisoner on a Mexican island. Roman went straight to Marlena, the love of his life, but she hadn't waited; she'd married John Black. Now everyone was all fucked up and no one knew who was supposed to be with whom.

———

"He should have called by now," I moaned to my sister on the phone. "I must have some fucked-up karma to have to go through this again. I must have been horrible in my past lives."

Or maybe it had been in this life. Maybe I was being punished for being with Grant.

Every moment of every day, I calculated how long it should have taken the guys to get up and down the mountain, pack up base camp and walk out to the nearest phone. Would that be in Gilgit? Or would they have to get all the way to Rawalpindi? At first I could convince myself they'd been delayed by weather, or more road closures, that they weren't dead. But now panic bore down on me like rockfall. Every time the phone rang, I expected it to be some government official with a Pakistani accent telling me my husband of almost four months was dead.

"What are your chances of being widowed twice? Maybe your karma will protect him," my sister said.

Every day I prayed to Dan and Ian to keep Grant safe. The other day I'd accidentally said to myself, *Please, please, Dan, come home*, instead of Grant. Three thousand feet. How long had Dan been alive on the way down? Had he had time to think of me? Would Grant think of me and our baby while he fell?

I phoned my parents collect and my father didn't gripe about it. "Sometimes I feel like it's my fate to keep losing everyone I love until I learn to survive on my own."

"Don't be ridiculous," my mother said, as though that were helpful in some way. My father was at a loss for words. He'd written to me after Dan's death: *This will eventually make you stronger.* I wanted to ask him when exactly he thought that strength might kick in.

At six a.m. the phone startled me awake and I risked premature labour falling off the futon to reach it. I picked up on the third ring.

"Jan, it's Yolande." Yolande. Kevin's wife. Kevin who was with

Grant on Nanga. Her voice sounded hoarse, like she'd been crying. Dread plunged through my body and I wanted to hang up the phone quickly, before she could change my world.

"Jan, something's happened."

"Yolande. Don't."

My hand was out in front of me, as if to ward her off. It was Alaska all over again. The phone call. The word *avalanche* knocking the wind out of me. I couldn't do this again. Not with a baby.

"It's not the boys, Jan. I haven't heard from them. It's BJ. He's dead."

Relief flooded through me. It wasn't Grant! And then I thought of Kevin.

BJ was Kevin's best friend. He'd taken a long fall on Mount Lougheed. His partners Jeff (Dr. Risk) and Steve had tried to resuscitate him for hours, but the head injury had been too severe. They'd spent the night hanging from the vertical mountain face in a storm, then the next day they'd left BJ behind and rappelled to the ground. The wardens would retrieve the body by helicopter. The guys were planning to finish the climb and name it in BJ's honour. We'd have to tell Kevin when he got off the plane.

Words of sympathy by rote. I'd done this so many times. There was a family out there grieving, but all that registered was: *It's not me this time. Grant is still alive.*

On the first day of August, twenty-one days after the guys were supposed to have started up the mountain, nine days before my due date, I got the call from Rawalpindi, the one that had never come from Alaska. As soon as I heard Grant's deep, gruff voice, I started sniffling, the last thing I wanted to do. He sounded so familiar. He would land in Calgary in five days. Four days before my due date.

"We should be dead," he said, his voice expressionless. "We barely made it off the mountain. I'm not going to be much use for a while. I'm pretty fucked up."

Yolande had warned me to keep my expectations low. The boys would be trashed when they got home. She'd been through this many times.

After I'd hung up, and after I'd made about a dozen excited calls to let everyone know the boys were alive, I sat back in the cool quiet of my basement and my elation started to wane. In three weeks, Grant was supposed to be heading back to Everest.

Dunkin Bancroft

Me in 1975, at age fourteen, around the time our family bought a dilapidated little cabin in the Laurentians, where I did my first "rock climb." After that ascent I wrote in my diary, "I'm going to be a mountain climber when I grow up."

Dave Stark

Tending to our blistered feet in the Canyonlands, Utah, during my three-and-a-half-month semester course at the National Outdoor Leadership School (NOLS) based in Lander, Wyoming. The Beast, my eighty-pound backpack, is in the background. I had just turned twenty.

El Capitan, on my first trip to Yosemite in the spring of 1982, with Saul and Geoff. On my next trip, that fall, Rik and I were rescued off this wall. I went on to take a total of five trips to Yosemite.

The summer of 1982 at our trail crew camp in Kananaskis Provincial Park in Alberta, beside my first car, a '67 Dodge Dart I bought for $300. I lived in the tent cabin in the background with five others.

Skiing across the Columbia Icefields with a couple of friends in the spring of 1982, on our way to climb Mount Columbia, seen in the background. As we made our way through the glacier's crevasses we discovered none of us had actually done a crevasse rescue, though I had read about it in my earmarked copy of *Mountaineering: The Freedom of the Hills*, the climbers' bible.

Leading the pendulum pitch on the Royal Arches Route in Yosemite. The route is easy but long, about seventeen pitches. Here the sky is blue, but not long after this picture was taken it poured, creating waterfalls on the route. We managed to get down the tricky descent before dark.

Gary Bocarde

Here I am looking very cheerful while suspended over 1,400 feet of nothing, on a classic climb in Yosemite—Lost Arrow Spire. We rappelled two rope lengths down into a notch and climbed three aid pitches up the spire, then set up a Tyrolean traverse back to the rim. I was being pulled on a haul-line by my buddies but they got a bit too enthusiastic and smashed me into the rocks on the other side a few times.

Gary Bocarde

One of the members of our group going across the Tyrolean traverse of the Lost Arrow Spire. We were a group of eleven, including Gary from Alaska, and the friends I'd travelled south with from Alberta—Doc, from North Carolina, and Niccy.

My first season of ice climbing in the winter of 1983, near Field, BC, with Jim. I'm leading here, but my ice climbing skills were by no means stellar, so it's a wonder I never fell.

The summer of 1983. Camping at the base of Yamnuska, a fin-shaped mountain of limestone, more than 1,000 feet high with well over a hundred routes, between Canmore and Calgary. My hair hadn't been cut in a couple of years, and my lip is fat with chewing tobacco.

Practising jumarring up a tree in Yosemite, fall 1983, in preparation for my first big wall climb. Jumars are metal ascenders that slide up the rope, but won't slide down when weighted. This way you can ascend the ropes without touching the rock when it's too hard to "free climb."

Here I am cleaning the Kor Roof on my first and last big wall climb in Yosemite, late fall 1983, with Karin, a friend from Sweden. Because I'd only jumarred one route (and had to be rescued) and one tree, it rated high on the terror scale. The two people above me are the Parisians who snuck up past us after we'd slept out on Dinner Ledge. They were so slow we had to bail, knowing we'd run out of water.

In Fernie, summer 1984, patching up the fibreglass kayak I inherited from Brad. Instead of leaving it shattered on his lawn after he broke my heart (my first impulse), I strapped it to my Dart and drove away.

In the Bugaboos, summer 1985, with the Howsers in the background. On this occasion, my friend Kevin and I were climbing the Northeast Ridge of Bugaboo Spire. I've done five trips to the Bugs, one of my favourite areas.

Dan Guthrie, pumped after a climb. This is about the time I first met him in Yosemite, fall 1985, when we were both nursing broken hearts.

The Professor Falls, near Banff, Alberta, in winter 1985. This was one of my first dates with Dan. He'd soloed the whole waterfall earlier in the season, and his crampon kept popping off. He'd hung off his tools, without a rope, snapped the crampons back on, and kept going. He could solo the route in two hours and forty-five minutes, doing the approach on a mountain bike.

Here Dan and I are posing at the base of the Professor Falls. The beaten-up blue vest is the one piece of his clothing I still have. He used to wear it everywhere.

Here we are in spring 1986, in front of my uncle Dunk and aunt Ruth's house in Vancouver, on our way to Squamish. This was one year to the day before the avalanche that killed him.

Taking a wee rest on a ledge in Yosemite in my classic patched-up red climbing garb, around 1987. Those rugby pants finally disintegrated in the washing machine.

Mount Aberdeen, near Lake Louise in June 1986. Niccy Code and I bragged that we didn't place one ice screw all the way up that tongue of ice. As Dan said, we were lucky we didn't fall.

Larry Stanier

Niccy in the summer of 1986, after we'd been climbing together for about five years.

Niccy at the Banff National Cadet Camp, summer 1986. I always felt braver climbing with Niccy. She had a way of instilling confidence.

Hamming it up for the camera with my tough-guide pose at the Banff Cadet Camp, summer 1986. As climbing instructors, we took the fifteen-to-seventeen-year-old cadets rock climbing and mountaineering. I worked with the French-Canadian cadets because I was "bilingual" after my month-long high school Quebec exchange, and my nine months with Katimavik. I did a lot of gesturing, including throat slitting.

Niccy, Doug and I taking our cadets to climb the 9,740-foot Saint Nicholas Peak, summer 1986. We went up the obvious line of snow to the summit, the northeast face. With four cadets on my rope, all of them heavier than I was, the likelihood of my being able to hold a fall was slim.

Dan and Ian in Seattle, May 1987, just before we headed for the airport to put them on the plane for Alaska. The paper bag was Dan's carry-on luggage.

Dan in Seattle, on his way to Alaska, tolerating one last photo. I'm glad I insisted.

Mount Foraker, in a photograph taken from the plane by Dan's parents. Ian's family also flew over the mountain. The boys' bodies are still in the avalanche debris on the lower right of the photo. They had been acclimatizing on the descent route of their ultimate objective, the bigger, more serious route—the Infinite Spur.

Climbing with Grant at Devil's Tower, Wyoming, two and a half months after Dan's death, when smiling was still a struggle. I'd just finished a stressful season of guiding on Valium at the cadet camp, and was about to move to Calgary to go to university.

With my parents, Jean and Ron, at my wedding on the banks of the Bow River in Canmore, Alberta, April 1988. My pink wedding dress, a hand-me-down from my mom, billowed over my five-month pregnancy. The jacket hiding the dress was borrowed from Barb, a friend and fellow guide at the Banff Cadet Camp.

Near Calgary with Jenna Danielle, a few months after she was born. Grant got back from the Himalayas just in time for her birth. He was such a proud dad he decided to stay home with us instead of heading off to Everest.

Our home on almost ten acres in the Blaeberry Valley, north of Golden, BC, in 1990. I expected to work in my huge garden, get dogs, cats, goats, possibly a horse, pop out a few babies, and live happily ever after.

Chaba, our golden Lab, came with me every day when I worked with the Ministry of Forests. We had to give him up when I went back to school, but he eventually went to a couple who loved him so much they shared their bed with him and fed him cookies and cake.

Samuel William, a few months old, in the Blaeberry. My list of the pros and cons of having a second baby (two pros, ten or so cons) went right into the wood stove after I brought this perfect baby home.

My dream job, hiking around in the bush with a bunch of amazing women. I worked in forestry for three seasons until I went back to university in Calgary. My only regret was having to return to work to keep my seniority (and sanity) when Sam was only five months old.

Working on a burn near Golden, a very grubby, exhausting job. I could barely hold on to the hose when the water was turned on. This photo I took of Nona and Bonnie won a photography contest with BC Ministry of Forests.

Sam helping with the weeding in our garden in the Blaeberry. He was the kind of baby who smiled with his whole body, a natural ham.

Jenna climbing near Canmore when she was five years old. My two kids had completely different reactions to growing up surrounded by climbers. Jenna adopted the lifestyle wholeheartedly and became a very strong climber, but Sam, who thought we were "hippies," got into golf, then mixed martial arts. Like me as a teen, he had to be whatever his parents weren't.

Doing a lead in El Potrero Chico, Mexico, in 2013 after not climbing much for several years. I went on this trip intending to rediscover the "rock warrior" within, and though I did manage to push myself well out of my comfort zone, I decided I'm more comfortable these days on my mountain bike.

With Dan Redford in front of the Stawamus Chief in Squamish, BC, our home since 2010. My second Dan, a second chance.

20

MIRACLES

"Welcome to the show, Barry and Grant."

The voice of the CBC interviewer, Linda, crackled from the transistor radio beside me on the couch in our Canmore suite. I double-checked the record button on the tape deck and moved the microphone closer to the speaker, keeping the volume low to avoid the squeal of interference, careful not to jiggle my tiny sleeping bundle. Jenna felt solid in my arms, like a six-pound sand bag.

Across the room, Grant sat hunched over the kitchen table, the phone pressed hard against his ear. In his kitchen in Calgary, Barry also waited on the phone to tell his story.

The interviewer gave the listeners some background about Nanga Parbat, that it was the second highest peak in Pakistan after K2 at

26,660 feet, and that its Rupal Face was the biggest wall in the world, with 15,000 feet of climbing. The boys had attempted the Messner Route, which had been climbed in 1970 but never repeated. Two Messner brothers had summited; only one had returned. Then four years ago, in 1984, a Japanese team lost four of its climbers on the route. They disappeared without a trace.

Grant gripped the receiver like a handhold fifty feet up a wall. This was his first time on national radio.

"We'll start with Barry," Linda said.

Grant's grip on the phone loosened and he leaned back in his chair.

"Let's get right to what the listeners want to hear. The 'miracle,' as you put it, that brought you boys home alive from one of the most extreme alpine climbs in the world. Barry, could you tell us what happened up there?"

Barry's voice sounded relaxed and personable. He was used to speaking in front of big crowds—he was a legend in the climbing world, as much as a Canadian could be.

"We got to 25,800 feet by day four, just 1,200 feet from the summit. We'd done the most difficult climbing and it was just a slog to the top. That's when everything started crapping out. All four of us were hanging off one ice screw in the Merkl Gully when a storm hit, blasting us with hundred-mile-an-hour winds, spinning our bodies around. Flipped us upside down. Thunder and lightning exploding. The whole time we were waiting for the ice screw to fail."

My arms tightened around Jenna as I listened to the tale I'd heard a hundred times since the guys had returned home. Barry, Grant and I, being Aries, were prone to drama, but Barry didn't have to embellish this story.

"And then the avalanches started," Barry continued. "There was nowhere to go. Being in a gully is like being in a funnel."

Grant, his eyes bright blue against the dark bags underneath, smiled at me, shrugged, like he was apologizing for almost dying. His face was emaciated from the expedition. His bleached blond hair, in need of a haircut, fell straight and shaggy over his forehead. It only enhanced his craggy good looks.

I looked down at Jenna. I hadn't known a baby could be so beautiful. Her skin was so pale it was almost translucent, and her hair was already lightening up, like Grant's, after two weeks in the world.

The interviewer jumped in. "Grant, I've been told you were near death up there, that you would have died of pulmonary edema and hypothermia if the guys hadn't gotten you down when they did." Grant's trench foot had kept him in base camp and on smaller peaks at the beginning of the trip, so he hadn't acclimatized as well as the other guys. "What was going through your mind?"

"Well, Linda," Grant spoke too loudly into the phone. Almost shouted. As though he could bully his nerves away. I motioned to him to keep his voice down. "We were being pounded by avalanche after avalanche, and I was suffocating from both the snow and the fluid in my lungs. There was also a lot of pressure building in my brain, and I was hypothermic." He sounded rehearsed, uncomfortable, until he added, "To tell you the truth, nothing went through my mind except how to get it over with quickly. I wanted to unclip from the carabiner and jump off the mountain."

I tore my eyes from Jenna again to watch Grant as he spoke so calmly about his near-death experience. That couldn't be true. What should have been going through his mind was that if he didn't get his ass off that fucking mountain he would never meet his daughter, Jenna Danielle. He'd never see me again.

"When we finally started rappelling I passed out partway down. The guys hauled on the rope to wake me. Then I passed out again on the ledge."

Marc had said, "An average man would not have survived that long."

There was certainly no mistaking Grant for an average man. None of these guys were average. They were like a special forces team—highly skilled, single-minded, tough beyond the norm. But they weren't fighting for any altruistic cause like the protection of their country. They created their own war zone, then launched themselves into it.

"Then the fun really began," Barry jumped back in.

"Marc threw the tent off the ledge," Grant said.

"An accident. So he started to dig a snow cave. We had to get Grant warmed up fast. He wasn't going to last much longer. So Kevin and I started to set up a rappel for the next day. I don't know what happened. We were screaming at each other through the wind. Could barely see each other. I thought Kevin would hang on to the end of the rope; he thought I would. We both threw our ends of the rope off."

Linda whistled. "So no ropes."

"And we were out of food."

"So no ropes, no tents, no food, stuck at what, 23,000 feet?"

"With 12,000 feet left to rappel," Grant added.

"Yeah, we were pretty much fu—er, goners."

Fucked. They were fucked. Even if they couldn't say it on CBC. What had I been doing while they'd been struggling so hard to hang on to their lives? Knitting. Watching soaps. Growing a new person.

I pulled Jenna closer, tried to breathe away my growing anger. They'd suffered up there, I knew that, but it's not like I'd found Jenna under a fucking cabbage patch. She'd ripped out of me, and no one was lining up to interview me on CBC.

"So Grant, can you tell me what happened next?"

"The next day we started to downclimb, unroped. I was perking up now that we were a bit lower down, but still pretty messed up. We were hoping we could tie together bits of old rope left behind by a Japanese team. They were the last ones up there. Four climbers disappeared in the gully we'd been avalanched in. Their team never found their bodies."

"Barry, can you tell us what you found up there?"

"We downclimbed to a pack we'd seen on the way up. It was off route so we hadn't bothered to check it out. Grant knifed it open and found two ropes, dozens of pitons—"

"And chocolate bars," Grant cut in. "All of our favourites. We couldn't believe it."

"It was our ticket down. The Japanese team had left it for their teammates, hoping they'd get down that far and find it."

"That's quite the experience."

"Like having sex with death," Barry said.

"Well, that's one way of putting it." Linda laughed.

Then they talked about how, after they'd gotten down, the storm blasted Nanga for another twelve days. They'd waited it out in base camp, where they still had a good supply of food, and then, when the sun came out, they'd headed back for another less dramatic failed attempt on the mountain. While I hung out by the phone awaiting the verdict: dead or alive.

"Grant, I hear you've just become a father."

"Yup. Jenna was born a week after I got home. I cut the umbilical cord."

In the hospital, in the early part of my labour, Grant had flipped through my books on pregnancy to figure out how to coach me, since I'd done my prenatal classes solo. Then he held my hand and applied his newfound knowledge for the rest of the nineteen hours. The only time I'd felt like killing him was when the anaesthetist arrived and, lo and behold, he was a climber Grant had guided up a mountain in Peru a few years earlier. So while an epidural needle was being inserted between my vertebrae, I had to listen to them talk about climbing Aconcagua.

"I bet your wife is happy to have you home."

"I hope so." He looked over at me.

I smiled at him. I was. I was so grateful he'd survived.

"So, when do you boys head to Everest? I've been told that Nanga was just a warm-up climb."

"We're off in a couple of weeks. Long enough to get a bit more meat back on the bones," Barry said.

Grant looked out the window so he wouldn't have to look at me, and I looked down at Jenna so I wouldn't have to look at him. I knew he was desperately embarrassed by his performance at altitude and wanted to redeem himself, but I'd been trying to muster the courage to tell him I'd be gone when he came back from Everest. But gone where? That was the problem. I had no money, barely a grade-twelve education, bleak job prospects, a newborn baby, and thirty-five extra pounds. No man would swoop in to rescue me this time. And I didn't want another man. I wanted Grant. A living, breathing Grant.

Jenna started to mewl like a kitten and I tensed up. My nipples were cracked, so nursing was like clamping them in a vise.

Grant hung up the phone and I turned off the tape recorder. Neither of us spoke. Jenna opened her eyes and stared up at me. Dark blue rings around light blue irises. I'd had her two weeks and already I couldn't imagine life without her. It horrified me to think she had almost not existed, and it horrified me to think her survival was almost solely up to me. When I gave Jenna her first bath in the hospital, with my mother, an RN, looking on, I'd scrubbed her back, not realizing her face was submerged in water. She'd choked and spluttered and I'd sobbed for hours. That was the moment I realized how much I had to lose.

Grant walked toward me. His jeans hung off him.

"I've been thinking." He sat on the couch, put his hand on my bare knee. My leg was tanned and still looked vaguely like a part of my former body, while the rest of me seemed to have succumbed to some strange flesh-creating disease.

"I've decided to stay home with you and Jenna. My little family's the best thing that's ever happened to me. I won't go to Everest."

My body slumped in relief against his. With my head resting on his shoulder, I closed my eyes. Jenna, tucked between us, squirmed against the tight walls of her receiving blanket.

21

INTO THE SHADOWS

A small gurgle came from Jenna's car seat in the corner of the empty living room where the couch used to be. It was a cute sound, like she was blowing spit bubbles, or about to murmur *mama*. I froze in the middle of the kitchen, a can of Ajax in one rubber-gloved hand and a rag in the other. The gurgle became a grunt and the flannel receiving blanket started to heave. I held my breath. How could she be awake? She'd been asleep for only half an hour after screaming the whole hour here to Canmore from our new house in Field.

Two days ago, we'd moved into a tiny duplex about the size and shape of a single-wide trailer, the same size as this basement suite, but with big windows. This was our compromise: I'd be an hour away from my friends in Canmore, and Grant would be an hour away from work in Golden. Mountain limbo. But this way we wouldn't actually have to *live* in Golden. I was not prepared to move to a logging town.

Field was a CP railway town with a population of about 150 colourful mountain people. Living on the same street was my good friend, Jeannette. We used to kayak together and still got out climbing when neither of us was pregnant. Now we had ski passes for Lake Louise, twenty minutes away, which had a daycare. She'd had her third baby a couple of months before I had Jenna, and I was hoping she'd be my guide into motherhood. Both of us would be on our own much of the winter: her husband, a heli-ski guide, was at a remote ski lodge, and Grant was in a logging camp.

A small wail came from under the blankets. I looked around the little basement suite, dingier and smaller now that it was devoid of furniture. I was only halfway through cleaning the kitchen. I hadn't even vacuumed. Sharon had new tenants moving in so this was my last chance.

The small wail turned to screams that echoed in the emptiness, bounced off the walls. Jeannette had told me the vacuum cleaner lulled her kids to sleep, and she would know, so I peeled off my rubber gloves, plugged in the vacuum and dragged it into the bedroom, started passing it over the thin, brown, glued-onto-concrete carpet. But Jenna's screams almost drowned out the sound of the motor. I dragged the machine back into the living room. She was kicking and screaming, the blanket all twisted in her pink-fleece-swaddled legs, her little earflap hat pulled down over her eyes.

I turned off the vacuum and scooped her out of the car seat. She was hot and red and sweaty, so I undid the zipper of the fleece bunting suit I'd sewn myself, slid it off her shoulders, pulled off her hat. She twisted and pumped her arms and legs, screaming as though her hair were on fire. I settled on the floor, leaned against the wall and pulled up my shirt, tried to tempt her with my nipple. She arched away, turning almost purple-black. My breasts were bloated and throbbing, double As mutated into Ds, blue veins almost bursting through the skin, but she wouldn't latch on. I finally gave up, laid her down on the floor on her blanket and slumped back against the wall with my eyes squeezed shut. How was I ever going to finish cleaning?

Jenna had been colicky from the beginning, but this was different. Last night she'd screamed for six hours, until midnight. She wouldn't nurse. I'd tried to feed her with a dropper, then had to squish her face against my breast until she started sucking. She'd finally fallen asleep.

The floorboards creaked above me. Sharon and Chris must have thought I was torturing her. I pressed my hands against my ears to block out the screams but they somehow managed to increase a notch, so I crawled back over to her, looked down on her little face, all contorted and swollen. Now I was crying too. I wanted to curl into a ball and wail with her. This couldn't be normal. Jeannette's new baby just lay on his receiving blanket smiling and looking around. Or sleeping. I hadn't heard him cry yet.

Ripping sounds spewed out then quickly got sucked back into tiny windpipes. She was only ten pounds. How could so much noise come from something smaller than a Christmas turkey? The noise seeped under my skin, into every pore, and the stress of the past week finally caught up to me—the sleepless nights, the colic, the move to Field with a borrowed pickup while Grant was in a logging camp.

I clenched my fists, pounded them into the floor on either side of my baby's arching body and screamed, "Just shut up, goddamn it!" then quickly scooped her up and put my wet face against her tummy, mumbling, "I'm sorry," over and over into the fleece.

"She screamed for six hours last night. Non-stop. I fed her breast milk with a dropper. I finally had to squish her face onto my boob until she nursed. I almost had to suffocate her."

The doctor looked at me impassively, professionalism plastered all over her face. "When babies scream it sometimes seems longer than it actually is."

"No, I timed it." My voice cracked. "She screamed from supper at six until midnight. Non-stop."

Dr. Jenkins scribbled something on her chart. Jenna was fast asleep in her car seat on the examination table, her lips sucking at the air. She looked angelic. I could almost see the bloody halo hovering over her head.

"As I told you the last time you were here, she has colic. Not much we can do about that."

"Colic. It can't just be colic." The doctor kept her eyes down, kept scribbling on her chart. She hadn't even taken Jenna out of her car seat, hadn't examined her, had barely glanced in her direction. "What about the blood in her diaper?" The tears started to flow. I swayed and grabbed on to the side of the examination table to steady myself. I felt like I might pass out.

"That's normal for newborn girls. It's similar to menstrual blood."

I put my hands over my face, no longer able to preserve my last bit of dignity. "But she isn't a newborn. She's three and a half months old."

I wanted to tell this goddamned woman to look at my baby. Check her tummy. Do some tests. But I didn't. She was the doctor.

"She screams and screams. Until she turns purple. I know she's in pain."

Dr. Jenkins finally looked up from her clipboard and watched me for a moment, seemed to really see me for the first time. I felt a smidgen of hope.

"Have you considered getting some counselling?"

Maureen started to cluck as soon as I walked in the door and she saw my unwashed, tangled hair and wild, bloodshot eyes. Maybe it wasn't such an uncommon sight. She was the public health nurse extraordinaire who had headed our Lamaze group. A big, hardy Scottish woman who'd raised her twins on her own, working full-time in a new country, after the father ran out on them. She could easily have told me, "Chin up!" but she never did.

Maureen rubbed my naked Jenna's distended tummy, oblivious to the death screams filling the tiny cubicle, and murmured softly in her ear in her beautiful, lilting accent. "Oh you poor, poor baby."

Jenna slowly calmed until her screams turned to big, shaky inhalations and hiccups. Maureen's soothing voice penetrated my exhaustion and I slumped into a chair, tears and snot squeezing through my fingers. She handed me a Kleenex without taking her eyes off my little girl.

"The child has a bladder infection. She's lost weight since I last saw her. The blood in her diaper means the pain must be excruciating."

The one time I'd had a bladder infection, I'd sat in a hot bathtub all night groaning, the only way I could tolerate the pain in my gut until I could get on antibiotics.

"I'll phone Dr. Jenkins and she'll have you back in her office as soon as you set foot in the door."

Within a half hour, in the doctor's small examination room, I sat with my arms folded triumphantly across my throbbing boobs while Dr. Jenkins wrote out requisitions for blood and urine tests. When she found out I'd just moved over an hour away to Field, with no clinic, she phoned the hospital to have us admitted pronto.

Bugs. Her urine was full of them. A full-blown bladder infection. They pumped my baby full of antibiotics and when we woke up the next morning in the hospital, she latched onto me hungrily, draining one boob to leave me lopsided. She looked up at me with a milky smile and fell back asleep.

Jenna and I descended the long, winding hill into the Yoho Valley, toward the braided channels of the Kicking Horse River. Field sat nestled deep in the shadows of the surrounding mountains: Mount Stephen, Mount Dennis, Mount Burgess. We wouldn't see much of the sun till spring. The waterfalls on both sides of the highway were already starting to freeze, almost climbable in November. It was so cold that the Honda had barely started that morning at the hospital. After three days in that place, I would have ditched the car and hitch-hiked home with Jenna in a Snugli. I'd spent ten days in that hospital with Jenna under the jaundice lights after she was born. I'd had enough.

Our white duplex was easy to spot, halfway up the hill in the town site at the base of Mount Stephen. Jenna and I had only spent two nights in Field before the hospital. Grant would be home from camp tonight, our first night all together in our new home.

As I turned off the highway and started to cross the bridge, I heard the train whistle off in the distance.

"Shit!"

I stepped on the gas. There was no way I was going to sit for half an hour behind the train while the CP Rail personnel had their staff changeover, blocking the only entrance into town. Jenna had been asleep for the whole hour from Canmore but I could feel my luck running out. I ripped over the tracks and continued up the hill. The train clanged and whistled as it ground to a stop behind me, cutting the town off from the rest of the world.

"Can you say 'dada'?" Grant held Jenna close to his face. "Come on. Say 'dada.'"

"She's a bit young for that, Grant," I said as I pulled a steaming fish casserole out of the oven, a recipe from the *Homemakers* magazine my mother-in-law had signed me up for. I'd been cutting out the good ones and pasting them onto index cards to put into a little pink plastic box with headings, grateful my climbing girlfriends in Canmore weren't privy to my mutation into a non-practising feminist. This recipe was simple: just pour a can of cream of mushroom soup over a frozen block of cod on veggies and potatoes. It was amazing how versatile Campbell's creamed soups were.

"Hmmm. This looks great." Grant grabbed his knife and fork and dug in. He loved to eat, and for some reason, I loved to watch him eat. Must have been part of the whole nesting syndrome. I smiled as I sat across from him. Jenna was nodding off in his arms and I was starting to feel all mushy inside. Maybe I was ovulating again. Maybe it was just my intense relief at finally having some peace and quiet, and adult company.

"Let's do something tomorrow." I leaned forward across the table.

"Like what?" He shovelled a potato into his mouth.

"I don't know. Ski around Emerald Lake. There's enough snow now. Go for a Jacuzzi." I smiled and put my hand on his arm, hoping he'd get the hint. "Maybe Jeannette will take Jenna for a couple of hours."

"We can go Sunday, for sure. That'd be fun. I already told Pete and Jim I'd do Professor with them this weekend."

I snapped my hand from his arm as though it had turned into a rattlesnake. "I thought we moved to Field so you wouldn't have to do that drive anymore. And now you're going to drive to Banff?" *And leave me here alone.*

"You know I have to climb."

"With Jim? You never climb with him." Jim was a Calgary climber who'd been to Everest several times.

"Yeah—well, looks like we might do a bunch of climbing together. He's invited me and Pete and Jeff to Nuptse this spring."

Pete was Jenna's godfather. Jeff was Dr. Risk. Nuptse was in Nepal.

I dropped my fork onto my plate. The walls of the tiny kitchen started to close in on me.

"It'll mostly be sponsored. I'll get a free Nikon camera, all the lenses, film for the whole three months. Think about it. This is my big chance to get into mountain photography. And it's not until March."

I pushed my plate away, stood up from the table. "You move me to Bumfuck, BC, and then jump on a plane to Nepal?" I pulled a knife out of the drawer and sank it into the banana bread I'd baked while Jenna had slept instead of doing my Jane Fonda workout video.

When I slammed the dessert on the table in front of Grant he said, "Look, you can be married to a grumpy prick who wastes away in a logging camp, or you can be married to a happy climber."

"How about divorced from both?" I stomped a few feet away into the bedroom, where I couldn't even slam the door because there wasn't one.

Two weeks before Grant's flight to Nuptse, I pulled off the highway into Field from Golden with the car loaded with clean laundry and Jenna fast asleep in her car seat. I didn't have a washing machine, so had to drive an hour every time I needed to do a load—which was often. I'd lost my zeal for the cloth diapers Wendy and I had sewn together over countless hours and was now a staunch supporter of landfill-clogging Pampers.

An ambulance, two Yoho Parks trucks and an emergency rescue vehicle were parked near the train station. Headlamps bobbed down the railroad tracks away from town, toward the ice climbs. I stepped on the gas but the hill was too icy to speed.

When I pulled up to our house, Grant's truck was in the driveway. Tension eased from my neck. I knew he'd gone ice climbing up the Icefields Parkway today, not near Field, but it was hard to control my dark thoughts.

I stepped in the door and there was Grant at the stove stirring refried beans, veggies all chopped and ready for burritos. I placed Jenna's car seat on the floor and put my arms around his waist, rested my head on his back and squeezed. He patted my hands, as though he understood what was going on.

"What's happening out there?" I asked.

"Avalanche on Guinness Gully. John Owen's dead. His partner got out."

My initial relief that it wasn't a close friend was short-lived. "Oh no. Didn't he and his girlfriend just get married? Sandra? I used to kayak with her old boyfriend."

"Yeah. She's staying at Graham's. I guess she's pretty fucked up."

"No kidding." I started to pull Jenna out of her car seat.

"Why don't you go over there? You might be able to help her."

"Right, and what do you want me to tell her? That everything's going to be all right?" I spat the words out, surprised at my anger.

"Hey, it was just a thought. You don't have to go. I'm sure she's got lots of people around."

That night, I barely slept. I slipped back to Burns Lake, to the first night after the news of Dan and Ian's avalanche, when I lay awake curled in a tight ball, heaving and choking, until Wendy pumped me full of Valium.

I wondered if anyone had thought to take Sandra some Valium. She was going to need it.

"I've been thinking," Grant started.

We were on the way to the airport once again. His duffle bags for Nuptse were piled up in the back of the Honda, pushing against the plastic sheet, a replacement for the back window. Barry had shattered the glass earlier that winter when he slammed the door down on a box of ice tools. I'd have to duct-tape it again when I got home.

Grant kept his eyes on the road. "Maybe we should move to Canmore when I get back from Nepal."

My smile was so big it split open the crack in my lip from the dry winter air. I could taste blood.

I felt like I was turning into Gollum in the dark depths of Field. We'd inherited enough money from his grandmother for a small down payment on a house, but we hadn't figured out in which town.

Grant had been set on Golden. I wanted Canmore. After this winter, I was ready to go back to school.

"I can get into photography, maybe get good enough to sell some stuff while you waitress."

My smile drooped.

"We can buy a cheap trailer with my grandmother's money," he added.

"A trailer? I don't want to live in a trailer." With all our friends in Canmore buying houses and condos, there was no way I was going to raise my daughter in a trailer court. Obviously this plan would need a bit of tweaking.

"It's the only way I'll be able to get out of logging. I finally feel alive again now that I'm climbing."

It was true he was a different person these days. All winter I'd locked horns with the logger, but now I was living relatively harmoniously with the climber. Ever since he'd quit work to climb for two months in preparation for Nuptse, it was as if someone had performed an exorcism on him. Instead of monosyllabic grunts, he was talking to me again, and making eye contact. He cooked and cleaned and played loud music and sent me out the door to go for a run or cross-country ski while he played with Jenna. We had so much sex it was hard to believe I'd escaped another pregnancy. Those two months had convinced me he had to get out of logging. A move to Canmore was in the right direction. Toward Grant the climber. A move in the other direction, Golden, was toward Grant the logger.

"We shouldn't fight," I said. He turned toward me and his grip on the steering wheel loosened. He nodded and turned back to the road. He understood the unspoken *In case you don't come back.*

The first turnoff for Canmore whizzed by. The car felt empty and light without Grant and all his duffle bags, just Jenna fast asleep in the back seat. I was surprised to be dry-eyed. Maybe I was a better Himalayan-climber wife than logging wife.

The second big green exit sign for Canmore approached and I pictured my eight-hundred-square-foot-duplex in Field, and the three months of waiting that lay ahead. I couldn't lean on Jeannette. I'd barely seen her all winter, except to clean her house and help with her kids, trying to make her life a bit easier. She'd been diagnosed with postpartum depression, a convenient label for the real problem—being all alone with three kids in the shadows all winter. Her mother had finally arrived and they were waiting for the medication to kick in, or the sun to come out, whichever came first. I knew I'd end up like Jeannette if I stayed in Field.

At the exit I turned the wheel sharply, left the highway and drove straight to Babs and Christo's. They had two-year-old Logan, so they'd have spare baby clothes. I could buy diapers and a toothbrush.

In my friends' kitchen an hour later, while Jenna played with Logan, I looked up the number for a real estate company and picked up the phone.

The first offer on a townhouse fell through because the owner didn't like my unusual conditions: *Pending financing, a house inspection, and approval of the husband upon his safe return from Nepal.* Everyone in Canmore was familiar with the death rate in the Himalayas. I went back to Field and waited for the realtor's phone call.

The second townhouse backed Spring Creek and was also within our price range. My agent suggested I get rid of at least one condition. I wanted to ditch the last one, it reeked of the old love-honour-and-obey crap that I had made sure wasn't in our marriage vows, but she insisted we needed Grant's signature on the deal when he got back. I had to get rid of the *pending financial approval.*

Wearing my wedding ring and armed with Grant's employment records and a letter from his boss, I left Jenna with Babs and Christo, along with our crappy car so there'd be no risk of the bank manager seeing I was driving a beater.

My palms began to sweat as a woman led me to a cubicle at the back of the bank. I sat, rehearsing my lines, until the bank manager walked in, shook my hand and sat behind the desk. She saw that Grant had worked more months this year than he had collected unemployment insurance, looked at our almost $20,000 worth of Canada Savings Bonds, and signed the papers giving me financial approval for a mortgage of $50,000. I almost did a pirouette as I backed through the door.

The owner accepted my offer, and Spring Creek Townhouse number 29 was mine. Pending my husband's survival, and approval.

22

BACK ON THE SHARP END

"You're sure you're okay for the whole day?"

My new neighbour, Caroline, sat across from me at her kitchen table. It would have been easy to mistake her townhouse for mine. Her floor plan was identical, as was the view out her window into the parking lot. She and Lorne had the same chocolate-brown shag carpet in the living room, which Grant called shit-brown, and up the long narrow stairs, where it turned into pumpkin-orange shag on the second floor.

Caroline took one last drag of her cigarette, stubbed it out in the glass ashtray. "Don't even think about it. I've got four of the little buggers, I might as well have one more."

Caroline had been babysitting for a couple of hours here and there all summer while I went for a bike ride or run. I would have used her more but three dollars an hour added up fast on one income now that we had a mortgage.

I took a sip of coffee. I hadn't had Nescafé since high school. It wasn't half bad if you put enough sugar in it. In high school my typical breakfast had been instant coffee, a spoonful of peanut butter, and Du Maurier cigarettes to keep my weight down. These days, trying to keep up with a one-year-old tornado was doing the trick.

Just as I got up to leave, a high-pitched scream blasted down the long stairway. We raced upstairs into the kids' room.

Caroline's two-year-old, Chrissy, was straddling Jenna, pinning her to the floor, but even if she had wanted to release her she couldn't; Jenna had two handfuls of her hair, on either side of her head. The scream had come from Chrissy, not Jenna.

I kneeled beside them and pried open Jenna's fists while Caroline hauled Chrissy off by the arm.

I picked Jenna up, looked over her head as she wriggled and tried to free herself from my grip. Caroline sat Chrissy into a chair for a time out.

"You sure you want to do this?" I asked again. But I knew the question was directed at myself. Maybe I should just go for a hike with Jenna instead.

Jenna squirmed and twisted till I put her down.

"Just go. The kids will settle down."

I kissed the top of Jenna's blond head. Lingered in the doorway. Whenever I was away, all I thought about was my little girl. But I needed to climb.

"Go! Have fun! She'll be fine." Caroline laughed.

I slipped down the stairs and out the door.

"Jesus, Niccy! What have you got in your pack?"

I lifted Niccy's climbing pack by the shoulder strap with two hands and let it fall back into the scree. Grey limestone dust puffed up, resettled.

224 9 JAN REDFORD

Barb grabbed the pack and tested the weight. Her biceps bulged with the effort.

"Niccy!"

Niccy looked up from sorting gear, pushed her helmet off her forehead. "It's just a first-aid kit and a few other emergency things. Space blanket. Extra clothes and stuff."

"What, like your parka?"

Niccy nodded.

Barb and I looked at each other and groaned. Normally I wouldn't care if she had packed in eighty pounds, but we'd be taking turns carrying it on the route so the leader wouldn't have to climb with a pack.

"It's July! We're doing three pitches of rock, not a bloody expedition in the Himalayas," I said.

"Can never be too careful." She grinned and started to calmly uncoil her rope.

Niccy was being extra vigilant because her mountain guide exam was coming up. She'd failed the first time. Still, maybe it was a good idea to have a big first-aid kit on a climb called Die Young, Stay Pretty.

I started to uncoil my rope. It was quiet, just the sound of the *clink clink* of metal on metal as Barb sorted the rack. She'd take the first lead, I'd take the second, and Niccy would get the hardest, most enjoyable pitch. A thin finger crack. We'd be up and down and pulling our chilled beers out of the reservoir below in a few hours.

As I belayed and Barb started up the crack, Niccy squatted beside me to watch. "How's the new home?"

"It's great. There's a woman next door with four kids who actually loves to babysit." I fed out the rope. The pitch was easy so Barb was cruising up it.

"I can't believe you did that. Bought a whole house without even telling your husband." She laughed and shook her head.

"He was still in the Himalayas. He couldn't get to a fax machine." My voice sounded more flippant than I felt.

After surviving Nuptse, Grant had signed the papers, but when we'd moved in two months ago, he'd accused me of taking advantage of him in a weakened state—dehydrated from dysentery, trashed from altitude sickness, and severely depressed. He had hoped Nuptse would be the start of his dream career as an outdoor photographer, but he'd injured his back on the first day and barely got to climb, let alone take brilliant mountain photos. At thirty-six he was the optimal age for alpine climbing, and he was fit from logging, but maybe it was the wrong kind of fitness.

"Well, it's nice to have you back in Canmore," Niccy said.

She worried about me, I knew that. Not about my climbing, but my love life. She had never directly said anything about Grant, but I knew through the grapevine that she thought I'd jumped out of the frying pan and into the fire.

"How's Grant feel about the new place?"

Grant hated everything about it: the eight-by-eight concrete pad of a back yard, the brown and orange shag carpet, the closet-sized kitchen, the mortgage, being sandwiched between neighbours he couldn't even be bothered saying hello to. He said it was like living in a fish bowl. I knew he felt like a piranha amongst the goldfish. He went out every day to destroy trees while our Canmore friends campaigned to save them. Niccy and Barb were very involved in the Save the Bow Valley Corridor Society.

"He's getting used to it," I said.

I wanted Niccy to know that I hadn't fucked up this time; I wanted her to know how honourable and loyal Grant was for staying with me. Many climbers I knew would have ditched me after I'd gotten pregnant.

"I'm all registered at the university," I said.

"Good for you. You'll be a great teacher."

The other day, when I visited the University of Calgary, I'd felt so alive and free walking around campus with Jenna gurgling and bouncing on my back, charming everyone with her white-blond hair, little chipmunk cheeks and four new teeth. I'd thought I'd feel like a freak, but there were moms and dads and little kids everywhere. When I went to the registrar's office I found out I was still in their system as a student, and all I had to do was register for classes. But if I didn't enrol now, I'd have to apply all over again next year.

About a hundred feet above us, Barb pulled herself onto a small ledge, then a couple of minutes later leaned out from the rock.

"I'm safe!"

"Good job!" Niccy and I yelled in chorus.

Once Niccy and I had finished the first pitch and the three of us were crammed together on the narrow ledge, Barb handed me the rack. My lead. I dipped my already sweating hands into my chalk bag, slapped them together to get rid of the excess, enveloping my head in a white cloud.

"Sure you've got enough chalk there?" Niccy said.

"It's just 5.8, Jan. You'll do great," Barb said.

That was two grades of difficulty easier than the standard I was sometimes leading before I got pregnant, which was 5.10. But I was a fair-weather 5.10er. I could lead easy-to-protect routes as long as I was with the right partner, at the right time of the month, with the wind blowing at the perfect velocity and direction.

My first lead as a mother. With my palms on the rock, I studied the pitch. I saw only one bolt, way above.

"Shit, I hope I can get something in before I get to that bolt."

The last thing I needed was a long, nasty fall on low-angled limestone when I was trying to get my head back into leading. Falling didn't seem to deter Niccy. She'd had a spate of bad ones lately, including a thirty-foot screamer on her first guide exam, which was why she'd failed.

I dipped my hands into my chalk bag again, perched my fingers on small, sloping holds, then placed my foot on a little edge.

"Have fun!" Barb said.

My feet were above my friends' heads when I started to look around for somewhere I could place gear. Nothing.

"This doesn't look good."

"Just keep going. You'll find something."

Another body length up the rock, I stopped, looked around. Still nowhere to place protection. I looked down. If I fell, I'd hit the ledge. But fifteen feet wasn't really that far. People survived that all the time. Or became paraplegics.

I closed my eyes and took a deep breath. Jenna's little face appeared before me. She smiled and showed off her new teeth. My foot started to shake.

"I really don't like this." There was that snivelling whimper in my voice, the one I usually reserved for guys I was sleeping with.

"Remember it's just 5.8," said Barb.

"I can die as easily on 5.8 as 5.10!"

I pulled my body up another move, looked down again. Big mistake. Niccy and Barb were getting uncomfortably far away and the bolt was still more than ten feet above me. That would have made it a very long fall to the ledge. We were definitely getting into quadriplegic territory. *What if I never see Jenna again?*

My leg started to shake wildly, like it had some kind of palsy. I shook it out, looked down at the ledge. I couldn't downclimb without falling.

I pulled on another hold and stepped up on an edge less than an inch wide. There was a flake of rock at eye level, and a small space behind it that might take a piece of protection. Maybe enough to slow a fall.

I groped at my rack, unclipped the tiniest piece I had, an RP, and wedged it into the space. The pebble-sized metal plugged up the crack. When I yanked to test it, it held. It was only psychological protection—it probably wouldn't have held a fall—but the feel of my rope running through the carabiner was reassuring.

The bolt was only five more moves away. If I could just get to it, I'd be protected from hitting the ledge. Dan's voice sprang out of nowhere: *Fake it till you make it.* Yeah, right. And look where that got you.

Dan had come to me before on a climb, a few months after his death. I'd been on Yamnuska, that fin-shaped mountain of crumbling limestone. I couldn't get any protection in and I'd frozen, hundreds of feet off the ground. All of a sudden I'd felt his presence. It had been unmistakable. Just like when he used to walk into a room and change the whole atmosphere with his big personality. He'd been right beside me, urging me on, till a calm flushed through me and I started climbing with a confidence I couldn't attribute to myself. He'd stayed with me until I'd reached the anchor, then slipped away.

Niccy yelled up, "Hey, Jan. Think of the cold beer in the reservoir!"

Obviously it was only me who thought I was on the verge of death. They assumed I'd make a few moves, clip the bolt, make a few more moves to the anchor, and bring them up. They still considered me a climber.

With my eyes closed, I pushed every negative thought out of my head, pushed away the sounds of Niccy and Barb's chatter, the souped-up motor of a diesel truck way down below on the road. Pushed away the images of Jenna.

I'm a climber.

My feet stepped up. Now I was only three moves away. I didn't look down and I didn't look past the bolt to the rest of the route. I found my next handholds and pulled up. Only two moves away. I pushed thoughts of the growing distance between me and the ledge out of my mind. Just focused on the narrowing distance between me and the bolt. Breathed in and moved upward. Breathed out. Breathed in and moved again, until I was finally there. I clipped a quickdraw into the bolt, slipped my rope through the carabiner. Allowed myself to look down. A good forty feet to the ledge.

I climbed past the bolt, the rest of the way to the anchor, with another long run-out, but not a hint of paralysis, like some guardian angel was guiding me up the rock. But it was just me.

"Good job!" Niccy rubbed her neck and shrugged the kinks out of her shoulders.

A few minutes later I reached the bolts. "I'm secure!"

Leaning against the rock, I soaked up the view, the deep blue reservoir, Chinaman's Peak wavering in the heat, the three emerald-green spots of Grassi Lakes.

I'm still a climber.

"I led the second pitch of Die Young, Stay Pretty. It was great. I had so much fun!" The memory of my terror had curiously dissolved, like the pain of childbirth.

Grant grunted but didn't look up from the television. I snuggled into his hard body, slipped my hand through his arm. It was already nine o'clock, Jenna was asleep and Grant was still awake. A rare occurrence on his first night home from logging camp.

"Aren't you proud of me? It's good that I'm getting right back into leading."

"Yeah, it's great." He wouldn't look at me, but he shouldn't have been pissed off. He climbed at least a day every weekend.

I leaned back on the couch and studied his profile. He was almost back to his normal weight after Nuptse but he couldn't seem to shake his depression. I tried to keep my expectations low on Friday nights, just like Yolande had advised me to keep my expectations low after expeditions, but sometimes I couldn't hold back.

"What's wrong?"

"Nothing." He took another swill of beer.

"I know something's bugging you."

"Jesus Christ," he said, reaching for his cigarettes. "Why do you always think something's wrong? I'm just tired and I want to watch TV."

He pushed himself off the couch, slid open the patio door and stepped onto the concrete pad to have a smoke in the backyard.

I tried to watch the movie but I couldn't keep track of who was shooting whom and why. After another car chase, I headed into the kitchen. Sauce from the sweet and sour ribs was still stuck fast to the casserole dish like dog shit to a Vibram sole, even though I'd been soaking it for two hours.

I squeezed out more dish soap and started scrubbing. I knew what was wrong. Grant was turning back into a logger. I'd tried to convince him to go to carpentry school now that we were so close to Calgary. I told him I'd even put off university if he'd go, but he kept getting drawn back to the bush. He wanted to become a faller, because fallers made more money. But I was starting to think he was drawn to the suffering, like he was drawn to the suffering of alpine climbing.

A couple of nights ago I'd called my mother and complained about our weekends, how I was walking on eggshells, scared to open my mouth. Rather like living with Dad. She had told me how, now that my father was retired and they'd moved to Victoria, he was softening up, getting a bit easier to live with. So it *was* possible. If my prickly father could become a relatively pleasant human being, anyone could. I just didn't know if I could wait twenty-five years.

Sunday night, I slipped out of my clothes, crawled into bed and snuggled against Grant's back. Ran my hand down his biceps. All his muscles were tense so I could tell he wasn't asleep. I moved in closer. I wanted him to touch me so badly. My body felt good these days: strong, bursting with energy.

"You asleep?" I whispered.

"Not anymore I'm not."

I draped my arm over him but he rolled away onto his stomach, let his arm hang off the bed. We'd put the mattress on a slab of plywood and raised it with milk crates so he could hang his right arm over the side. It went numb in the middle of the night from the vibration of the chainsaw.

"I have to get up in five hours," he mumbled into the pillow.

On Mondays, he left at three in the morning to make the two-hour drive to Golden to meet his crew at Humpty's Restaurant. Then they drove another two hours out to the block. He was scaling and bucking—measuring the logs and cutting them the right length, then cutting off the branches. It was the first step toward becoming a faller, and he'd be a lot happier as a faller. He'd told me the best thing about that job was everyone had to stay two tree lengths away from him. But it meant he had to buy a chainsaw for seven hundred dollars. A year's tuition.

I rubbed his back for a couple of minutes to help him sleep, rolled onto my side away from him and wrapped myself around my pillow.

Jenna's screams started at one in the morning. I groaned and pushed the covers off. I couldn't remember the last time I'd slept through the night.

"I can't sleep with that kid wailing all the time," Grant said as he sat up and swung his feet to the floor.

"She's teething."

"She needs discipline. You're coddling her."

"She's only a year old! You can't coddle a year-old baby."

We were just like my parents: my mother waving her Dr. Spock parenting book around, my father waving his dad's old cane.

"Fuck this." He stood and pulled his grey Stanfield's undershirt over his head, tugged up his faller pants, dragged the orange suspenders over his shoulders. The smell of Christmas trees and chainsaw fumes filled the air.

"What are you doing?"

"What do you think I'm doing? Going to Golden."

"It's only one o'clock. You don't have to leave for two hours."

"You can sleep with Jenna."

A few minutes later, with Jenna sucking her fingers contentedly in my arms, I watched out the window as my husband backed the truck out of our parking spot and drove through the complex toward the road.

When the ultimatum came, the next weekend, I still wasn't prepared, even with all the warning signs.

"I can't keep commuting eight hours a weekend. It's killing me."

I didn't know what to say, so I kept my head down, kept washing the dishes.

"We're going to have to move to Golden."

"Golden?" The slippery casserole dish slid out of my hands and sank in the soapy water. I turned to face Grant, who was sitting in the tiny alcove of the kitchen at the table. Beside him, Jenna finger-painted with her creamed corn on the tray of her high chair.

"I can't move to Golden. It's too far away from the university!"

"I work five days a week, drive four hours, climb one day, see my family one day, then drive another four hours. I can't even train for a big climb. Barry wants to do the North Twin with me but I can't get in shape in time." He pushed away his plate of half-eaten apple crumble. "I can't believe we're playing the same game our parents played. I've avoided this all my life and now look at me."

"But I'm already signed up for all my courses!"

"And how the hell do you plan to pay for these courses?"

I hadn't figured that out yet. The price of tuition had gone up in the past two years and we'd just depleted the account to buy my friend Geoff's Subaru.

"It's only two courses."

"Jan, I can't climb and log. I'm exhausted." He put his head in his hands and rubbed his eyes. I could see the exhaustion in his shoulders, hear it in his voice. I took a step toward him.

He looked up. "And you knew I was a climber when you married me."

His words were a rock wall erupting from the floor between us. I wanted to scream: *What about me? I'm a climber too!* But I wasn't an alpinist. A Himalayan climber. A "real" climber. I still shit myself on easy pitches of rock.

"And you knew I wanted to go back to school when you married me," I threw back.

"Well, how 'bout you just tell me where to send the money."

Jenna looked up from her messy art work, swivelled her head from Grant to me.

A familiar panic tightened around my rib cage like a muscle spasm and shallowed my breathing. What if he left us? Even though I often toyed with the idea of leaving him, I knew I never would. I had no money. I couldn't haul Jenna around in her baby backpack while I ski-patrolled or taught climbing, or drag her off to a pesticide-laden tree-planting camp. I could waitress, but I'd probably make more on welfare once I factored in childcare. I didn't want to be a single mom on welfare.

Grant's voice broke through my panic. "You can do distance courses. Then when Jenna's older you can go back to university. She only just turned one. She needs her mother."

As he talked my heart stopped racing. He wasn't planning to leave us. And it was true. Jenna was still just a baby.

I slumped against the counter, stared down at my bare feet. They were getting tough and calloused again from my climbing shoes. "But we just bought this place."

If we moved again, this would be the fourth house I'd cleaned for the next occupants. Just like my mother, following my father all over Canada, leaving clean houses in her wake. I'd sworn I'd never end up like her, just like Grant had sworn he'd never end up like his father, and here we were, sixteen months into our marriage. We'd had our first wedding anniversary in April, while he was on Nuptse.

I looked around my house. The first house that really felt like mine. There was so much space. A stream going by in the backyard. A university an hour away. Here, I could be a student. I had a babysitter. Here, all our friends were climbers. Grant was a climber. In Golden, Grant would turn into a logger, and I'd turn into a logger's wife.

"I hate this house!" The harshness was back. "You tricked me into it. I couldn't see straight when I signed those papers."

"Mama!" Jenna stood in her high chair, put her arms out for me. Grant lurched toward her—she'd tumbled to the floor once—but I reached her first. I scooped her up and propped her on my hip, let her wrap her arms and legs around me tightly.

I turned my back on Grant, tried scouring the casserole dish with my free hand but it kept slipping away from the scrubbie.

Golden. The only people I knew there were Ted and Diane, Grant's friends. He and Ted used to climb together and now Ted was a logger too. He worked in the bush and Diane stayed at home with their two kids on a property south of town. She cooked and cleaned and made his lunches, but she seemed happy.

Grant took Jenna out of my arms. "We've got to be realistic here. I'm a logger, and the work is in Golden. And we could buy a whole house on a big piece of property. Real estate is so cheap there. You could have a huge garden. We could get a dog."

In Canmore so many of our friends were professionals: doctors, physiotherapists, psychologists, teachers, university professors. We didn't measure up. In Golden, maybe I could be like Diane, happy to be a mother and wife.

I started scrubbing harder. I had to fight this urge to turn back the clock to the 1950s. If I moved to Golden it would be like giving up the sharp end of the rope. I'd be following again. I had to go to school.

When I didn't respond, Grant added, "Let's just try it for a year. One year. We don't have to sell the townhouse—we can rent it out."

I stopped scrubbing and stared into the bubbles I'd churned up. "I'll think about it."

23

YODEL VILLAGE

Bent over a tape deck, I sat cross-legged in our makeshift front yard—a ten-foot-square section of sod thrown down at the end of our dusty driveway. I strained to understand the garbled Acadian French. The narrator—an old man from New Brunswick—stared up at me from my textbook. His face was shrivelled like a dried-apple doll; he didn't seem to have teeth. No wonder he was unintelligible.

This was my very first university distance course. When it had arrived in the mail, about the same time we'd moved to Golden in the fall, it had been like unwrapping a Christmas present. Every day, all winter, stranded here in yet another, bigger, Bumfuck, BC, I'd waited for Jenna to nap so I could squeeze in some precious time on

236

the next lesson. At this pace it would take approximately thirty years to get a degree.

Grant had been excited to move here to Yodel Village, as he called it. It had seemed fitting for us, being climbers, to live in a house built in 1911 for the original Swiss mountain guides, but the novelty of an eighty-year-old home had worn off quickly. The bugs were the biggest problem. Dormant flies that crawled all over the carpet every time the weather heated up, and worse, squiggly stunted wormy things that popped up everywhere, even in the bed. I'd taken one in a mason jar to the landlord, Al, and he'd said, "Those are cupboard beetles. Everyone has cupboard beetles," and looked at me like I was on something. Or from the city. Soon after that I found empty shells everywhere, like tiny snake skins, and suddenly there were brown beetles in the flour, the cereal, everywhere. Not just the cupboards.

A semi roared by on the TransCanada below, drowning out the dialogue, and I had to rewind the tape. The house was a few hundred feet up a hillside, just above Golden, and sounds rose, something I hadn't known until after we'd moved in. So did smells. Whenever the mountain passes on either side of town were blocked by avalanches or landslides, semis lined up on the highway, engines idling for hours, sometimes days. The exhaust—mixed with emissions from the lumber mill and smoke from the wood stoves—flowed up and into our house.

A scream pierced the highway rumble. I wrenched my eyes off my work. In the sandbox a few feet away, my friend's daughter, Tanya— her white-blond head submerged under a bucket-shaped pile of sand—turned toward me. Her little pink tongue darted in and out of her mouth, pushing out black, gritty saliva. Jenna was holding an empty plastic bucket.

We were in the throes of the terrible twos and our kid wasn't even two yet. Last week Jenna had pushed another little friend down three stairs and I'd automatically slapped her hand. Me, who'd always sworn I'd never hit my kids, slapping my twenty-month-old's hand.

I'd tortured myself, imagining her following me into therapy when she grew up, or writing a mountain version of *Mommie Dearest*. So now I had a stack of books on parenting on my bedside table along with my books on creative visualization and relationship rescue.

I shut off my tape recorder. I had to get Tanya cleaned up before her mother got back. Patty was at a counselling session at the Women's Centre. Last week she'd started packing to leave her husband. This week she'd found out she was pregnant. It could turn out to be an extra-long session.

After Patty and Tanya had headed home, I put Jenna down for a nap, poured myself a cider and surveyed the damage. Sand from the back door, through the kitchen, across the red shag carpet in the living room, and up the stairs. Toys from one end of the living room to the other: plastic monkeys from the barrel, wooden puzzles, teething toys, stuffed animals, Mr. and Mrs. Potato Head. Dishes from breakfast and lunch still on the kitchen table. Two bloated wet diapers beside the garbage pail.

I had about an hour before Grant got home. I poked some potatoes, shoved them in the oven, then grabbed my cider and Shakti Gawain's *Creative Visualization Workbook*, sat cross-legged on the blood-red living room shag carpet, and opened the book to my goals.

For most of the winter, I'd worked hard on my "relationship goal." I'd written out an affirmation, in present tense, to trick my brain into thinking I'd already achieved it: *Grant and I are now feeling very close and getting along well. We have begun to express our love for each other verbally.* Then Grant had announced that he and Peter were planning a trip to Alaska to climb the Infinite Spur in Dan and Ian's honour, and that put the kibosh on my relationship goals. I started visualizing going to school. Real school. Not a mail-order school. I sent my application in to the University of Calgary again and just last week my acceptance letter had arrived.

Jenna's singsong voice, dragging out the vowels in her favourite word—*Mommy!*—brought me back to Yodel Village. I opened my eyes, groaned. Drained my cider, stood up. How could I love my child so much, yet feel so free when she was asleep? I'd forgiven my mother countless times in the last two years when I thought of her in Inuvik with a newborn, a two-year-old, a four-year-old and my father.

Jenna and I looked up from our tea party when we heard the diesel engine of the Crummy as it pulled into the driveway. "Crummy" was what they called an extended cab pickup stuffed full of smelly loggers; it was not a description of how they felt. But Friday seemed to be the only time they *didn't* feel crummy. Grant had told me some of the guys drank beer all the way home on the logging roads, pissing in the cans and throwing them out the window so they wouldn't have to stop.

When the basement door slammed, I tensed up. Was that an angry slam, or just a regular slam? In Canmore, Grant had blamed his moods on the long drive, but our move to Golden hadn't made him any less cranky. He'd shaved four hours off the commute, but still had to drive a couple of hours to camp, spend all week in an Atco trailer an hour or so from their block, then drive two hours home to listen to "the wife" bitch and complain all weekend.

"Dat Daddy?" Jenna jumped off the couch and ran to the door leading to the basement with me following close behind. Even though she couldn't yet turn the knob, I was paranoid about the steep stairs down to concrete. I picked her up and plunked her on a chair at the table with a bag of pink homemade play-dough. Grant would put away his chainsaw and take a shower before coming upstairs. I had a bit more time to work.

I poured Shake 'n Bake into a plastic bag, added pork chops, shook, popped them in the oven. The smell of baked potatoes filled the kitchen and I realized they'd be done long before the meat. I spun the lettuce, threw it in a bowl, put bread in the toaster for instant croutons. *Voilà.*

Grant emerged from the basement, his blond hair wet and slicked back.

"Daddy!"

"Jenna!" Grant used a voice he reserved for his daughter—animated, exaggerated, loving. She was in his arms, squealing, flying above his head. Grant pressed his face into her tummy, his deep voice rumbling like a train. She giggled and squirmed, her head thrown back.

"How was your week?" I put my arm around him in a half hug, but I couldn't squeeze in.

"Fine."

Since the arrival of my acceptance letter he talked to me mostly in monosyllables. Our one discussion of school had ended with him saying, "Just tell me where to send the money." At least it was better than what Patty's husband had said when she'd wanted child support: "Good luck finding me in Mexico."

But our deal had been to spend one year in Golden, then, if it didn't work out, we'd kick the tenants out of our townhouse in Canmore and move back in. And I'd go to school in Calgary. That year was almost up.

"Dinner'll be ready soon."

"Good, I'm starving." He pulled a beer from the fridge.

"I made Shake 'n Bake and Caesar salad."

"Great." He made eye contact with me briefly, then turned and squatted low to get into the living room with Jenna on his shoulders. He kicked a toy out of the way.

"What the fuck happened in here? It looks like a bomb went off."

"I watched Tanya all afternoon for Patty. She went to the women's centre to talk to Rhea. She's pregnant."

"Oh, Christ." He turned on the TV. Grant was not a fan of Rhea, who was now my counsellor too. He knew we talked about him.

I stepped back into the kitchen. Scheduling the news at supper-time must have been part of the patriarchal plot to keep women uninformed.

The anchorman's voice on CBC, the only channel we could get with rabbit ears, filled the house. At least I could listen to it.

Jenna started to whine.

"Go see what Mommy's doing!"

Jenna wandered into the kitchen, stretched her arms out. "Up!"

I put her on my hip, opened another cider, headed back into the living room. "Could you take her for a few minutes? I've got to get dinner finished."

"She wants *you*."

"She'd be fine if you played with her."

"I'm trying to watch the news."

"I'm trying to get dinner on the table." He took her out of my arms, eyes still on the TV.

She wandered back into the kitchen as I was pulling the pork chops and shrivelled potatoes out of the oven. There was something black in the corner of her mouth. I took a closer look.

"Shit. Grant! You're supposed to watch her! She's eating flies again."

I swirled my finger around in her mouth and scooped out a black fly, still wiggling, then threw the wet blob into the sink and turned on the hot water, full blast.

"Yukky, Jenna! Yukky!"

"Ukky, Mommy! Ukky!" She opened her mouth wide, showing her widely spaced baby teeth. I picked a leg off her tongue, muttering, "I hate this goddamned house."

I stomped into the living room. "What is wrong with you? All I ask for is a few minutes to get supper on the table. You've got to watch her. You can't let her out of your sight."

"What's wrong with me? I'll tell you what's wrong with me. I come home to a fucking pigsty after working my ass off all week . . ."

He brushed by me, grabbed his pouch of tobacco off the counter and headed outside, slamming the screen door behind him.

When Grant came back into the kitchen, supper was on the table and Jenna was in her high chair playing with Cheerios. He closed the door quietly. With my back to him, I tossed the salad. I tossed and tossed all my anger and hatred up with his favourite food, Caesar salad. The last time I'd made it he'd choked out a compliment, said I was a pretty good cook.

He came up from behind, circled his arms around me. I stopped tossing.

"I'm sorry for being such an asshole."

I couldn't remember him ever apologizing. I leaned back against him. I just wanted us to be a happy little family.

The next morning, I opened my eyes to a hint of daylight softening the dark room and a pair of big hands groping at my pajamas.

"Why do you wear all this shit to bed?" My "armour," he called it.

I groaned and looked at the alarm clock.

"It's six o'clock. Go away." I pulled the pillow over my head, but he was curling into my back, pushing against me. It felt good to have his heavy arm draped over me, anchoring me to the bed. It felt safe. I moved toward him. He peeled off my pajamas till they were bunched at our feet under the covers. I wondered for a moment if Jenna would wake up. Should I close the door?

I melted into him. We didn't speak. Didn't look at each other.

Lying with my head on his damp shoulder, I couldn't remember why I'd been so pissed off. I traced my fingers over his lean stomach while my head rose and fell with his breathing. This was what I needed. Connection. Harmony. But we could never hold on to it for long.

"I think we should buy the Morrises' house."

I rolled off him. Sat up. "But I just got my acceptance letter."

The Morrises were climbers who'd moved to Revelstoke. They were having trouble selling their house on ten acres. Most of Golden's climbers lived on rural properties either north or south of town: generally, the more redneckish hippie climbers settled to the north, and the hippie-ish hippie climbers to the south. It made it hard to know where to move when you had one of each in a family. The Morrises' house was to the north, in the Blaeberry Valley.

"Let's get a real estate agent to take us out there next weekend. At least take a look."

"What about university? I don't want to be fifty when I get my degree."

"You aren't even thirty yet. We can go to Calgary later, when the kids are older."

"What do you mean, 'kids'? You said *kids*, with an *s*."

"I've been thinking. Jenna needs a sibling."

A baby? Intense feelings flooded through me, horror or joy, I couldn't tell. It was that same sensation you got when you put your foot in water so hot you could almost mistake it for freezing.

"What?" he said. "I think it's a great idea."

My mouth must have been hanging open. I'd hinted at another kid a few times, always pretending to be joking, but I'd never expected he'd actually go for it.

"I couldn't have survived without my brother Nate," he added.

I could never have survived my family without siblings either, and it was looking more and more like Jenna would need a sibling to survive us.

"We should focus on the family right now," he said in his world-according-to-Grant voice.

I stiffened, crossed my arms. "The family. You say it like it's a disease. Or the mafia. *The* family, not *our* family. It's like the guys you work with who say, *the wife*. 'I was talking to *the wife* the other day—'"

"Where do you come up with this crap? I love my family."

I needed to hear him say he loved *me*, not an idea, a collective. But him saying he wanted another baby was almost like him saying he loved me.

"Just phone Barney at Re/Max this week and make an appointment. If we don't like the place we won't buy it."

I'd already quit university once to have a baby, then last year I'd cancelled my registration to move to Golden. In ten years, some admissions officer was going to open my tenth application and say, "Oh, Christ, it's that woman again," and put me in the reject pile.

"What about Alaska?" I said.

"We couldn't afford a climbing trip if we bought the house. The family comes first."

All along I must have known that the acceptance letter was just a bunch of words typed on paper. That it was the easy part. There were still a lot of loose ends to take care of: affordable housing, daycare, reliable transportation, money, Jenna and Grant. Guilt. All the moms here stayed at home with their kids. When I told one of our friends I was planning to go back to school, he said, "We decided Nancy would stay at home because we didn't want someone else raising our kids." In Canmore the moms were motivational speakers, adventure consultants, physiotherapists, doctors, teachers, mountain guides, all with their kids in daycare. No one questioned them. Moving from Canmore to Golden was like reversing twenty years in a time machine.

"You're planning to look at a house? Just last week you were ready to get a divorce. Again! And what about university?" My sister sounded exasperated through the phone from Vancouver.

Susan wasn't married. She wasn't a mother. She didn't get how hard it was to just pick up a kid and go to university.

"We're just looking. But I'm wondering if maybe I've been so miserable here just because of this house. If we had our own place . . ."

When Susan had come for a visit in the spring, the squiggly wormy bugs were right in the bed she was supposed to sleep in, like they'd dropped from the ceiling. She'd slept with me for a week while Grant was in camp.

"Jan, it's not just the house."

"But he was back to the nice Grant again last weekend. By Sunday, anyway. And he thinks he's been so miserable all winter because *I've* been so negative and miserable. And if he's unhappy because I'm unhappy, that means if I change *my* behaviour, maybe he can change *his* behaviour."

Silence on the other end.

"You still there?"

"Yeah, I'm still here. It's just that, I don't know, you seemed your perky self on my last visit, until Grant came home. Then you could have cut the tension with a knife."

"Don't worry so much. Anyway, you wouldn't believe how funny Jenna is these days. She's constantly bringing me the book you gave her. I'll point to a picture of a dog and she'll go, 'Woof, woof!' Then I'll point to a cat and she'll say, 'Meow!'"

"Really? That's nice." My sister sounded distracted. "So, did you read my essay? I was a bit worried about what you'd think about the section on you."

Susan had written an essay about our family dynamics titled "And a Rock Feels No Pain" for one of her social-work classes at UBC. It was about our father's little drinking problem. Dad was the villain of the story, and the only one who hadn't read the essay. She wrote that I'd learned early to ignore anything I didn't want to hear or see. How Eric and Dad would scream at each other, and I'd tune them out by getting down on the floor to do sit-ups and push-ups. How surprised I was during my annual visits home that I didn't have a nice family.

"I'd forgotten I told you all that stuff—about blocking everything out."

"It seemed like you just didn't want to live in a family like ours so you made one up."

In Whitehorse, in the park across from our house, I used to etch lines in the dirt for my fantasy home—bedrooms, kitchen, living room—then wander through the rooms talking to my fantasy family, the famous singing Partridge Family. Keith was my big brother, Shirley my perfect mother, and there were all those cool siblings. The father was conspicuously absent. Conveniently dead.

"Well, we were no Partridge Family, that's for damned sure," I said.

"Just don't forget how badly you want school."

"Um. There's one more thing. Ah . . . Grant's thinking it'd be good to have another baby. . . ."

"Oh, Jan. You'd better phone Mom."

My poor mother. She and Dad would probably have to remortgage their house to pay the phone bill. We had a special system. When I needed to talk, I'd call her collect, she'd refuse the charge, then call me back. She tolerated Dad's bitching about the bill to keep Grant off my back about ours. In Munster she'd listened to Dad's sister, crazy Aunt Helen, for hours and hours with my dad muttering in the background to get off the bloody phone. Now she had to listen to her crazy daughter.

The highway wound and twisted, hugging the Columbia River as we headed north of town. I had to look straight ahead so I wouldn't lose my Raisin Bran. We were on our way to look at the Morrises' house. My brain hopped from one affirmation to another, from *I am now a university student* to *We now own a beautiful house in the Blaeberry and I am pregnant with my second child*, till I felt like I was playing pinball with the universe. Two opposing affirmations probably cancelled each other out.

A fully loaded logging truck came around the corner toward us. My fingers clamped down on the armrest like a claw.

Grant watched the truck recede in his rear-view mirror. "Shit, that's big cedar. Wonder where that's coming from?"

"I hate those trucks. I'm always scared a log'll roll off on us."

"That's why there's all those squished cars on the side of the road." He looked over at me and laughed.

I punched him in the arm. My happy Grant was back and it was only Saturday. Maybe it wasn't a degree I needed. Maybe I needed to be more committed to this marriage. Rhea had told me that Adult Children of Alcoholics are always defining themselves through externals, meaning, for me, climbing, mountain biking, skiing and Grant. She'd think this house was an external. But what if a degree was as external as a house? And Jenna? How could she be an external? She was my life.

"What about Al?" I said. "He'd shit if we told him we're looking for a house. We promised we'd stay a year."

"Fuck 'im. We've been in that hole for eight months. That's close enough."

That's what I wanted to be able to do. Tell the world where to go. Not give a shit what anyone thought. Sometimes I felt like Grant and I would be fine if we could live in our own little bubble, with no outside influences.

"We're just looking, remember?" I said.

Ten minutes out of town the highway straightened and the Columbia River widened into the Wetlands. Acres and acres of marsh that attracted almost two hundred species of birds—and billions of mosquitoes. We turned up a dirt road and rattled up the freshly graded hill in second gear.

Past an intersection, we turned off into a laneway that ran through some woods. We followed two tire tracks with tall grass down the centre toward a house sitting on the highest point of land in a clearing. The backdrop of mountains grew and grew, filling our view as the Subaru groaned up the steep, potholed dirt, past rows of raised garden beds and raspberry bushes, a woodshed and chopping block, a small greenhouse. We pulled up on a gravel parking spot, Grant turned off the engine, and we took it all in: the cedar salt-box house on cement Sonotubes—like little stilts—the steep red metal roof, the 360-degree view of three mountain ranges: the Rockies, the Purcells and the Selkirks. There was a miniature version of the main house that the owners had lived in while they were building.

"Oh my God," I said, letting my breath out with a sigh.

This was my dream home. I wanted to skip though the chest-high grass, spin around and sing the theme from *The Sound of Music*. University and the city seemed very far away.

"Look." Grant pointed. "There's a shitter."

An outhouse squatted below the house, facing the mountains.

While Grant pulled Jenna out of her car seat, I wandered up a path lined with bright orange lilies and blood-red poppies covered in ants. I climbed weathered cedar steps to a deck and stared down into the valley at a bright, meandering thread of silver, the Blaeberry River.

Grant tried the front door. It was locked. We'd have to wait till Barney got here to see inside. Grant and Jenna peeked through the window.

"Look, Jenna, this is our new home." He was better at creative visualization than I was and he hadn't even done the workbook.

Jenna was so tiny in Grant's arms. She was almost two and I'd been with her almost every second since she was born except to occasionally climb, bike or ski. If I went to university, I'd have to put her in daycare. Someone else would take care of her. She'd be in the city, away from the mountains, away from her father.

During my last counselling session I'd told Rhea how safe I felt with Grant. How if there were a major disaster and we had to escape into the mountains, I knew he could protect us. She'd said that in this day and age there were more important characteristics in a husband and father than being able to protect a family from disasters. How many disasters came along in a lifetime? But that wasn't the point. The point was I knew he'd die for us, even if he wasn't all touchy-feely about it.

Jenna's hands were splayed on the window, her nose pressed against the glass. Her blond hair shone white in the sun. When she pulled her face back, laughing, she left two tiny handprints and a smudge from her breath on the window. Marking her territory.

As I watched Grant heft her onto his shoulders, I realized, *I do want to have another baby with this man. He's my home.*

24

YOU LEAD, I'LL FOLLOW

I lay naked on top of the comforter, palpating my breasts and watching the pink glow on Redman Peak through the northeast-facing window of our new bedroom. Grant, lying beside me with his hands laced behind his head, glanced over at my chest.

"What are you doing?"

"My boobs are getting bigger, don't you think?"

He looked back up at the ceiling. He was still here only because I'd told him I hated it when he jumped out of bed after sex. I could almost hear the calculations in his head, as he wondered if enough time had passed.

"They hurt. I wonder if I'm already pregnant?"

"Maybe you're poking at them too much." His eyes crinkled with his slight smile. His face was scabbed from above his eye, over his cheekbone to under his chin. A log had rolled over him the week before at work, leaving a path of ripped skin. He'd been lucky. It could have been a lot worse.

We lay still, listening to the silence. It was so quiet this far from town. No more semis blasting or idling for hours at the bottom of the hill outside Humpty's restaurant. No more trains banging in the switching yard. Now all I heard was that hum that was always in my ears, the absence of noise.

"Guess how long it's going to take me to get my degree by distance taking two courses a year?"

He didn't answer.

"Nineteen years."

"So, take more courses."

That was impossible with Jenna. She used to go to daycare two mornings a week but I'd cancelled to save money. We were barely getting from paycheque to paycheque with the mortgage. I tried to squeeze in my studies after she fell asleep and before I nodded off myself.

"I've been wondering if we should have another baby right now. I feel like a climber with a kid, but with two, I'm going to turn into a dumpy housewife, a real mother."

"You're already a real mother."

If I'd gotten pregnant right away, I wouldn't have had all this time to think, but we'd been trying for two months. Enough time to change my mind.

"It's going to suck to be fat again. I'm the perfect weight for climbing."

"You won't be fat, you'll be pregnant."

Good answer. I turned toward him to snuggle into his side but he was sitting up, reaching for his underwear. The Crummy would be here soon.

He shoved his feet into his socks with his back to me. He was getting tired of my waffling, but when my period arrived he looked suspiciously relieved.

He was moving stiffly. His ribs were in worse shape than his face. Nothing broken, but his chest was a mass of purple and green and red, fading now after a week or so. I put my fingers lightly on a bruise.

"How's your body?

"I'll survive."

With Grant climbing mountains and felling trees, the most dangerous job in Canada, I never knew what to expect when the phone rang. Not long ago a logger he worked with died in the bush, and another died in a collision on the drive home. Maybe this contributed to my waffling about a baby. Being a widow with a toddler was rosier than a *pregnant* widow with a toddler.

I burrowed back under the covers to sleep until Jenna woke up.

"Come on, Jenna, let's go for a bike ride!"

"Just a minute. I busy."

Jenna was trying to squeeze Gus, her new kitten, into a pink lacy doll dress. His grey body hung limp with defeat between her knees, like a dead rabbit's. A little mewl escaped his mouth.

When I moved toward her, she reassured me quickly, "I be gentle, I be gentle."

Grant had been gone a couple of hours. The dishes were done, the laundry was folded, the toys were picked up, the play-dough scraped off the walls and floors, and the kitchen linoleum was lit up like gold where the sun streamed through the front door.

I finally coaxed Jenna outside, clutching her ratty old "special blanket." She wouldn't leave the house, wouldn't sleep, wouldn't do anything without it. I strapped her facing backwards into the black, missile-shaped bike trailer we'd picked up in Calgary out of the Buy and Sell—my freedom machine—straddled my bike and headed down the driveway. Jenna let out a long moan so she could listen to her voice jiggle and bump with each pothole as we zoomed through the thick scent of cedar, pine and freshly cut grass. There was lots of room for a baby brother or sister in the trailer. It'd be heavier for sure. But it would keep me in shape.

A heavier bike carrier. There was another pro for my Pros and Cons of Having a Baby list. I had nine cons: no freedom, more housework, no time to ski or study, work postponed for three more years, school put off forever, expensive, fat and out of shape, alone with two kids instead of one, labour. I had two pros: companion for Jenna, never have to do it again.

In my lowest gear, I turned onto the road. Burl was in his tractor beside their house, a big split-level right beside the road. I waved and he gave me a big grin and waved back. The first time we'd gone over to their house to introduce ourselves no one answered the door, so we walked around to the back to see Burl with a newly killed deer dangling by the legs, blood pouring from its neck into a bucket. But he'd been all warm and friendly, and welcomed us to the neighbourhood. He was going to plough our driveway during the winter and his wife, Anne, had offered to babysit.

I stood up on my pedals and pumped my legs. This steep hill went on for a few miles. Boot camp.

After only half an hour on the back roads, Jenna's happy chatter turned to whining, which I knew would downgrade to screaming in no time, so I turned around before we got to our destination, the Blaeberry River, and cycled home. As I approached the house, I heard music coming from the shop. Grant was not supposed to be back until Friday, but there was his gear—his chainsaw, oil-soaked backpack, hard hat, toolbox, axe and red gas jug—all piled on the lawn. He usually stashed his chainsaw and gas jugs at his last tree so he wouldn't have to haul them all the way up the steep slash the next day.

Jenna and I pushed open the heavy door to the "little house," as we'd dubbed the workshop—the miniature version of the big house. A blend of cigarette smoke, cedar, gas and oil rushed to greet us; Bruce Springsteen crooned on the ghetto-blaster. Grant looked up from sharpening his chainsaw, grinning through cigarette smoke.

"Yarder broke down." He grabbed Jenna, plopped her on a chair and continued his sharpening.

"Shit. How long?" We needed a new car to replace the rusted-out Subaru, there was the mortgage, and we were supposed to be working on a new baby.

"Won't be that long, and I'm totally fried. I need a break. Look at the weather." He waved his arm toward the window to take in the cloudless blue sky, the Purcell and Selkirk mountains with only a light dusting of snow at the end of September.

Grant had done some interior decorating to the shop. He'd hung a big-boob Husqvarna-chainsaw calendar above the desk and an old painting on the opposite wall—a faded acrylic of Banff's Mount Norquay. Centre stage was a Stoney Nation chief in full headdress on a chairlift. The last time I'd seen that painting was on the wall of his grungy basement room in Banff when we first got together. His last bachelor pad. He'd told me once that it reminded him of his old life.

"Barry called. He wants to go climb Mount Alberta."

A sharp intake of breath. My arms crossed my chest. Mount Alberta had been climbed only a few times, and it was a several-day commitment. The kind of mountain you couldn't afford to fall on.

"I've got to climb, Jan."

I stared at the calendar, my hackles rising. I wanted to ask him what big boobs had to do with chainsaws but I couldn't afford to be a feminist right now. I was either ovulating or pregnant. And I knew it wasn't about the big boobs. It was the climbing. If he climbed more, he'd work less, or die, and any wage I brought in wouldn't even cover the mortgage.

"Let's go climbing tomorrow—just cragging at Lake Louise or something. It'll be good for us. Anne can babysit."

I nodded, my prickliness dropping away. I'd barely climbed this summer. I could use a day feeling like a climber instead of a mom.

Grant navigated the hairpin turns while I stared out my window at the thousand-foot drop into Kicking Horse Canyon. I tried not to think of the car rolling down the embankment and landing upside down in the river I used to paddle with Brad. I turned my focus to our destination—Lake Louise. This would be our first day of climbing together in weeks.

"You really think Jenna's safe with Anne?"

Grant took his eyes off the road long enough to glance at me and nod. "Jenna will be fine."

"She seemed too keen to babysit. Didn't she seem pretty keen?"

When my fears came in contact with air, they started to multiply. Anne had tried for years to get pregnant and had finally adopted two little boys. Brothers. Maybe she wanted a little girl to complete the picture.

Grant glanced at me. "You need an off button for your mind."

Grant climbed easily, his movements smooth and fluid, placing protection as he went, but not nearly as much as I would have placed.

"Shouldn't you put a piece in there?"

He looked down at me, flashed a tolerant smile. His eyes looked glacial blue against his rough, tanned skin. We'd always been drawn to each other's eyes.

He was the kind of guy who could get up off the couch and do hard leads without a warm-up climb. Without climbing for weeks. Nerves of steel.

As he climbed, I fed out the rope, then realized I was swaying back and forth as though there were a baby on my hip. I forced myself to stand still.

As Grant approached the crux, I widened my stance and kept a close eye on him. He grunted under a steep overhang, pulled himself up and over and rested for a moment on a big foothold, shaking out his arms. A few minutes later, he was at the anchor, looking over the treetops at the emerald green water of Lake Louise and yodelling. No need for an exorcist to get rid of the surly logger. He just needed to go climbing.

Once Grant had me on belay, I climbed toward him, my forearms getting pumped with exertion. The holds were big but the rock was steep, overhanging. I used to want to lead this route, but never tried.

I crouched in a little ball under the overhang, shook out my arms, then chalked up and felt around blindly for a hold around the corner. It was just out of reach. The rope tightened as Grant pulled up the slack. When I looked down fifty feet to the ground, I got a flash of my body, bloody and mangled on the rocks below, even though I knew I was safe on a top rope.

Focused on the huge chalk-covered handhold I was aiming for, I moved out on the face. The hold was still out of reach of my white, groping fingers. I looked down again. I didn't remember this move being so hard. I was just about to yell up at Grant to tighten the rope while I made the move (in other words, hoist me up a bit), but then noticed he was staring out at the water, smoking a cigarette. He wasn't even looking. A PMS-like irritation injected me with energy and I pushed off on my foot, lunged for the hold. My whole hand clamped down and my feet lost contact with the rock momentarily till I matched my other hand on the hold and got my feet firmly back on the rock. I did a mantel move, which thrust me up onto the small ledge below the anchor.

"Nice going!" Grant said.

I looked up. He'd been watching.

———

Back on the ground, Grant coiled the rope while I sorted the gear.

"I could get logging out of my system with a few more days like this," he said. "I'm coming alive again." The tension lines and frown etched in his face were softening. "Hey, you should lead a pitch."

"No, not today." The thought of leading even one foot away from my protection made me feel ill.

"Come on, you're climbing great. You've gotta get back on the sharp end. Just do one of the routes we did with the cadets."

Anxiety, like heat, spread up my neck. "No, I'm not in the right headspace." The last time I'd led had been at Tunnel Mountain near Banff with Jeannette, on a route so easy I should have been able to do it without a rope. I'd taken so long on it Jeannette had finally said, "Jesus, would you just climb?" I couldn't even keep my shit together with women anymore.

"You're a way more graceful climber than me. You should be pushing it." That was what Dan used to say. It hadn't helped much then, and it wouldn't help now.

"No! I'm fine following."

I have a two-year-old daughter now. I'm a mother. What if I don't come home?

"Okay, okay. But you'd feel way better if you did."

He avoided my glare and put extra-special attention into coiling the rope.

The red light was flashing on the answering machine when we got home.

"Good news, Grant." It was Dale, his boss. "Yarder's good as new. I'll need you back at work tomorrow morning. Got a big block to open up. I'll pick you up at the regular time." A dial tone replaced his voice.

Grant's shoulders slumped. "Well, that's that." He pushed a button to erase the message.

25

CARSICK

The faded blue '67 Buick Skylark station wagon looked like it hadn't moved in twenty years. The hood was buried under heavy, wet snow. Grant and I stared at the fins on the back end while Jenna did calisthenics off my body, stretching her hands over her head like I was her diving board and she was about to do a back flip. We were standing in inches of mud and slush and she had insisted on wearing her black shiny party shoes, so I tightened my grip, but stumbled backwards and almost tripped over Chaba. Three months ago, just before Christmas, Jenna had picked the tiny, pug-nosed golden Lab out of his litter of siblings because he was the runt. She was drawn to the underdog.

"Looks pretty good to me," Grant said to his friend Ted, and rubbed his hands together like the Grinch. Ted and Diane hadn't used the car in years. They'd told us if we could get it out of the snowbank, it was ours. Grant liked free stuff.

Our Subaru was sitting at Petro-Can where the mechanic was waiting for the okay to haul it off to the wreckers. I'd been going a little too fast down the driveway in my haste to get to the ski hill and had broken the suspension. But maybe it was a blessing in disguise. We were long overdue for a new car. I'd seen the Subaru up on the hoist. The underside was completely coated with a layer of orange rot.

But a '67 Buick Skylark, manufactured when I was six years old, was not exactly what I'd had in mind as a replacement.

Ted shivered in his wheelchair, almost disappearing into his heavy down parka. A year earlier he'd been felling a skinny lodgepole pine when a branch dropped the whole height of the tree and landed on his neck. He spent his thirtieth birthday at the Calgary Foothills Hospital. After our first few visits, Grant had stopped going—Ted was too much of a reminder of what could happen to him—but now he was back to doing odd jobs for them and keeping Ted company. They went too far back for him to stay away. Ted and Grant had climbed together in their twenties, then both got into logging, so Ted was one of the few who could understand how Grant could kill trees and still love the mountains.

Ted had always been lean and tough, but now he was gaunt. Everything about him was dark—his straight dark hair, the shadows under his hollowed-out cheekbones, the sagging bags under his eyes. He'd grown a bulky moustache that made him look like a little boy disguised as a man. Technically, because of where the break was in his neck, Ted was a quadriplegic, but he could push himself along in a wheelchair with his wrists and was able to drive a modified van.

"It's American. You'd need a car compactor to stop that engine." Ted seemed to be trying to sell me something he was giving away for free.

"I know American cars," I told him. "My first two cars were Dodge Darts." I wanted something less than ten years old, like the '84 Toyota Corolla I'd circled with grape-scented marker in the classifieds of the *Golden Star*. But spring break-up had come early this year, so all logging was shut down until the ground firmed up enough to haul. Possibly as long as two months. Last year we hadn't received an unemployment cheque for six weeks.

I turned my back to Ted and tried to glare at Grant hard enough that he'd look at me but he was oblivious. He kicked the tires, saying, "Tires are a bit worn, but we can get new ones."

I peered in the back window. Garbage bags were stacked to the ceiling. I did not want to drive home in this big, ugly heap of metal. I was tired of feeling like a welfare mom.

"We've been using it as storage till Diane can get to the dump."

"Can you help me here, Jan?" Grant said.

I resigned myself and lowered Jenna to the edge of the muck beside Chaba so I could help hook up the car to Ted's tractor. Ted yelled instructions to Grant and the blue beast slid easily out from under the snow.

I stood guard over the patch of black left behind so that Jenna and Chaba wouldn't wade through it. "I think it might be leaking oil," I said.

"Why don't you pull the garbage out, Jan? I'll come back tomorrow with the truck and haul it off to the dump for you, Ted."

While Grant hooked up the jumper cables from one of the tractor batteries to the car, I opened the door to the back seat and covered my face with my hands against the stench of soft banana, mould and rotten meat. I started to haul out the bags.

"Sorry. It didn't smell as bad when they were frozen." Ted backed his chair away from the bags.

"Shit, I'm not complaining. Free's free." Grant slid behind the wheel, stuck his head out the window and added, "Too bad it doesn't have that fake wood panelling." His laugh unleashed like a foghorn.

I crossed my fingers. *Please, please don't start.*

It blasted to life with the first turn of the key. It spluttered and then it roared. I clamped my hands over my ears. Ted yelled over the noise that there was a small hole in the muffler, but he knew someone who might be able to weld it. His moustache quivered on top of his smile and I wondered for a second if this car was his revenge for my lending his wife my "feminist" books and feeding into her fantasy of going back to school.

I grabbed Jenna's hand and pulled her away from the clouds of blue smoke. "I'll be up at the house with Diane."

With Jenna on my hip and Chaba at my heels, I trudged up the long driveway toward the double-wide trailer. I slowed near the top of the hill, more exhausted than I should have been.

Diane was pulling cookies out of the oven when I stepped into the kitchen. Jenna ran over to the table to join Lee and Katie who were bent over colouring books. Two dark mops of hair contrasted with my pale blond Jenna. I looked more like *their* mother than my own daughter's. Jenna looked so much like Grant. The hair, the strong jaw, the light skin.

"How're you surviving, Diane?"

"You know, same old same old." A tired smile.

That was as close to complaining as I'd ever seen her come since the accident.

Diane scraped the cookies off the pan with a spatula and placed them on a wire rack to cool. Her face was pale and there were streaks of grey in her hair that I hadn't noticed before. Until their Workmen's Compensation claim came through, she had to do all of Ted's care— he couldn't feed himself or take care of any of his bodily functions.

"Jesus! How the hell do you find time to bake?" I said, trying to be cheerful. "That gives the rest of us a bad name."

Diane rolled her eyes. "So, did you get it yet?"

"Nope, not yet. But the pee test came back negative." Diane knew my period was a week late.

"That doesn't mean much. Too early. You have to get a blood test." She looked up from the cookies and smiled. "You have that pregnant look about you."

"Does it resemble *The Scream*?"

It was rewarding to hear her laugh. I hadn't heard that for a while.

We bundled up the three kids, filled their hands with cookies, poured coffee into a thermos, and headed down the driveway toward the rumbling noise.

I was close to tears on the drive home. The Skylark stank of garbage and it sounded like there was a Harley in the back seat with Jenna and Chaba. I hadn't wanted to put her back there but the seat belts up front didn't work.

Grant was driving too fast, playing chicken with the ditch at every curve. He'd crank the wheel and nothing would happen till he'd gone a quarter of a turn, then the car, as an afterthought, decided to do as it was told.

As we approached another curve, I pulled a sharp, hissing breath through my teeth.

"Jesus, would you quit doing that?" Grant's forearms bulged as he tightened his grip on the steering wheel. I realized I'd probably been hissing through each turn.

"I can't help it. And it's better than screaming." I braced myself for the next curve.

"I'm going the speed limit. It just feels faster in a bigger car."

"I had that much play in the steering wheel of my '73 Dart—then found out the steering was about to go."

"Quit being so negative. It's not the steering, it's the tires. They're bald. I'll get new ones put on. This car'll last for years." He patted the dashboard.

"Oh, joy." Those were my mother's words coming out of my mouth. It was happening more and more often.

I peeled my eyes off the road to check on Jenna. She was trying to suck her special blanket but it kept popping out of her mouth as her head ricocheted back and forth.

As we careened around the curves toward our turnoff north of town, my mind filled with scenes of me dying in a heap of twisted metal, leaving Jenna motherless. Or worse, Jenna flying through the windshield like in a horror movie I'd seen, and me surviving. I gripped the dashboard again. "Grant, would you just slow down?"

Grant turned his whole body toward me and roared, "Shut the fuck up!"

I clenched my teeth and stared out the window. I wanted to crawl over the seat and curl up with Jenna.

We turned off the highway, not saying a word. Drove past the Magnussens' farm, then Anne and Burl's, and up our driveway. Grant cut the engine in front of our house. We listened as the last of the exhaust rumbled through the hole in the muffler, both of us staring at our little cedar house over the crack that ran the whole length of the windshield.

With his hands still on the steering wheel, Grant, sounding defeated, finally said, "I know you won't believe me, but I'm doing the best I can."

26

DIE YOUNG, STAY PRETTY

When the phone rang in the middle of the night, I was awake instantly. I glanced at the red glowing numbers of the clock. Midnight. If someone was calling this late, it was probably with news I didn't want to hear.

Grant lay unmoving like a plank of wood beside me. I pushed away my extra pillows and heaved myself from my back onto my side with the grace of a turtle flipping itself over. I would have suspected triplets if I hadn't heard the single heartbeat with my own ears, or seen the ultrasound with only two little hands and feet. There was a good chance I'd surpass the forty-five pounds I'd gained with Jenna. At seven and a half months I'd gained thirty. I was so big I'd grown right out of my new job.

For four months I'd been working as a silviculture technician with the Ministry of Forests. It was my dream job, tromping up and down steep logging blocks in the bush with a bunch of women, but I'd only been three months pregnant when I started. The bigger I got, the harder the job became. One day I fell over in the middle of a plot on flat ground and punctured my butt on a stick. I'd just been holding the end of the measuring tape. Another day, I rolled down an embankment into a ditch. When word got back to the big boss, he'd suggested I finish up, go home and look after my family. I didn't like his tone, but was secretly relieved. I was ready to knit, drink tea and play Barbies with Jenna. The season was almost over till next year anyway.

The din of the phone pierced the air and bounced off the vaulted ceiling.

Grant groaned. "Just ignore it. They'll go away."

The phone kept ringing.

"What if it's one of our parents?" My father had fallen off a ladder a couple of weeks ago. He had broken some ribs and ended up in the hospital. I'd panicked when I got that call, realizing how much I didn't want anything to happen to him.

Grant pulled his pillow over his head.

The air was cold on my bare legs as I swung them over the side of the bed. It was only October and we were already burning through our stash of firewood. With a flannel blanket draped over my extra-large T-shirt, I padded along the wood floors in bare feet, down the stairs toward the phone. At least I didn't have to get up early for work anymore.

It was Dave, my friend from Canmore, who'd been my fellow Canadian at NOLS in Wyoming. I didn't see him often these days. Our lives had careened off in opposite directions. He was a mountain guide and the director of the Yamnuska Mountain School, and I was a logger's wife and mother in the wilds of BC.

His voice was husky, like he'd been shouting too much. Or crying.

My hand settled on my belly as though that would steady me. Dave wouldn't call from Canmore at midnight unless someone was dead. I wanted to set the phone back on the cradle. Go back to sleep. Pretend I'd never answered it.

"Who?" I said.

"Niccy. Niccy's dead. I'm so sorry, Jan."

I sank into the sofa, crushed the receiver into my ear against his words. I couldn't speak.

"It happened this afternoon, in Leavenworth. She was guiding. It's been a nightmare here. Her parents . . ." His voice broke. "She fell right past her students."

I couldn't breathe. But I had to breathe for my baby. I groaned and tried to put my head between my legs but my belly was in the way. Grant appeared at the railing above me in his underwear. I looked up at him, gasping.

"Who?" he said. He sounded resigned.

"It's Niccy!"

He lowered his forehead to the railing. "Oh, Christ."

The memorial service was at Camp Chief Hector, near Canmore, where Niccy and I had met ten years before. The dining area in the huge post-and-beam lodge was full, mostly of climbers. Many of them had been at Dan's memorial in Banff four and a half years earlier. And Ian Bult's, John Lauchlan's, Alan Deane's, Dave Cheesmond's, Steve Devine's, BJ's. The same ones who would come to Grant's if he fell off a mountain.

I saw James's long red ponytail and moved toward the group of guides he was with. James had been the head guide on the trip to Leavenworth with Niccy. He'd been one of our mentors when we'd started out. One of the mountain gods. He'd taught me how to ice climb. Now he looked small, defeated. He put his arm around me when I slipped in beside him.

"That's a pretty big belly you've got there." He smiled. His eyes were bloodshot. I smoothed Diane's maternity dress over my bulge.

"When are you due?"

"Month and a half. A Christmas baby."

He was staring at my belly the way the guys at the Forestry office did. As if he were terrified that something was going to erupt from me, like in *Alien*.

James and I talked about everything except what we were here for. Everyone in the room seemed to be doing the same. The laughter and chatter disguised the fact that this was a memorial service for a woman who'd loved life and had only managed to hang on to hers for thirty years.

"I'm so sorry you had to go through that." My voice cracked.

James's pale blue eyes glazed over. He'd been the first to reach Niccy's body. She'd fallen three hundred feet. His last image of her was a shattered one, while the rest of us got to remember her as our strong and bold Niccy.

"Yeah. Hasn't been a good week." He forced a smile.

Bruce—the original director of the Yamnuska Mountain School back in the early days when it broke off from Camp Chief Hector—stood in front of the stone fireplace, waiting to start the eulogy, so we all moved toward him. Grant and I leaned against a wood railing.

"Niccy and I used to sit in my cabin, or on the porch, right here at Camp Chief Hector, drinking red wine and talking about life."

As Bruce talked about Niccy, my fists clenched and unclenched at my sides and I realized I wasn't just sad, I was pissed off. At Niccy. Because she'd fucked up. She'd been climbing an easy route beside her students as they learned to lead and she hadn't roped up. She'd been too fucking cocky, just like when we'd worked at the cadet camp together.

One of the students had told Dave that just before she fell, Niccy had said, "Shit." Her last word. She hit the ledge headfirst, right in front of the other students, before she continued her fall to the ground.

It was so quiet in the huge dining room I could hear someone clear his throat on the other side. My own throat was aching from holding everything in.

Now Niccy would never meet my new baby. And she wouldn't meet Wendy's new baby, Zac, who'd arrived prematurely, twelve hours after Niccy's death. Wendy was still in the hospital with him.

Bruce swiped at his cheek. "I shared with her my own philosophy: 'Life is short. Do what makes you happy.' And she ended up practising it much better than I do." Bruce smiled, then looked down at his feet for a few very long moments. "In the end, she followed her heart. She was finally on her way, her dreams all coming true. She was a mountain guide."

Grant handed me a Kleenex. My anger was no longer able to act as a dam.

Students came up to the front, one after another, sharing their Niccy stories. She'd been such a good teacher. She'd made them feel brave, capable. I wanted to get up and tell everyone I'd felt the same way when I climbed with Niccy. She'd brought out the climber in me. Helped me get out of my own way. But my voice wouldn't work.

Niccy's father took his place in front of the fire. "My daughter was stubborn." Laughter and murmurs of agreement rippled through the room. "I'll tell you how stubborn she was," and he described how her mother had forced her to eat her peas, so she stored the entire serving in her cheek and got rid of them later. He told us how he'd wanted her to go to university to become a forester. "But Niccy wanted to be a mountain guide," he said. "So that's what Niccy did. We eventually worked things out." He chuckled and lifted the edges of his mouth in some semblance of a smile.

That was Niccy. She didn't let anything get in her way: not the sexism in guiding, not fear, not failure. Definitely not a man, including her father.

Niccy's mother spoke next. Niccy had been this woman's little girl. It didn't matter that Niccy was thirty. I suddenly wanted to phone my neighbour, make sure Jenna was okay. I wanted to go home. *Please. I can survive anything but that. . . .*

A sob erupted from me. Grant put his hands on my shoulders. I wanted my anger back. Anger was easier than this.

"If you could write me stories, any of your memories of Niccy, all the stories you've told tonight, please, I would treasure them."

What would Niccy have wanted me to tell her mother? We'd made some stupid, cocky mistakes together. And we'd laughed. Like on the way out from Aberdeen, miles and miles of empty trails in mountain boots and Niccy, a profuse sweater, had whipped off her shirt and bra and hiked topless. Her uninhibitedness surprised me. It had usually been me letting it all hang out. Then a bunch of guys came around the corner. I'd never heard her scream so loud. That would be a good story to write to her mother.

I looked over at Sharon. She wasn't alpine climbing anymore. Not since her son was born. Even though she'd climbed Everest. Three other women I used to climb with had kids, and none of them took big risks in the mountains now. Maybe a baby would have saved Niccy.

Niccy's mother ended by telling us how proud she was of her strong daughter, of her integrity. Of everything she'd achieved in a short, intensely lived lifetime. She spoke of Niccy in present tense.

At Dan's memorial so many people had said the worn-out, "He died doing what he loved." I hoped people were telling Niccy's parents she'd *lived* doing what she loved. She went after her dream and never gave up.

27

GRANT'S LUNCH

As Sam nursed, he clenched and unclenched fistfuls of my skin. His body was heavy and compact in my arms, already a little bundle of muscle at three months. He pulled back to watch me, smiled a milky smile. Thick, dark eyelashes ringed his huge, round, blue eyes—the whites so clear, so unblemished. I gave him my exaggerated mommy-smile back, then breast milk spewed like a geyser, spraying him in the face until he latched back on.

Jenna chatted away with Grant at the table. "Can I have more juice in my pwincess cup?" Grant's mother had given her a Cinderella cup with glitter floating in water between double walls of hard plastic.

"It's not 'pwincess,' Jenna, it's 'princess,'" Grant corrected her. His deep voice was rough with irritability. He wasn't pissed off at Jenna, though she wouldn't know that; he was pissed off at me. Again. This time it was because the Forestry office had called. I had my job back. I would start in May, two months from now, and I thought he would be celebrating, not kvetching. Over the winter we'd decided to take turns working and looking after the kids. But I'd made that deal with the climber, not the logger, and earlier today, the logger had said, *What kind of mother leaves a five-month-old baby?*

Grant's seesaw routine was making me feel like I was losing my mind. It took me right back to Munster, to my "breakfast" dad and my "after work" dad.

"That's how Haley says it," Jenna said.

"Yeah, well, that's not how you say it," Grant replied.

Many of the kids Jenna played with couldn't pronounce "r," and Grant wasn't convinced they'd grow out of it. Jenna could pronounce the "r" when she wanted to. She was just toying with him. The other day I'd passed by her bedroom and overheard her talking to herself. She'd said "fwog" and then immediately admonished herself, "No, no, Jenna! It's 'frog' not 'fwog,'" in the exact same tone Grant had just used, then she'd giggled.

Jenna's kitty, Gus, sauntered by me, rubbing up against my shins, then walked to the oversized, now defunct speaker, stretched out his grey body to place his paws near the top, and dug his claws through the blue material.

Something blurred through the air like a missile and exploded into sparkling pieces against the speaker. Gus ripped across the carpet, up the stairs, and Jenna launched herself at me, sobbing, "My princess cup!"

Sam popped off my breast, stared up at me, his mouth forming a tiny "o".

"What the hell?" I said, looking over at Grant.

"That goddamned cat." Grant pushed back his chair, grabbed his coat and headed outside, slamming the door behind him.

———

The next morning, the sun hadn't yet risen when Grant sat up in bed and reached for the lamp. Harsh light flooded the room. He could have found the bloody door in the dark; it was three steps from the base of the bed. This was his way of saying *If I suffer, we both suffer.* I did it all the time myself. *Passive-aggressive*, the new counsellor at the women's centre had called it, then rambled on about the importance of using "I statements" with Grant. "Like, 'I hate you'?" I'd asked her, only half joking.

I sank the tip of my cold nose into the duvet, then pulled my pillow over my head. The wood stove had gone out in the middle of the night.

"Did you make my lunch?" His voice was gruff.

I'd glanced at his metal lunch box as I'd carried my daughter, sobbing over her princess cup, up the stairs, but that's as far as I'd gotten.

"No. I did not make your lunch."

"Again?"

He didn't know it, but I was weaning him off my lunch-making. I couldn't come right out and tell him because it didn't make any sense. Why wouldn't I make his lunch if he was working in the bush and I was at home with the kids? But I found it degrading. Now that he wasn't in camp, every night he would sit with a beer or tea in front of the TV while I seethed over the kitchen counter slapping corned beef into buns, hacking up banana loaf, cramming pickles into a tiny Tupperware container, knowing damned well Gloria Steinem would sooner put her head in an oven than do what I was doing.

Part of the reason I wanted to go back to work was so I could feel justified *not* making his lunch.

I rolled over and watched his lean back as he sat on the edge of the bed. Wide shoulders tapered down to a narrow waist. Each muscle clearly defined, maybe 5 percent body fat. I'd look more like that if

I could get out of this goddamned house and get some exercise. Instead, I looked more like Jenna's Mrs. Potato Head.

Grant grabbed his work clothes and headed down the hall, stomping like an Irish step dancer right past the kids' room. I turned off the lamp, but moments later light streamed up through the cracks between the floorboards from the bathroom below, slicing through the darkness.

Grant banged around in the bathroom for a while, then moved to the kitchen and banged around there. Only after the front door had closed and I knew he was out in the shop waiting for the Crummy did I sit up. The duvet might as well have been wet cement; I could barely dig myself out of bed. But there wasn't much point in trying to sleep now.

In the hall, I leaned over the railing and looked down into the living room at the wood stove. We'd been so busy battling last night we'd forgotten to bring in some wood, and there was no kindling.

I slipped into the kids' room. A tangle of blond hair spilled out from under Jenna's ragged blanket, covering Gus, who was curled into the side of her head. I pulled the blanket off her face and tucked it under her chin. Between the cat and that blanket, I was terrified she'd suffocate in the middle of the night.

Sam was splayed out on his back in his crib, his chubby hands curled by his ears. I rubbed the backs of my fingers across his cheek: such soft, rubbery skin. His lips sucked instinctively at the air and I felt my milk drop.

Maybe Grant was right. Maybe I was being selfish. Unmotherly. Jenna had been almost three when I'd gone to work last summer. A little girl. Sam would be only five months old. He hadn't even taken a bottle yet. What if I caused lifelong damage?

But I couldn't imagine not working with my big group of silviculture women. They all knew what I was up against. They all had kids. They'd all expressed milk into logging slash. They'd all fought their husbands and their debilitating guilt to stay in the bush. And they were all encouraging me not to give up on university. They said it was easier to pick up little kids and take them with you than school-age ones. Most said it was too late for them, except for Laura, who was whittling away at her forestry degree while working full-time, year round, with two kids and a grumpy husband who hung out at the Moberly Pub. She made me think anything was possible.

The other day I'd found myself flipping through university calendars at the library while Jenna was at story-time. After spending a winter with a three-year-old, a new baby and a dried-up well—hauling drinking water from town, showering at friends' houses, using the outhouse, making lunch for a cranky logger—I was starting to dream about life as a single mom and full-time student in a city as if it were a vacation at an all-inclusive resort in Mexico.

My bare feet were silent on the wood as I tiptoed down the steep stairs. Chaba padded across the gold linoleum from his blanket in the corner of the kitchen to greet me as I pulled on my rubber boots and a jacket, then headed outside, closing the thick wood door softly behind me. He flopped his gangly blond body down the steps ahead of me.

The snowy peaks were soft pink in the early light, floating on a sea of valley fog. The only sound was the crunching gravel under my feet as I headed down the driveway, past my gardens. The melting snow had revealed a gloppy mess of weeds in each of the six raised beds. My rows of raspberries were tangled, bent over. Working in the bush, I hadn't had much time for gardening last year. I wouldn't have any if I went back to work with two kids.

I cut across the stiff grass to the woodshed, grabbed a piece of birch and balanced it on the chopping block. I swung the maul over my head and it sank into the wood with a hollow thud, stopping at a big knot. I wrenched it out, took two more thwacks at the wood before giving up and throwing the maul on the ground.

My breasts tingled then went rock-solid. Milk started to leak into my pajamas. I slipped my hand under my clothes and felt my belly, still soft and stretched in spite of four months of interrupted sessions in front of *The Firm* aerobics video with Janet Jones Gretzky. I wanted my body back. Not this one with the jiggly belly and boobs that spewed milk into the air like geysers. I wanted to hike up and down steep logging slash all day with the girls, bombing around logging roads in a four-by-four, picking huckleberries on our breaks. I knew my muscles would reappear—*I'd* reappear—if I could just get back to work.

I picked up the axe and started splitting cedar into kindling. An earthy sweetness released into the air, the same smell that hit me each time I opened our front door.

When I heard the sound of crunching gravel, my gut tightened with a fight-or-flight kind of feeling. Grant walked toward me down the driveway, crossed the little plank of wood over the ditch and leaned against the woodshed.

"I forgot that." He nodded toward the jacket I was wearing.

I'd thrown on his rough wool plaid jacket when I left the house. I loved the smell of the bush in the material: the sap, the newly cut timber, the needles. I even liked the smell of the oil and gas from his chainsaw, the faint smell of cigarettes.

"Looks better on you anyway."

I could tell he regretted our fight.

"Why don't you just take the summer off, go back next year? When Sam's older."

"You know why." If I lost my seniority, I lost my job.

"Just explain the situation."

"You promised you'd look after the kids."

"Jesus. I can't talk to you when you get like this." He picked up the maul and balanced my pain-in-the-ass piece of birch on the chopping block, took one swing and split it down the centre. "I wasn't thinking straight when I said I'd quit."

"I need that job. I need to save up for school." Just mentioning school to Grant was like prodding a grizzly with a red-hot poker.

Grant threw the maul to the ground. "Do what you want. You always do." He started loading wood into his arms. "I'll make the fire."

"How the hell am I supposed to work twelve-hour days in the bush with you in camp? I don't know if Kim will even babysit. She has her own kids to look after."

We could see Kim's house down on the Blaeberry River from our window. Her daughter, Haley, was Jenna's best friend, and her new baby, Ocean, had been born two months after Sam.

"I'm sure you'll figure it out." He headed back toward the house, his arms loaded with wood.

The house was quiet except for the occasional pop in the wood stove, and CBC Radio on low in the kitchen. Jenna crawled up on the couch beside me, where I was nursing her brother. She was holding the doll my mother had bought her. Kali Jean—which would have been Sam's name if he'd been a girl—was made of soft, spongy rubber. She felt almost like a real baby, even peed like a real baby when you gave her a bottle, and she'd helped Jenna finally accept the fact that Sam was a Sam, not a Kali. For the first month Jenna had told everyone she had a baby sister, and referred to Sam as "she."

Jenna pulled up her shirt, crammed Kali's face against her smooth chest. While her doll nursed, Jenna popped her thumb and the corner of her blanket into her mouth.

The phone sat beside me on the couch, stretched to the end of the cord. I had a call to make, either to the Forestry office to turn down my job or to Kim to see if she'd babysit for four months. If I went to work my kids might end up in therapy for the rest of their lives, but if I stayed at home I might end up on the psych ward or in prison for committing mariticide.

Gus jumped up on the couch and flopped against Jenna, bits of multi-coloured glitter in his grey fur.

28

FRACTURED

Our Forestry truck bounced over the wash-boarded logging road as we passed the white kilometre marker on the tree. Sixty-five.

Nona grabbed the mic and pushed the transmit button. "Loaded pickup, B65." Now anyone barrelling toward us around the blind corners would be alerted to where we were on Big Bend Highway, at kilometre 65, and what direction we were headed. Toward town. Finally. It was already almost six. The last block had been thirty hectares and we'd worked overtime so we wouldn't have to come back tomorrow.

"Kleenex?" Nona passed me a baggie full of tissue.

I looked down at my chest. It looked like I'd attached a water hose to my boobs and turned it on. Even though I left full bottles for Sam at home, I usually had to express milk into the trees a couple of times a day, but today we hadn't even stopped to eat. I took the Kleenex and stuffed a few pieces under my shirt.

The first two weeks had been the hardest. Leaving my baby had been worse than losing a limb; more like losing a torso. Grant had looked after the kids for the first ten days but Sam wouldn't take a bottle, so Patty and Kim had to wet nurse a few times. I came close to quitting every single day. When Grant went back to work and Kim started to babysit, things finally settled down. But Grant's moods had remained black. We barely talked to each other these days, no mean feat in a thousand-square-foot open-concept house.

But there was no way I would quit. Missing this season meant I'd lose my seniority, which meant I'd lose my job, and I could not let that happen. Grant and I had started to discuss separating. In the past, when we'd thrown those words around, they'd served more as a threat, but this time I'd gone so far as to check out the rental situation in town. He said he'd never give up the house.

"Loaded pickup, B55," Nona said into the mic. We were the only female voices on the radio, so even without Nona's heavy Spanish accent, everyone would have known *it was those damned Forestry girls again.* Grant had told me the loggers laughed at how often we gave out our location, but we were cautious for good reason. One time a logging crew had screamed around a corner and almost forced us off the road. When Nona lit into them, not bothering with radio protocol, the idiot had replied, "Gave you a bit of a scare, did we, ladies? Maybe you should learn to drive." We'd both said, "Fucking loggers," at the same time, though not into the mic, then burst out laughing when we remembered we were both married to loggers.

The radio crackled, then the voice of the dispatcher at the Forestry office broke through.

"Nona, Jan's with you, right?"

Nona unhooked the mic. "She's right here."

Even before the next words, fear flashed through me, right to my fingertips, like tiny shocks. *My kids! I should never have left my kids!*

"Jan, Grant has had an accident."

Relief flooded through me, as though I'd been on death row and given a reprieve, but it lasted only a split second. I grabbed the mic from Nona, my hand shaking. Pushed the button.

"What happened? Is he okay?" I wanted to say, "Is he dead?" but I couldn't say that word. My knuckles were white around the mic. This was my punishment. I should never have gone back to work. I should have been happy with what I had.

Nona's head swivelled from the road to me and back to the road.

"I don't have the details, Jan. They're taking him to Calgary by ambulance right now. Just get back to the office as soon as you can."

Nona took the receiver out of my hand, slipped it on the hook.

An image of Ted in his wheelchair flitted through my mind, his body useless from his armpits down, his hands curled and his atrophying legs pressed together at the knees.

I speed-walked down the hallway of the Calgary hospital with Sam on my back. His breath was sweet and warm on the back of my neck and he was blowing spit bubbles near my right ear. He and Jenna had been born on the floor above, on the maternity ward. Now we were back to visit their father lying in one of these rooms with a mangled leg.

When I got to Grant's room, I peered in before entering. There were four curtained-off sections, and I didn't want to stick my head into the wrong one, but Sam gurgled loudly and Grant's voice came from behind the furthest curtain. "I'm over here." At least he had the window, even if it was facing east, not west toward the mountains.

He was lying with sheets and blankets tucked up under his chin, his bare leg raised by a pulley off the bed. It was a swollen mass of colour—purple, pink and red—spreading from a line of black stitches and coagulating blood where the bone had broken through. Metal bolts protruded from the sides of his knee and ankle. A compound tib/fib. He'd had the first operation that morning. He needed one more.

Before I left for Calgary, Grant's boss had explained how the roots of the tree Grant had been bucking rolled right over him and pinned him. They'd had to cut him out with a chain saw, close to his leg, wedging the tree so it wouldn't shift and squish him. It had taken a long time.

I forced myself to look up from his leg, into his eyes. Shiny blue. What would I do if he cried? He cleared his throat.

"I didn't think you'd come," he whispered hoarsely. His wall was gone, replaced with a naked defencelessness I saw on the kids' faces when they were scared or hurt.

This is how he'd looked when we'd discussed splitting up. I'd tried to picture him living all alone, without his family, and it was worse than the thought of me and the kids in a trailer court in the toxic fallout of the lumber mill.

I squatted by the bed and took his hand. It was cut and scraped, like he'd ripped it apart in a hard crack climb. "Of course I came." My throat closed as I pressed his rough hand against the smooth skin of my cheek.

We didn't speak for a few moments, until Sam grabbed two handfuls of my hair and I had to let go of Grant's hand to unfurl tiny fingers.

"When I saw that log coming at me, all I could think about was Ted in his wheelchair," Grant said.

"Yeah, I thought the same thing."

After I'd dropped Jenna and Chaba with Kim, I had too much time to think on the four-hour drive to Calgary. While I thought of Grant and how close he'd come to having a life like Ted's, I'd also realized how close I'd come to having a life like Diane's. Washing and feeding a quadriplegic, emptying his catheter and bowels. Diane had wanted to go to school too, but now she never would.

"I've been doing a lot of soul-searching in the past few hours," Grant said. "I don't know what I'm going to do, but I've got to get out of logging. This is my wake-up call."

I took his hand again. Smiled. I'd always known that Grant the logger was not the same as Grant the father and climber. I knew we could make it if I could just convince him to get into carpentry or mountain guiding. But each time he was on the verge of change, he'd be drawn back to falling—the risk, the physical exertion, the mountains, the money.

He looked at me. Really looked at me. "We've gotta make some big changes."

The next day, Grant was sitting up in bed when Sam and I arrived.

"There's my little family!"

"Wow, you're sure perky," I said.

Sam picked up on his father's energy and wriggled on my back, growling. It was his new form of communication. I extracted a handful of my hair out of his fingers.

"Morphine." Grant grinned drunkenly and pointed toward his IV. "Nothing better than morphine."

"I got you a book." I handed him a paper bag.

A few months ago, Grant had drawn my attention to our bedside tables. On mine, a teetering stack of self-help books—*The Dance of Anger; An Adult Child's Guide to What's Normal; Co-dependent No More; Men Are from Mars, Women Are from Venus; Relationship Rescue;* and on his, *The Truck Trader.* We'd laughed, but I'd found it more sad than funny.

He pulled the book out of the bag. *Iron John: A Book about Men.*

He flipped it over, read out loud: "Get in touch with your masculinity. The wild man sleeping inside of us wakes up for good and helps us make peace with the dark and bright sides of our psyche." He flipped the pages, breathed in the smell of new book. "Cool. My very first self-help book."

"I've been thinking. I'm going to quit smoking. I already have a head start." Grant had made it through the second operation, they'd replaced the morphine with Demerol, and even though he was in pain, he was optimistic.

"That's a great idea." I thought of the money we'd save. No lung cancer. No cigarette breath.

"And I'm going to quit drinking."

I tried not to smile too hard. "It sounds like you've been reading your new book." *Iron John* was still on the bedside table.

"Not yet. I can't concentrate. I'll start it when I get home."

I handed him a bag of muffins from the bakery, a climbing magazine, the *Calgary Herald*. I had to drive back to Golden. I had to get back to work and bring Jenna home from Kim's. If she even wanted to come home. She'd told me she wanted Kim to be her mommy, wanted Haley and Ocean to be her sisters. I got it, but it didn't make it any easier to hear. She was fantasizing about a stable family, like I used to, not one that alternated between screaming at each other and freezing each other out. But if Grant could get out of logging, we could be a normal family.

"Also, I'm starting to think it's a good idea for you to go to school. Why don't you stop at the campus on your way home? Check out the rental situation there."

I wasn't sure if I should speak. I didn't want to break the spell. "Are you serious?"

"I could work at some crap job and look after the kids, or start apprenticing for carpentry. We have to get out of Golden. That place is destroying us. Logging is turning me into someone I don't want to be."

This was what I'd been waiting for. For him to see what logging was doing to us. I threw my arms around his neck, almost grateful for the accident.

"One more year of logging. Save up a bit of money, then we're out of there," he said.

Walking through the university family housing complex was like walking through a red brick maze. With Sam growling and trying to launch off my back, I wandered out of one court and into an almost identical one, then another and another. In each court, about twelve townhouses faced a grassy, treed yard with a big sandbox at one end that seemed to be party central. Mothers mostly, but some dads, sat on the concrete edge, and little kids of all shapes and sizes and colours flipped sand with shovels, pushed trucks and made sand castles, while older kids did laps on the pavement on bikes. I reached behind me, grabbed Sam's hand.

"What do you think, Sambones?" I said, using Kim's new name for him. "Wanna move to the city?"

With his feet on the frame and his hard little toes poking into my back, he bounced like he was in the jolly jumper and squealed.

Finally we found the housing office.

"You understand the wait list is long. At least a year. Sometimes two. People don't realize that. They come marching in here, asking for a unit just a month before their classes start. I hope you weren't planning to go to school this fall." The woman in the university housing office gazed at me over her reading glasses.

"No, no," I said and pointed to Sam on my back. "He's only seven months old. It'll be a year."

A whole year. Would Grant still want to come to Calgary in a year? And could I survive another winter alone in the Blaeberry with the kids while he worked one last season in the bush? Especially if the well dried up again.

"Good, good. When your name comes up, as long as you put down the deposit, we'll hold a unit for you. How many occupants? Just you and your baby?"

I looked at my ring-free hand. I rarely wore my silver ring. It made me feel like a possession.

"Four of us. My two kids and my husband."

"Great. That's wonderful. Wonderful."

Was it my imagination, or did this woman just suddenly start treating me like an adult? An adult with a real family. Not just some thirty-year-old single woman with a baby.

"Just sign here." She handed me a pen with *University of Calgary* stamped in gold letters.

As we wove back through the maze, I took a closer look at the units. Each had a living-room window, a tall narrow window by the front door, and two upstairs bedroom windows. Most were stuck to neighbours on both sides and at the back, and had a "private yard" consisting of a six-by-six-foot entrance area at the front door, enclosed by brick walls. No ten acres of trees, no garden, no picture window with a mountain view, no big deck.

Grant was going to hate this place.

29

PLAYING DEAD

A cloud of dust followed the car as I drove down the dirt road toward home. Sam faced backwards in his baby seat beside me gumming an arrowroot cookie, but I knew it wouldn't occupy him for long. He was staring at my chest and drooling. He'd only take the bottle if I wasn't around. His thick eyelashes were dark with tears because I'd only nursed him for a couple of minutes at Kim's before Jenna had started whining for supper. She was lying in the back seat, covered in grey silt from the pond, with her bare feet stuck out the window, munching on a granola bar.

My stomach growled. Nona and I had worked an eleven-hour shift in muggy heat, fighting mosquitoes and black flies, so I knew how the kids felt. But now I had two flex days. This was my Friday. For the next four days I could work in the garden, get the house liveable again, take the kids for bike rides in the trailer.

When I pulled up to our green metal mailbox, dust billowed in through the windows. I pulled out a stack of mail and flipped through bills and flyers. There was a big shiny brochure. I flipped it over. It was addressed to Grant.

We bumped up the driveway, then, with Sam on my hip and Jenna straggling behind me with her blanket, I climbed the stairs into the house. Grant was lying on the futon with his leg propped up on several pillows. He had a beer in his hand.

"Where'd you get the beer?"

"Dale popped in to see how I was doing."

"Should you be drinking with codeine?" Suddenly I was so exhausted I felt like I'd been hit by a logging truck.

"A couple beers never hurt a guy."

Maybe it was a good thing he was drinking. Put him in a better mood. The first few days back from the hospital had been fine; he'd been happy just to be home. Then boredom had set in. Then crankiness. Sometimes I wondered if that had anything to do with being taken off Demerol and morphine. He'd been on one or the other for three weeks. I dropped the stack of mail on the futon beside Grant. "Still no cheque from Compo."

The dirty dishes from last night and this morning were still piled up on the counter, so with Sam still perched on my hip, I started the hot water to get them soaking in the sink. Grant could hobble around enough to get to the bathroom or grab a beer, but not to cook or clean.

"I'm hungry." Jenna pulled at my dusty work pants. A tantrum was brewing.

"I know, baby. Why don't you play with Daddy while I nurse your brother?" Sam started to cry and bang his head against my chest.

"I don't want to play with Daddy. I want to eat."

"Oh, Christ," I whispered under my breath. Every time I swore in front of the kids I thought of my poor mother locking herself in her bedroom to curse us while my brother and sister and I listened quietly outside the door, thinking this time she was going to leave. How she had survived was beyond me.

I opened the fridge. Almost no food. I hadn't been able to take the time to go to Overwaitea after work. Kim had my two kids, along with her own two, for ten to twelve hours as it was, and I certainly couldn't expect her to feed them dinner. She must have been looking forward to Grant taking over for her in a few weeks, as soon as he could get around more easily.

I slapped together a peanut butter sandwich and milk for Jenna to hold her off until dinner, then sank into the couch to nurse Sam.

"What's that?" I asked. Grant had the large brochure I'd thought was junk mail in his hand.

"A photography school in Calgary. I'm thinking of applying."

"Photography school? What, like an evening class?"

"No, full-time."

"What are you talking about? What about carpentry?"

We had it all planned out. In Calgary next year, he'd either do a job as a labourer so he could be around to help with the kids, or we'd both get loans and he'd retrain as a carpenter.

"I thought if I have to get retrained I might as well do what I love," he said.

"Is this a joke?" Sam sensed my tension. He looked up with wide eyes and kneaded my skin harder as he nursed.

"I thought I'd log for another year then go to photography school. When I'm finished, you can go to school." He held the brochure up in front of his face, signalling the end of the conversation. He was using his ultimatum voice, a cue for me to shut up. He reached for his beer and it disappeared behind the brochure.

Rage rushed through me with such ferocity I was sure it would contaminate my milk. I stared at Grant for a few moments, the anger ramming against the back of my teeth, wanting to spew out of me like lava. But I kept my voice steady. "There is no way you're going to school before I do."

Grant lowered the brochure. His face was flushed. "You've been nagging at me for years to get out of logging. So now I'm planning to get out and this is the support I get? Fuck it. I'll just keep logging." He reached over and turned on the TV.

I popped Sam roughly off my breast and plunked him in the baby backpack. He stared up at me but didn't cry. I swung him onto my back. I needed to take a walk down the driveway to clear my head, get my heart rate down. But Jenna was about to freak out and I had to get her fed before she had a complete meltdown.

I pulled out the carton of eggs Jenna had collected from Anne and Burl's chickens. My hand shook as I passed one to her. I tried to keep my voice calm, motherly.

"Let's scramble some of your eggs. You can break them."

Jenna took the egg from me. I could tell she sensed the change, that she realized she had to be good.

When the kids' food was ready, Jenna spooned Pablum and puréed carrots into her brother's mouth between her bites of scrambled egg. As I broke the eggs for an omelette, I felt a prickliness on the back of my neck. I turned around. Grant was staring at me, an odd smile on his face.

"What? Why are you staring at me like that?" I'd had no intention of talking to him for the rest of my life, but it looked like he was ready to apologize.

"I'm just enjoying myself."

"What are you talking about? You enjoy watching me get run off my feet?" I poured the eggs into the pan. They sizzled and spluttered till I adjusted the flame.

"Yeah, I do. In fact, I get a lot of satisfaction from it."

I turned back toward him. He wasn't smiling anymore.

"If you hadn't gone back to work, I wouldn't be lying here. You might as well have picked up a maul and broken my leg yourself."

"You can't be serious."

"Well, think about it. I got hurt because I had to help you with the kids and around the house. I was exhausted."

I stared at Grant, his skinny white legs sticking out from baggy, worn red nylon shorts, the broken one—bruised, swollen and powerless—propped up on a pillow. This was the guy I'd let be the boss of me. Where to live. How to live. Whether or not to go to school. For four years.

The omelette started smoking. I pulled it off the heat, dumped it out of the pan with my lips pressed tight. If I opened my mouth, what would spew out would certainly not be an "I statement."

"How can everything crap out like that?" I half-whispered into the phone. "It was going so well and then—poof! We're right back where we started."

I looked out the window of our shop, across the dark yard to the lit-up window of the living room. The kids were asleep, but Grant was still awake. When I talked to my mother, I was always terrified he'd listen in on the other phone.

My mother murmured soothingly on the other end from Victoria and I was transported back to Whitehorse, Mom sitting on the edge of my bed, singing, "Que sera, sera."

"What is wrong with me? Why can't I just be happy with my little family and my gorgeous house?" I tried to rub the knots out of my neck. I couldn't turn my head in either direction more than about three inches. "Sometimes I feel like I'm going crazy. Making it all up."

"If everything was working in your life, you wouldn't have this turmoil. People don't feel this way for no reason."

"I'm so angry I could scream. Or murder someone. It feels like a cancer growing in me." I paced to the end of the phone cord, spun and paced back.

"Anger can be a good thing. It doesn't have to be a cancer. It can be a motivator. Help you push for change. When you're ready."

When I'm ready. But when would that be? Would I ever be ready? Or would I follow in my mother's footsteps to the bitter end. Settling, for the rest of my life.

"But why does it keep surprising me, every time he changes his mind?"

My father had done the same thing, back and forth, making promises, taking them back, and it had caught me by surprise every time. But my dad had been a drinker, my dad had had blackouts. It was different with Grant.

Before I phoned Mom I'd had one more brief conversation with Grant, probably the last one we'd have for a while. I reminded him that he'd agreed to my going to university in the fall, even suggested it, and he replied, "The only reason I said yes was because I didn't think you'd really go."

"Jan, you might not want to wait until he lets you go to school. You might never get there," my mother said.

"I don't think I can do it alone. Just working full-time with two kids is grinding me into the ground. I can't imagine school."

"Don't underestimate yourself, kiddo." She paused. "I've been thinking. I'd like to put a bit of money aside for your tuition. It won't be much, but I can give you a hundred dollars a month. I wish I could do more."

"You don't have to do that, Ma."

"If it gets you one step closer to university, it'll be worth it."

I looked at my watch. It was getting late and the kids would wake me at five.

There was a click on the phone. I looked out the window, my pulse thudding against my temples like someone was hammering to get out. *Has he been listening?* Guilt settled over me like a burka. Grant was lying there, all cut up with a broken leg, in pain, bored, unable to do anything, and I was in here as usual, complaining about him.

Another click and I realized it was probably the party line.

"I should phone you sometime when Grant's being nice so you'll realize he's not always a schmuck."

"Yes, that's a wonderful idea. Why don't you?"

"Probably because it never lasts long enough for me to get to the phone."

We had a little chuckle. I felt better. It was handy having a mother who volunteered for a crisis line when your own life was one big crisis.

Another click on the line. Seashell noise, like someone was listening in. Click, and they were gone. Definitely the party line.

"I've gotta go, Ma. Someone's trying to use the phone."

I choked up saying goodbye. For me *and* my mom. She deserved a better life than the one she got.

"I have a really shitty feeling about this block," I told Nona as I stepped out of the truck and peered into the heavily overgrown bush.

We knew the contractors' camp nearby had been destroyed over the weekend. Metal siding ripped off the trailer, the fridge stripped down to its insulation, windows smashed, puncture marks in cans of food. It must have been the problematic silvertip grizzly the Banff wardens had relocated to this area.

"We just have to do a quick walk-through," Nona said.

"Isn't that what you and Pam were doing? A quick walk-through?"

A few years ago, Nona and Pam had been working a block like this one. They'd come around a corner and almost bumped into a grizzly sow and her two full-grown cubs. They'd tried to back away but Pam had panicked, started to run, so Nona had run too. The sow charged, Pam tripped, and when Nona looked back, she could see Pam's hands sticking out from under the mama bear. Nona reached the truck, jumped in, and backed up while leaning on the horn. The bears took off, and Pam had been conscious enough to crawl into the cab, in spite of the hunks of flesh missing from her back and shoulders, the scalp missing from her head. The girls had told me this story on my very first day of work.

We headed into the bush with our dogs on leashes. Chaba and Rocky stayed near, didn't pull ahead like they normally did. We walked heavily, talked loudly and blew our whistles every few minutes. I put my flares in my shirt pocket and kept a hand on my bear spray. Nona looked around often, stopping every once in a while to listen, but we passed massive areas of dug-up dirt—bear diggings— without turning back. The bear had rolled good-sized boulders looking for insects. I felt very empathetic toward Pam and wished we'd never stepped out of the truck, but Nona just kept pushing on. The mauling had made her belligerent, almost territorial in the bush.

As we were crashing through the brush, she looked back and said, "So how's it going with Grant this week?"

This week. The girls were getting used to my marital problems. I tried to stop myself from spewing, but it was like trying to plug a punctured artery.

The more I heard the others' stories, the more I wished I could stop whining. Nona's husband's liver was on its way out; Shawna, with her two kids, had escaped a physically abusive husband; Jane had been unhappy for years but didn't feel she could take her three kids away because her husband was neither an alcoholic nor physically abusive. Sher, Pam and Bonnie were genuinely happy after years of marriage. Their men doted on them. If I ever worked with them, I'd grill them and take copious notes.

"I'm starting to wonder about school. I don't know if it's worth the fight."

"You have to go to school."

All the women said the same thing. That I had to go to school. Sometimes I thought they were trying to live vicariously through me.

"The kids are so young."

Nona sighed impatiently. "If you want to go to school, you'll go to school."

Irritation crept up my scalp. It wasn't that easy to just pick up and leave. I had two kids. A dog and a cat. A house. A husband who didn't even want me to go.

We walked on in silence, listening to the bush.

"I'm leaving John," Nona said.

"What?" I quickened my pace and came up beside her.

"I found a house in town and the boys and I are moving this weekend."

"Are you serious?"

There I was, so hung up with my own marital conflicts that I hadn't even noticed what was going on with one of my best friends. She and John had been together for fifteen years. They lived down the road from us on over a hundred acres with a couple of wood-lots, but it was John's. He had grown up there and inherited the property—Nona would never try to take it from him. I couldn't imagine her in town, down on the flats without her garden, without the woods all around her, without her little log home.

Nona stopped and put up her hand. "Did you hear that?"

I listened. Breaking branches. Something was crashing around out there.

I unsnapped my bear spray. "I vote we go back."

Nona veered away from the sound, in the general direction of the truck, but not as directly as I'd have liked.

"What are you doing?"

"We've hardly seen any of the block. I don't want to come back tomorrow. Let's take the long way back. Show him he can't push us around."

"But he can! That's the problem." Chaba pulled me toward Nona and Rocky so I took the safety clip off my bear spray and followed. We crashed around, blew on our whistles and made a wide arc in the general direction of the truck. I followed Nona, wishing I were half as gutsy as her. She had the balls to take two teenaged boys and move to town, leaving her husband and a property she loved, and she had the balls to stand up to a grizzly.

"If you see him, whatever you do, don't run," she said in a low voice, as if the bear were listening. The same thing she'd said to Pam.

My mouth was dry. I wished I'd brought some water. Our arc slowly got more in line with the direction I wanted to go, back toward the truck. Soon I saw the double track and knew the truck wasn't far.

"Would you play dead or fight?" I asked.

"Pam played dead and the bear kept chomping away at her. I'd never stop fighting."

More branches snapped. It was far away and the truck was near, but Nona's hand jumped to her bear spray. It rested there. Her fingers trembled.

She was scared shitless and she was going for it anyway.

With my paycheque, I headed to the bank to meet with the bank manager, Fiona.

"I'd like to open a savings account," I said, sitting on the edge of a plastic chair in front of her desk.

Fiona passed me a form. "You'll need Grant to sign if it's joint."

"I want it just in my name."

Fiona dealt with Grant for the mortgage and our joint account and measly RRSPs.

I looked up at her before I signed and said, "I'd like this to be confidential." Having an affair must feel just like this.

"Of course," she said. Her eyebrows rose only slightly.

I signed the papers, deposited part of my pay, and left quickly.

30

MAMA SPIDERS

"Mommy! Haley won't play Barbies with me."

Oh, Christ. I white-knuckled my pen and stared down at my list of things to pack for our trip to my parents' place in Victoria. The words blurred. I was so tired I could barely see straight.

"Mommy!"

I put my hands over my face and pretended not to hear. That old childish urge to stick my fingers in my ears and sing *la la la la* washed over me. I squeezed my eyes shut under my hands. *If I can't see her, maybe she can't see me.*

"I hate stupid Barbies," Haley said.

"Let's watch a video!" I said, getting up from the table. Bribes and threats, threats and bribes.

The two four-year-olds sat on the big overstuffed couch with their legs sticking out in front of them. As I pried *Insect World* out of the plastic rental box, I noticed its rating: PG. I always got G-rated movies but it must have been a typo; it was a nature film. I pushed *play* and the deep, male voice of the National Geographic commentator filled the room. *The caring mother spider spins a protective web around her babies . . .*

The kids were immediately enthralled. I had no idea how mothers had survived before the invention of television. How my mother had survived in the North, where we had only CBC-TV in black and white, starting at six in the evening. Wayne and Shuster and Walt Disney kept us out of Mom's hair, once a week. Videos hadn't even been invented.

The spiderlings are relatively helpless in their early days, and need lots of care.

I turned down the volume so as not to wake Sam. Once he woke up, that'd be the end of the packing. As I was pulling a tray of brownies out of the oven—more tools of bribery for the long drive—the phone rang. When I heard my father's voice I panicked.

"What's wrong? Has something happened to Mom?" My father never called; it was always my mother and he'd listen in only until I started complaining about Grant. Then all of a sudden there'd be something urgent he had to do in the garage.

"No, no, your mother's fine. She's at one of her bloody Newcomers' meetings. We've been living in Victoria for four years, for chrissake."

I calmed down and propped the phone on my shoulder, continued cutting brownies. "So what's up, Dad?"

"You're all ready for your trip?"

"All ready. Tomorrow we're going to blow this godforsaken Popsicle stand." The well was dry again. I was back to hauling water from town in big blue jugs, using the outhouse, showering at friends' places.

"You've got good snow tires? The conditions can get bad on the Coquihalla Highway this early in the spring."

He was worried about us. That's why he'd called. At thirty-two years old, I was still desperate for scraps of affection from my father.

"Yup. We've got good tires." And we finally had a reliable car. Just before Sam was born the heater had gone in the Skylark, so we took out a loan for a brand new Toyota Tercel in Calgary. A red one. Grant had almost missed Sam's birth because he'd had to go back to Golden to insure it.

"Good, good," my father said.

"Don't worry. I'll drive carefully. I'm used to the snow. And we only have to get to Kelowna tomorrow." Grant's mother, conveniently, lived halfway to Victoria. If we could survive a couple of days with her.

"So, how long are you planning to stay?"

"I don't know. Couple of weeks maybe. As long as it takes Sarah to fix my life."

Sarah was a counsellor in downtown Victoria who my sister had worked with in her social work program. She'd guided me through two previous upheavals, the first one being Niccy's death, and I'd decided I needed a counsellor you pay, not a freebie at the family centre for this next one. I'd just received a notice from university student housing. We had a two-bedroom unit for the fall and had to put a deposit down. I just had to convince Grant to move away from the mountains for four years, which would take my growing some big cajones. Sarah had her work cut out for her.

My father cleared his throat, paused. "Just want to make sure you aren't staying too long."

"What do you mean?"

"Well, look what happened last time, for chrissake."

"What happened last time? I thought we had a good visit."

"Those bloody kids were into everything. I had to rearrange the house so they wouldn't destroy all our stuff from the North."

How could I have thought he was concerned about our safety?

"That's called baby-proofing, Dad, and it was months ago. Jenna's over four now."

"I'm more concerned about Sam."

He had a point there. I, too, had been dreading what Sam would do to their house. Last fall he'd only been ten months old and just starting to walk. Now he was fifteen months and running, climbing and pushing stuff over, pulling stuff down. My friend Laurel called him Bamm Bamm, from *The Flintstones.*

"Dad, they're kids. That's what kids do. They destroy things and make life miserable." I didn't even get a chuckle.

"Those soapstone carvings are worth a lot of money, you know." I'd always attributed his attachment to stuff to his childhood poverty. As a kid, he'd had to work hard for everything, and then his dad would turn around and do something like sell the bike he'd bought with his own money. So as an adult he was incapable of putting up with atrocities like one of his kids leaving a water ring on his teak coffee table.

"And that bloody dog crapped all over my yard."

"I cleaned it up. And besides, Chaba's going to the kennel this time."

"Two weeks is a long time."

. . . *spiderlings start drinking blood from her leg joints and within a few weeks, she cannot move at all.*

"Eew! Gross!" The girls were close to tears. I looked at the screen and saw a fat, black spider sitting immobile, with millions of tiny spiders swarming all over her body.

At this point the spiderlings attack their mother just as they would prey, injecting her with venom and digestive juices and consuming her entirely.

"Jesus! Dad, I gotta go. I'll call you back." I slammed down the phone, raced around the couch, punched the power button and the screen went black, just as the fat, passive, nutrient-laden mother disappeared under her babies.

We hit the snowstorm about halfway up the first pass on the Coquihalla Highway. Big, white, wet flakes stuck to the car like spitballs. The plough hadn't gotten this far yet, so there were only two tire tracks to follow in the slow lane. The fast lane was covered in a pile of slush a foot deep. The windshield wipers thunked back and forth and I had to lean forward to squint through the narrow path in the ice they were clearing. Brown snow was glued to the back window, leaving me with only my side mirrors, which I'd never been good with. At least both kids and the dog were asleep. The kennel had been full.

Maybe I should have stayed in Kelowna—I'd known the weather report was calling for snow—but I probably would have committed matri-in-law-cide. Dorothy had been pickled when we'd arrived and was worse after supper.

"You're just using him for his money," she'd said, as though I were married to a billionaire philanthropist. "You'll let him put you through school and then leave him."

She couldn't believe I was serious about university. She had thought having a second baby would cure me of my subversiveness. She went on and on. ". . . You knew what you were getting into when you married a logger. . . . You have a duty to follow him wherever he has work. . . . You have a duty as a mother and a wife. . . ."

The same bile, almost word for word, that had been coming out of Grant's mouth. A few months ago he'd been talking about going back to the Himalayas with Barry, and now he wanted to move us all to Port Hardy, way up on the northern tip of Vancouver Island, so he could work in big wood. Away from family, friends, my job, school.

The next day Dorothy apologized, was contrite for an hour, then picked up where she'd left off—a pattern I'd noticed in her son. So I packed up the car and left. Now Dad would get us four days earlier than planned. With the dog. He'd be overjoyed.

Crawling along, the needle barely reaching sixty K, I came up behind a semi-truck with its four-way flashers on, going about fifty. I eyeballed the passing lane, imagining all that heavy snow sucking at the tires and throwing us into a 360, right under the semi, crushing us all to a bloody death. But the truck was kicking up snow, like a bombardment of sloppy snowballs coming one after another, and for seconds at a time, everything went dark as night, even though it was just past noon. I almost wanted my '67 Buick Skylark. At least it had been more of a contender than a tiny Toyota Tercel.

I steered the car into the passing lane to make a break for it but didn't notice another semi coming up behind me. I would have seen his lights in my side mirrors if I hadn't been too terrified to take my eyes off the road. I almost jumped out of my seat belt to the deafening blast of his horn, and my foot slammed automatically on the gas. The car started to fishtail. *Think think think!* Was I supposed to turn the wheel into the slide like I did with my Dodge Darts? But they were rear-wheel drive, not front-wheel. Maybe I was supposed to step on the brake! But the semi on my ass was having trouble slowing, so I stepped on the gas again. The car straightened and kept us a few feet in front of death. I pulled in front of the semi I'd been tailing, and the idiot behind me blasted past, leaning on his horn and spraying a huge tidal wave of slush.

I slowed right down to forty, too terrified to go faster, and the semi I'd just passed flashed his lights. In my side mirror I could see more headlights coming up quickly through the snow. I wanted to put my head between my knees.

"Mommy, I'm hungry."

"Not now, Jenna." *Please, please, not now.*

In response to the insistent flashing behind me I managed to get my speed back up to fifty. At least that driver didn't use his horn.

"Mommy, I'm really, really hungry."

"Jenna, I can't talk right now. Please, just wait a few minutes."

Another semi passed and pulled in front of me to let the next one pass, and we were hemmed in on all sides, like a tiny ladybug engulfed by big cockroaches.

"I'm going to wake Sam," Jenna teased in a singsong voice. I looked in the rearview mirror and Jenna was poking her little brother. His head rolled to the other side of his car seat.

"Jenna, no!" If he woke up and started crying, I'd lose it.

She kept poking at him. He rolled his head again.

"Jenna, if you wake your brother I'm going to pull over and drop you on the side of the road and drive away. I swear to God!"

She withdrew her hand like it had been slapped, tucked her blanket under her chin and stuck her two fingers in her mouth. Self-loathing gripped me like a bout of food poisoning. I wanted to take my words back, tell her, *I'm so sorry! It's not you! It's me!* but my throat clenched up.

I needed her to stay quiet.

31

REMEMBER THE LILAC

"Ron!" My mother shook my father, who was slumped on the couch in front of the TV.

"Ron. Get up and go to bed."

He grunted angrily and swiped at her hand, then opened his eyes, looked around, got up and staggered up the stairs without saying goodnight.

For a moment I was back in our living room in Munster, classical music cranked, watching my father pretend-conduct the orchestra—arms thrashing, sweat dripping, black hair flopping over his bald spot. Even now, when I heard classical music, I felt queasy.

"He didn't last long." I looked at my watch. It was only nine.

"He's had a big day."

"What, he pruned the stupid apple tree?" Why was I angry with her? She hadn't done anything. No one seemed safe from my smouldering irritability these days, even my own mother.

"You know what I mean."

"Why don't you just tell him to fuck off?"

She didn't react to my choice of words, though I knew it irked her. She used to wash my brother's mouth out with soap when he said the F-word, now here she was with a daughter who swore like a logger, and worse, was married to one.

"He seems to drink more when you're here," she said.

"Why would he need to do that?"

"I don't know, Jan. He seems to need to thump his chest around you."

Just like me showing off for him when I was a kid, doing chin-ups on the shower curtain bar. "Well, I don't know how you live with him."

"It's much better than it looks. He's mellowed with age."

"Mommy, I'm scared." Jenna, in her pink nightie, sucking on her blanket, stood at the top of the stairs between the kitchen and TV room, looking down on us. "I need you to sleep with me."

She seemed traumatized from only two days in her nana's spotless beige condo. She and Sam and Chaba had been confined like goats behind a baby gate in the TV room so they wouldn't empty bowls of smelly potpourri onto white carpets, or get fingerprints on mirrors, or tip over the antique family coffee table, which was "priceless" but unstable. Having her mother threaten to abandon her on the side of the highway probably hadn't helped.

I pushed myself up out of the chair. "Night, Ma. Sorry for being so cranky."

In the bedroom, Jenna and I snuggled under the covers and started reading her favourite Robert Munsch book, *The Paper Bag Princess*, where the princess gets dirty trying to save Prince Ronald from the dragon and he tells her to clean herself up before he'll marry her, so she turns up her nose and dances off into the sunset, all by herself, to live her own life.

Sometimes I wondered if it was Jenna's favourite book because she knew it was *my* favourite.

"So, what brings you back?"

Sarah swivelled toward me in her chair with her clipboard full of papers, notes she'd taken during my previous counselling sessions. It looked thick.

I shifted on the leather sofa, trying to assume the appropriate facial expression under her scrutiny. Instead of meeting her gaze, I let my eyes wander around her office. We were in a heritage home near downtown Victoria. The room was huge, with dark hardwood floors and windows on three walls with wide ledges full of plants. There was a slight smell of incense, possibly jasmine.

Last spring I'd paced this office, vibrating with anger, recounting how Grant was trying to sabotage my attempt to go back to work after sabotaging my multiple attempts to go to school. Instead of sympathizing, Sarah had said, "You must be getting something out of it or you wouldn't stay. What do you think is your payoff?"

I'd looked at her as if she were in the throes of psychosis. How could she have thought any of this was my fault? Couldn't she see it was Grant? Couldn't she see how stuck I was?

"We all make choices," she'd said. "And if you don't believe that, you'll never have any control over your life."

I'd been trying to figure it out all winter. What *was* my payoff? Money? Stimulating conversation? Safety? Nope. Nope. Nope. Familiarity? Was that enough?

Sarah rephrased her question. "What do you want out of these next few sessions? We have to be specific since we don't have much time."

I almost said, *Make me satisfied with what I've got. Cure me of this obsession with school. It's ruining my marriage.*

She looked harmless—small and plump in her billowing flowered hippie skirt, her long grey hair tied back in a ponytail. But her softness hid boundaries like chain mail armour. She knew where she ended and I began. She didn't sit there wondering if I liked her or approved of her. Some day, I wanted to be on her side of the room.

I sat up like I'd been given a couple of pumps of air. Now I knew why I'd come back.

"When I'm around Grant I give up, turn to mush. I need to stay awake. I need to stay angry long enough to get to school. The good anger. Not the kind that keeps me in limbo."

She watched me for a moment, nodded, wrote something down.

"Grant's always telling me how negative I am, always asking why I can't focus on the good parts of the marriage instead of the bad."

I wanted to stop telling Sarah what Grant said and did and felt and thought, but it was like he was implanted in my head, jabbering away at me. I couldn't get rid of him. I knew the name for what I had. I'd read many books on it. Co-dependence. In one survey, out of 237 characteristics of co-dependence I'd checked off 220.

Sarah looked up from her clipboard.

"What *is* good about the marriage?" She looked genuinely curious.

"Good? Um . . ." I pulled my legs up on the couch to sit cross-legged while I gave that some thought. "Well, he's a hard worker. Like my dad. And a good provider."

"And?"

"He's really strong, really physically fit. He's an excellent climber." She waited for more.

"He loves the kids. Loves having a family. Well, he at least loves the *concept* of family. And he doesn't show it, but I'm sure he loves me."

"How do you know?"

"Well, he married me. Didn't screw off on me when I got pregnant. That couldn't have been easy for him, at the height of his climbing career. And he's stayed with us. Sort of. Not emotionally, but physically. Well, I guess he's only there a few days a month, but he wouldn't be working as a logger if he didn't love us. . . ."

"Most people work for a living, you know. It isn't an act above and beyond the call of duty."

"It kind of is with climbers."

She didn't laugh. My former counsellor Rhea once told me I used humour to deflect.

"Do you think your mother loves your father?"

"Of course she does." My mother loving my father seemed as indisputable as my mother loving me. Or my father loving me. It was just the natural course of things.

"How do you know that?"

"I guess because she stayed with him?"

My sister and I had often discussed what kind of person Mom could have been if she'd left. What kind of people *we* could have been.

"So you're with Grant because you love him?"

"I must be. Why else would I put up with so much shit?" My love for Grant, for any man, it seemed, stood between me and some dark abyss I'd only come close to on a few occasions. Like when I lost Dan. But having this knowledge didn't make it any easier to leave.

She gave me homework. I was to describe an "intimate relationship." I asked her if I could look it up at the library or if that would be cheating.

"That would be cheating." A tiny smile.

"Mom, do you love him?" I looked up from the pile of clean laundry on the bed.

"Who, your father?" My mother kept folding Sam's tiny T-shirts.

"Yeah. Dad."

"What kind of question is that?"

"Well, do you?"

She stopped folding. Looked at me. "Of course not. How could you think I loved your father?"

I glanced at the door, suddenly afraid Dad was just in the other bedroom, or coming up the stairs. He had the hearing of a bat. Shame, like the ash of Pompeii, settled over me just for being part of this conversation. Me, of all people. "You're the only one who loves me," he'd told me when I was a kid. A familiar mixture of anger and protectiveness churned around inside me.

"Why would you stay with him then?"

"People didn't just leave their husbands. What would I do? I had you three. And *now* what's the point? We're comfortable." I could hear the words she wasn't saying: "What would the neighbours think?" It had always been more important to her for us to look like a normal family than to be one. To eat supper at six o'clock, with a tablecloth and place mats, the cutlery properly placed, and a father at the head of the table.

I turned my back on my mother to put a stack of folded sleepers in the drawer.

"Well, *I* love him," I said, partly in case he was listening.

While Sam slept, Jenna watched the first cartoon from the foot-tall stack of videos that my parents' neighbours, Mike and Liz, had brought over. I was prepared to insert them into the machine, one after another until we left, just to keep the kids out of their grandfather's hair, but he was already moaning about losing his television privileges. He was in self-exile in his office off the TV room, with the accordion-style doors closed.

I popped my head through his doorway, scanned the desk. No Scotch. Mom had talked to him about his drinking, made it clear it was unacceptable. She had sounded proud of herself, as though it wasn't thirty years too late.

"I'm going to grab a beer. Do you want one?" Beer was okay. Beer wasn't Scotch.

"It's about that time, isn't it?" There was a hint of conspiracy in his voice.

No one else in my family drank anymore except my dad and me, but thankfully I was well past my high-school drink-till-you-puke phase. My mother would sip wine on occasion, my brother had been sober for years, and my sister couldn't drink anything except the occasional straight vodka. She'd discovered she was allergic to almost anything she put in her body, including most food. Apparently it had something to do with our upbringing.

"Yeah, thanks. I'll have a beer. Just keep those goddamned rug rats quiet, will you?" Dad chuckled. I chuckled with him. I loved it when we got along.

"So, do you think you have an intimate relationship?"

Sarah had just read my list of characteristics: supporting one another's dreams, communication, conversation, respect, eye contact . . . Eye contact! I couldn't believe I'd had to put something as basic as eye contact on my list.

"No."

Not a single one of the twenty characteristics on my list existed in my marriage.

"Do you want one?"

"Of course I do. Doesn't everyone?"

"No, not everyone. Do you think Grant does?"

"Yes, he just doesn't know how."

Maybe Sarah should come to Kelowna with me sometime for a reunion with Grant's family. Then she'd understand.

"Do you think he can learn?"

"I don't know."

"Can you stay without intimacy?"

"I hope not."

"So, you can leave?"

"No."

"So, where does that leave you?"

"In limbo. Making no decision as usual. Just letting life do to me as it will." I put my head in my hands. I was so tired. I wondered if it would be rude to curl into a ball and take a little nap.

"You *are* making a decision. That's the whole point. You are making a decision to flop around and not make a decision. That's a decision."

I looked up. That last statement had sounded a bit rude. Sarah looked exasperated. Were counsellors allowed to look exasperated? I didn't blame her. I was getting tired of me too.

"I didn't say it was a good decision," she said. "It is the one you are able to make right now. But it is *your* decision. Not Grant's. It's your decision."

I stared at my clenched fists on my lap. My breathing was shallow, moving in and out too fast. My head was a ball of fluff, floating somewhere above my shoulders, detached. I wanted to reach up and pull it back down, cram it onto my neck where it belonged. I should have eaten something before I came.

"So, you told me he blamed you for his broken leg."

"Yeah," I said warily.

"So, you find it unreasonable that he's not taking responsibility for the things happening to him?"

"Of course. It was his choice to log in the first place. It was his choice to go back to work while I was working. . . ."

Jesus, what is she getting at?

"So, what do you blame Grant for?"

"Everything! For sleeping with me after Dan died. For making me move to Golden, for stopping me every year from going back to school . . ." My anger was back.

"Does that make any more sense than him blaming you for his broken leg?"

She paused for a moment, letting me make the connection. A tiny light tried hard to flicker on in some far-off corner of my consciousness.

"If you float," she said, "you have no power. If you take responsibility for your decisions, you have power. Because that means you can make other decisions. If you believe Grant keeps you stuck, or your father keeps you stuck, you'll stay stuck. You only have control over your own actions."

My father had once said to me, "You can't keep blaming me forever." But apparently I could. I split the blame evenly between him and Grant.

Jenna and Sam sprawled across my bed, asleep. I closed my journal on my pen. I kept seeing the look on Jenna's face in the rear-view mirror after I'd told her I'd abandon her on the side of the road in a snowstorm.

I threw the journal on the floor and curled around my kids. Jenna's mouth was lax around her two fingers.

Sarah had said, "You're doing the best you can in the circumstances." Grant had said the same thing to me: "I'm doing the best I can." But I wanted our best to be better.

I untangled myself from my kids' sleeping bodies, pulled on my housecoat, slipped down the carpeted stairs. Maybe if I heated up some milk I could sleep. When I'd been plagued with insomnia as a child, sure I was dying of cancer and would roast in hell for eternity, or worse, that my family would roast in hell, Mom had drugged me up with warm milk and Gravol.

The TV was still on. Dad looked up from the couch. He was empty-handed. No Scotch. "Trouble sleeping?" he asked.

"Yup. You too?"

"Yup."

"What are you watching?"

"Late news."

I sat beside him on the couch. We watched quietly together. His news-watching had been sacrosanct when we were kids, just like the morning newspaper. No talking.

My dad smelled faintly of aftershave. Old Spice. My suit-and-tie-and-briefcase morning dad.

My throat tightened. I'd been crying every day these past couple of weeks, usually several times. Almost as much as after Alaska.

"So, your mother tells me things are still rough with Grant."

I nodded. Tried to hold back the tears. I didn't want him to head upstairs, or out to the garage. "I feel like I'm going crazy."

He patted my leg briefly. Made the growly sound in the back of his throat that I'd liked so much when I was little. It used to make me feel special, even though he made the same noise to the dog and cat and gerbils. Sometimes he'd wink at the same time, like we shared a secret.

"I think school's a good idea," he said.

I sniffled quietly as we watched the rest of the news.

I drove toward downtown, turned onto Sarah's narrow, tree-lined street and parked the car around the back of her office. This was my last session. I'd barely slept, worried that Sarah still hadn't cured me. Worried that maybe this was as good as it got. Was I really as unhappy as I thought I was?

Sarah seemed more relaxed, and I wondered if she'd set up the past sessions like boot camp, or basic training. Break me down to build me back up again. Maybe she'd be easier on me today.

"Why do you want to go to school so badly?"

School. For years school had been dangling in front of me like a massive carrot. Education led to meaningful work, which led to money, which led to independence, which led to confidence—and it all led to freedom. Education was something I could take with me everywhere because it'd be inside me. It would transform me. Education would save me.

"I feel like if I can take this step, I can do anything. I can turn into someone who can't live with someone like Grant. I can turn into the person I know I can be."

"Don't worry about leaving him at this point. If it's going to happen, it'll happen when you're ready. Just get yourself to school."

"I'll never convince Grant."

Sarah leaned forward, her elbows on her knees. "So when he didn't want you to go back to work, what did you do?"

"I went back to work."

"And when he didn't want to move back to Canmore, what did you do?"

"I bought a townhouse. I'm actually pretty proud of that." I smiled.

"So, it's selective. You let him tell you what to do sometimes, and not others."

"It's not that easy. I can't get a student loan. Grant makes too much money now. I have kids. A house. A cat. A dog. Chaba can't come to Calgary with us."

Just the thought of leaving Chaba made me want to stay in the Blaeberry and make Grant's lunch for the rest of my life. Chaba was part of the family.

"No one said it would be easy."

I leaned forward with my elbows on my knees. Sarah had approximately ten minutes left to save me. I could not dick around. "Sarah, I can sit here in this room and think, *Yes, I'll go to university*, but what about when I get home? How do I hold on to this conviction? How do I hold on to *me*? When I start to explain to Grant why I need to go to school, he gets pissed off and I start to shrink. Then poof! I'm gone."

"What are you the most afraid of?"

I thought of the chilly silence in our house. When he wasn't in camp it was like walking through a minefield.

"His anger. His disapproval."

"So you have his approval now?"

"Nope. I don't. I don't have it at all."

"But you had it before?"

I tilted my head. "No. Not really. Maybe sometimes. When I buy into the 'me Tarzan, you Jane' lifestyle. But no. Not even then." The only time he seemed somewhat happy was when he was climbing, with no interference from me or the kids or the logging industry.

"You could stay at home with his anger or go to school with his anger. You can blame him until you're eighty if you want, and even if you're right, you still won't have gone to school. And you still won't have his approval."

There was a little click in my brain, like the switch in a railway yard that makes a train head down a different set of tracks.

"So what if you had his full approval? Is anything else stopping you?"

I pictured myself sitting in a classroom, handing in assignments, doing a presentation in front of a roomful of strangers, opening and closing my mouth like a guppy, nothing coming out. Trying to learn how to use a computer like the ones we had at work. Nona and I had gotten hysterical trying to control the little arrow with the mouse.

"What if I've been fooling myself all along? What if I don't really have a brain? If I try and fail, I won't have my dream to keep me going."

"So it's not really about Grant. It's about you. About your fear."

Christ! Am I still playing follow-the-leader? Hiding behind Grant?

I felt strange. Like I'd been floating around watching until now, and I was finally there in the room, in my body.

"You've done everything right. You're further along than you know. You've taken courses, you have a job and you've saved money, you're on the lists for housing and daycare. Now put in your application. You don't have to make decisions about your marriage just yet. One step at a time."

Out in the parking lot, a thick perfume enveloped me and I looked up into hundreds of heavy purple lilacs. This was the first time I'd noticed this tree, after parking four times in this exact spot. I took a deep breath, sucked in the sweetness. I didn't ever want to forget this moment: the clarity, the certainty, the surge of power. It was the same feeling I'd had on the Calgary campus with Sam hopping up and down on my back. I knew I'd go floating off again but this moment was mine. "This turmoil is uncomfortable, but it's what will get you to school. Don't run away from it," Sarah had said. "Run into it."

I picked one tiny blossom. Back at my parents' house, I pressed the speck of purple into my journal and wrote, *Remember the lilac.*

32

POWER SURGE

Hiking along the shoreline of Lake Louise, Doc and I wove in and out of the crowds of camera-clad tourists like slalom skiers. They gaped at us and the ropes hanging off our packs as if we were exotic pandas in a zoo. Some of them even swung their cameras from the blue glacier of Mount Victoria and the milky turquoise lake to point them at us.

As we approached the back of the lake, the tourists started to thin out.

"Hey, Jan, where's the fire?" Doc said, and I slowed down so he and I could walk side by side.

It was hard to drop my sense of urgency. At home I had to race to keep up with the house and kids with Grant in camp, and at work

I had to race around with all the women who were trying to be the best, the fastest, the most efficient, so they wouldn't be the first on the chopping block. Huge cutbacks were coming to Forestry. It was a good thing I'd finally made my decision. In two weeks we'd be in Calgary.

"Hey, you're used to tromping around in the mountains all year," I said.

Doc and I had met in Wyoming, at NOLS, and our lives had been intertwined ever since. We'd taken an epic trip to Yosemite with Niccy, all three squeezed into his tiny car with everything he owned, including the monster-sized stereo and speakers I had to sit beside in the back seat. These days, Doc worked for Outward Bound.

"I have to coax my clients along gently. Not the best thing for my own fitness."

Doc had my dream job: using the mountains to help women find their long-lost gumption. He worked with women coming out of abusive relationships. A far cry from the testosterone-drenched Banff Cadet Camp where my cadets had been less concerned about personal growth than submachine guns, napalm and who could get up a climb the fastest. The totally opposite end of the touchy-feely spectrum.

"I like Annie. She's a real sweetie," I said.

Doc's girlfriend had gone for a hike and would meet us at the end of the day. She was a sparkly blonde from Louisiana with a Southern drawl and lots of positive energy. An Outward Bound instructor too.

"Yeah, I think this might be it. And how are you and Grant?"

"We're still married!" There was my perky, upbeat voice, but the truth was Grant now slept in the screened-in room out back. He was pissed off that in two weeks we'd be moving into student housing in Calgary, pissed off that we had tenants set up for our house for the next four years, pissed off that I was ruining our lives and our little family.

"He's not impressed that I'm climbing on Jenna's birthday."

Guilt seeped through me when I thought about my kids, but this was the only day Doc could climb. He and Annie would fly home to the States tomorrow. And I couldn't count how many family events Grant had missed in the past four years to be in the mountains.

"I hope I'm not causing problems." His North Carolina accent dipped and dragged out his vowels.

"You kidding? A slight change in wind direction causes problems. And tomorrow's her big party, not today."

Jenna knew tomorrow was her special day. Ten friends, a water-slide, a Pocahontas Dairy Queen cake and a big piñata that the four- and five-year-olds probably couldn't even dent with a big stick. Every day I'd been putting a new layer of papier mâché on a big balloon after work, and tonight Jenna and I would paint it and hang a little yellow bear in a basket below to make it look like a hot air balloon. As long as Grant didn't make a big deal of my absence, Jenna wouldn't care that today was her real birthday.

"You should come back for birthday cake. Break your teeth on a few silver candy balls."

I'd baked a chocolate cake after work yesterday and let Jenna cover it in M&Ms, sprinkles and silver candy balls. It was a two-cake birthday.

"Would love to. I can finally meet Grant."

Bubbles of unease started to percolate. Grant hadn't come out of the house when Annie and Doc picked me up. I'd told Doc he was busy with the kids.

He hadn't met Grant three years earlier when he visited me in Canmore either. I'd asked Doc and his friend to move from our guest room to a campground before Grant came home because I was worried about Grant's reaction to someone like Doc—someone with a brain and Southern manners, and a gentle disposition. Someone who wrote poetry.

We headed off the main trail into the trees and hiked up a narrow path toward the steep cliffs of quartzite. I threw my pack down at the base of the climb.

"This is it."

Doc put his hands on the rock on either side of a fist-sized crack set in the corner and looked up. The route started off vertical and got steeper after that, running through two roofs, which would take some serious Spiderman moves. We'd climb up the wall, then through a horizontal ceiling, then back up the wall—twice—before reaching the bolted anchor.

"You want this lead? It looks way harder than it is. There's lots of huge holds."

I wasn't sure how I wanted him to respond. I hadn't climbed much over the summer with work and the kids, but I knew the best thing for me was to lead right away. Not give myself the chance to snivel and chicken out.

Doc peered at me over his thick glasses as though I'd asked him if he'd like to take a leap off the top of a thirty-storey building. He declined the lead.

I felt a surge of excitement, like I'd won the lottery. I'd done this route many times, so it was the perfect way to get back into leading.

With my rack around my neck, I started sorting gear. The weight pulled on my neck muscles. I'd barely been able to turn my head all summer. It seemed the more Grant and I fought, the more my neck seized up.

"That's my style!" Doc laughed when he saw all the gear I'd brought.

"Hey! It's a very long pitch." The route was about 130 feet, almost the full length of the rope.

I kept sorting gear, from smallest to biggest so I could grab the right size quickly while I was hyperventilating a hundred feet up.

When Doc had me on belay, I reached up and grabbed a huge hand-hold, pulled myself up. Once both feet were off the ground, firmly positioned on large footholds, I paused and took a deep breath. The ground was still just a jump away. I hadn't committed to anything yet.

With my hand crammed in the crack, I stepped up again. I felt light, even with the rack of metal hanging from my neck and the rope dragging from my harness. My shoes were about level with Doc's head, so I placed a piece of protection in the crack as high as I could and clipped the rope.

"Lookin' good," Doc said.

I moved up steadily, putting protection in the crack every eight feet or so. Not too much, not too little. I waited for that familiar panic to plant itself in my belly, then expand outward until it grabbed hold of my arms and legs and tried to shake me off the rock, but I felt calm, in control. I felt the clarity I was always looking for.

Under the first roof, I bent out backwards from the rock, reaching for an edge to grab onto. As my hand groped around, I had one of those *what the fuck am I doing here?* moments and then my palm fit perfectly around a huge hold. I pulled myself up and over.

"Nicely done!"

The bigger roof waited for me, thirty feet up. With my eyes fixed on the next rest spot, I climbed away from my last piece of protection, farther and farther from the ground. Placed another piece of protection. Repeated the process. Ropey tendons popped up on the backs of my hands, white with chalk as I clamped down on each hold like a vise. There was no noise in my head, no voices telling me what I could or could not do. Just the sound of my breathing.

When I scrunched my body under the big roof, preparing myself to commit to pulling up and over the edge, I looked down at Doc, eighty feet below. It was a long way away. My two blond children danced in front of my eyes for a moment like fairies. *Your children will be okay if their mother's okay,* Sarah had said in Victoria. Did I want my kids to see their mom bake cookies all day and make lunch for a logger, or climb steep cracks and go to university?

Which mother would they believe when she told them, "Follow your dream!"

I was up and over the roof and cramming another piece of protection in the crack. With my feet stemming the wall on either side of the corner, hands sunk deep in the crack, I felt like a climber again.

As we hiked down the trail toward the Chateau, I could feel the heat-sensor missile of Grant's anger and resentment raging through the passes and valleys of the Rockies to home in on me, here in Lake Louise.

"We'd better boot it," I said.

I'd be home by six. We'd done one more route than we should have. Grant had "suggested" I get home at five and I'd wanted seven, so I was compromising. He just didn't know that yet.

Doc matched my pace, looked over at me and said, "You're amazing."

"Right. I used to take my cadets up some of that shit. Grant could probably solo them without a rope."

Doc put his hand on my arm. Stopped me. We stood in the middle of the trail, tourists flowing around us like we were rocks in white water.

"Don't do that to yourself. You can do anything you set your mind to. I've seen you."

"Four years of school is a very long time."

"Hey. Remember the chewing tobacco? You were wild. If you can chew that shit, you can do anything."

"Oh, God," I groaned. "Pig shit in a can." I slipped my hand through the crook of his arm and we walked arm in arm the rest of the way. In front of the Chateau, Annie was waiting for us, smiling and swaying in time to the guy in lederhosen playing "Edelweiss" on the alpenhorn.

Doc bumped the rental car up our driveway, pulled up in a cloud of dust in front of the house. As I dragged my pack out of the trunk,

Jenna flew down the steps from the deck, wrapped herself around my leg. I ruffled her hair.

"Hey, sweetie-pie. You having fun with Daddy?"

"It's my birthday. Daddy said you should have been here for my birthday."

Doc and Annie came up behind me and Doc introduced himself to Jenna.

"The last time I saw you, you were turning one."

"I'm five now." She held up five fingers.

Annie squatted down beside her. "Five! Wow. That's pretty old. You'll be going to kindergarten!"

Grant stomped down the steps toward us, scowling. He held Sam out toward me with straight arms. I lifted him above my head and he giggled and drooled. He was teething again. Before it splatted on me, I lowered him to my hip. At twenty months, he was getting too heavy to hold for long. Jenna hadn't been this weight until about three.

Grant stood in front of me with his arms crossed. Sam peeked around me at the two strangers.

"This is Sam," I told Doc and Annie.

Doc wanted to acknowledge Sam but Grant's body posture was too overwhelming.

"Grant, this is Doc. Doc, Grant." Doc extended his hand but Grant just glared.

"I know who you are."

I didn't bother to introduce Annie.

"We finally ate without you."

I looked at my watch. "It's only six."

"But we saved the cake, Mommy." Jenna's voice was too cheerful. She grabbed my hand and guilt jabbed at me. Maybe I should have stayed for her birthday, or at least found a phone booth in Lake Louise. But I wasn't that late. He could have held off.

"Thanks, baby. And we'll have your real party tomorrow."

"Her *birthday* is today." Grant stood over me. I took a step back.

He grabbed Jenna's hand and said, "Come on, Jenna. Let's go light your candles." Jenna ran after her father, looking back at me, tripping a bit as he pulled her along. He slammed the door to the house. Hard. Sam snuggled his face into my shirt.

Doc let out a long whistle. "Wow."

"Sorry, you guys. He's not always like this." I didn't sound convincing. He'd been like this in Canmore four years ago too.

"I'm not sure if I feel comfortable leaving you here," Doc said. "Will you be safe?"

My sister had said the same thing. I'd waited to tell Grant about my savings account until her visit a month ago, thinking he would moderate his response. He hadn't.

My laugh sounded forced. "I'm okay. He's just being a jerk. I figure he owes me about 210 days' worth of climbing for his two expeditions, and I haven't even come close."

We hugged goodbye, then I watched Doc and Annie slowly bounce down the driveway in the rental car and turn onto the road. They honked, two little beeps on the horn.

In a couple more weeks we'd be in Calgary. I'd meticulously and intentionally burned every bridge behind me. I'd quit my job, the house was rented, deposits were paid, Jenna was signed up for school, Sam for daycare, and me for university. There was no backing out now. I just had to get Grant away from logging, then he'd lighten up, he'd see this was the right direction for us. We just needed a change.

Weighted down by my climbing pack on one side, my twenty-month-old on the other, I trudged up the grey weathered cedar steps to the house. As I scootched Sam up my hip I said, "Did you know your mommy's a wild woman?"

33

LEAVING CHABA

"Come on, Chaba!"

I patted the tailgate of the truck and Chaba backed up to take a run at it, hoisted his thick, blond body up into the box where he sat and panted heavily, his tongue dripping down his white chest. He thought he was going for a walk.

"Why can't Chaba come with us?" Jenna asked.

"I already told you, Jenna." I'd explained this to her over and over, all summer long. She knew they didn't allow pets in family housing.

I slammed the tailgate shut. Chaba plunked his head over the side of the box and Jenna reached up, scratched behind his ears. Her face was impassive, too impassive for a five-year-old. She was learning to cover up so young. But she'd forgotten to wipe the soft powdering of salt from her face, dried-up tears from her goodbye earlier with Gus.

"I don't want to leave him either, and I don't want to leave Gussy. But I didn't make the rules. They don't let people have cats or dogs at the university."

"I hate that stupid university."

She hated our new life before it had even started. So did Grant. So much so that he wasn't coming with us. I wasn't surprised. In fact, I'd been wondering when he'd get the guts to tell me. But our house was rented out to a couple from Montreal, so he was homeless. He would rent a room from a friend of ours, a mountain guide, and try to visit us on weekends. We were hoping to smuggle Chaba in once in a while.

"I'm gonna drive with Daddy to Calgary in the big truck," Jenna said in a singsong voice, looking over at the loaded U-Haul.

The words were intended to punish, and they did. My eyes started to sting. I'd been a blubbering mess all week, cleaning the house for the tenants. Scrubbing out our claw-foot tub after three winters of sharing bathwater. Washing crayon and markers off the cedar walls and getting that familiar whiff of home. Weeding the garden and imagining our tenant with her Montreal makeup, picking my carrots and zucchini and raspberries with her long red fingernails.

Grant came toward us with Sam on his shoulders, his hands encircling grubby bare feet. Sam had hardly worn shoes all summer, let alone clothes. Getting him into his diaper and T-shirt was like trying to dress a giant eel.

Grant passed off our son without a word and everyone crawled into the pickup. We headed up the valley, toward Kim and Dick's house by the Blaeberry River, where Jenna had spent the past three summers playing in the pond with Haley, and Sam and Ocean had transformed together from small blobs who could barely hold up their heads to walking, talking little people.

Chaba's doghouse waited for him on the dirt driveway; Grant had brought it a few days ago. There was a metal stake in the ground for the rope. Chaba had never been tied up in his life. He'd never even used the doghouse because he slept inside with us.

"Their van's not here," Grant said, looking through the windshield.

I pulled Sam out with me and propped him on my hip. "Kim said to just tie him up if they weren't home."

Grant grabbed the red Hudson's Bay blanket from the back seat. He spread it out in the doghouse, smoothed it, tucked in the ends so they wouldn't get wet when it rained. My throat throbbed and squeezed shut as I watched him set up Chaba's new home.

I dropped the tailgate. "Come on, Chaba!" He looked at me but didn't move from his spot in the corner of the box. Jenna peered through the rear window, her fingers crammed in her mouth, her special blanket balled up in her fist.

"Come on, Chaba." I patted the tailgate. My voice quavered, came out in almost a whisper. Chaba didn't move. I tried again, but he only looked at me and whined.

"Chaba, come!" I started at Grant's booming voice beside me.

Chaba stood slowly and paused.

"Come on, baby," I said softly. I was crying now. I couldn't help it. With my twenty-month-old pressed against me, and my five-year-old glaring from the truck.

Chaba lumbered toward me, licked the hand I extended to him. For three years we'd been in the bush together, tromping up and down logging blocks. I'd screamed at him when he'd chased after a fawn, held him while the neighbours pulled porcupine quills from his muzzle with pliers. Guilt needled into my gut like bark beetles and I buried my face in his fur, sobbing. Sam stopped squirming. His hand crept into my hair and he stroked my head.

Grant's hand was on my shoulder for a moment, brief enough that it could have been my imagination, or an accident, then he was lifting Sam out of my arms. I pulled my face out of Chaba's fur and my eyes locked with Jenna's. Her mouth was open, her fingers forgotten, the blanket dropped out of sight. Shock had replaced her anger, and I saw what she saw reflected in the glass. Wild, dark hair sticking out in all directions, my face shining wet in the sun.

I stepped back, my reflection disappearing from the glass, pulled Chaba's collar till he was on the ground beside me. I walked him over to his doghouse, knelt down, clipped the carabiner to his collar, put my arms around him.

"Come on, Jan. You're just torturing yourself. We've got to get driving." Grant's voice had lost its edge. He sounded defeated. He'd told me I was ruining everything we'd built together. Our home. Our family. That we had a good life. I stumbled to the truck and crawled in beside my silent children. Chaba yipped and whined.

As we started down the driveway, I twisted around in the seat, peered through the back window. Chaba charged after the truck but got jerked back when he reached the end of the rope. I put my face in my hands and choked out big, heaving sobs.

34

ONLY FOUR YEARS

"Please, Jan, just leave. Sam will be fine. Really."

Tina, the daycare worker, tried to peel my son from my hip but he seized my shirt and wouldn't let go. I watched her hands pry one tiny finger open at a time.

"Come on, Sam. Let's go to the window and wave bye-bye to Mommy!" Tina finally got the last of Sam's fingers unfastened, took his bottle from me. "Then we'll have story time! You love story time, don't you, Sam!" Her voice dripped with enthusiasm, exclamation after exclamation.

She pulled him from my hip, then turned and walked toward the front room with Sam howling and twisting in her arms, reaching for me. His blond hair stood straight up, his face seeped snot and tears and saliva.

"Thanks, Tina," I called after her. My voice broke. What was I thanking her for? Ripping my child from my arms? I took a deep breath. I could not afford to cry now. I had to get to school.

In approximately two hours, after my first class, I would run straight to the pay phone in the Education building, phone the daycare, and they'd tell me he was just fine, playing happily with the other kids. Settled down as soon as I'd left. I'd been phoning them after class for two weeks, and I'd probably phone every day for the next four years. I wanted to set up a video camera in each corner to see if they were telling the truth.

The screams followed me out the door. I looked back to see his face glued to the window. I forced a smile, curled my fingers in another wave. There should have been a course at the university called Mother Guilt 101.

I looked at my watch. *Shit! Late again.* Wiping my face on my sleeve, I hurried to the car. Jenna was in her booster seat in the back, clutching her blanket and sucking her fingers. She looked at me through droopy eyelids with her best pissed-off look. At least she suffered quietly.

"I'm going to be late for kindergarten," she slurred through her spit. She was all dolled up in her pink princess dress and multi-coloured knee socks from her auntie. I wasn't sure how she'd turned out like this—I lived in fleece sweaters, jeans and hiking shoes—but I'd given up worrying what her kindergarten teacher thought of me. I was picking my battles.

We headed west, toward the red-brick school a few blocks away. In a couple of hours one of the daycare workers would pick up a half dozen morning kindergarten kids, including Jenna, and lead them all in a row holding on to a rope back to the daycare, like little ducklings behind a mother duck, or the Pied Piper.

At the door to her classroom, Jenna handed me her blanket. Her class was seated in the story corner at the back of the room. There were so many of them, a wriggling sea of four- and five-year-olds. The teacher counted, *un, deux, trois, quatre,* and tapped her wooden pointer on the calendar, then reached out to gently pull one little boy, who seemed to have no idea of personal space, off the legs of another. She looked up, smiled and greeted Jenna. This would be me in four years. A teacher. I'd have to keep a stash of Valium in my desk.

Jenna's little friend, Breanne, one ponytail planted on the top of her head like a water fountain, wiggled her fingers at us. In the first week of school, this harmless-looking child had told Jenna she was going to chop off her head if she didn't play with her.

"Breanne wouldn't chop off your head," I'd told her, trying to picture a five-year-old with a machete sticking out of her pink Pocahontas backpack. "She's your friend."

"She said she'd get her big sister to do it," Jenna had wailed. I didn't know how much was true and how much was a stall tactic, but it had led to our first meeting with the teacher—in week one of her first year of school.

As Jenna walked away from me, her face deadpan, I said, "I love you, sweetie," quietly, so she wouldn't be embarrassed. She sat down next to Breanne, turned back and saw me lingering in the doorway. She raised her hand in a little wave.

My attempt to sneak into the classroom, *quiet like a bunny,* failed. The heavy door slammed shut behind me like it was loaded on lead springs, and about thirty heads turned to watch me take my seat. The silver-haired professor paused and looked up over his glasses from his papers, smiled briefly. My face felt hot but everyone's attention was already on the front of the room.

"Could you please pass your essays to the front?"

I took the stack of papers from the guy behind me. They were all typed up on computers. I looked down at my own white-out-blotched handwriting on lined paper. I hadn't been able to get to the computer lab at the library to type it. When I passed the pile to the girl in front of me, I noticed she had written hers out too.

"Thank God I'm not the only one with a handwritten paper," I whispered to her. She looked at me like I was a bug, or worse, a thirty-two-year-old mother in a first-year education class. She could easily have been in grade ten.

"How long did you spend on it?" I continued, wondering what I'd do if she completely ignored me.

"On what?" Her voice exuded boredom.

"On your paper."

"I wrote it on the bus on the way here. It's only worth one percent. I wasn't even going to write it."

I stared at her. I'd spent hours on it: a conservative guess would have been about eight. It was a critical review of a chapter on "school culture" and I could barely understand what the author was going on about, let alone critique it. It made me think I should study factual content like geography so I wouldn't spread my stupidity around for the whole world to see.

"What kind of moron assigns eight one-percent papers?" She didn't bother to whisper.

I forced a smile and slouched back in my seat but I wanted to shake the little sloth and scream, *Do you realize how lucky you are to be here?* She was probably living at home with parents who paid her tuition, bought and cooked her food, and did her laundry.

". . . oral presentations will start next Monday. . . ." The prof described another assignment.

Hummingbird-sized butterflies slammed into the walls of my stomach. *An oral presentation? In front of all these people?* I got a flash of eight-year-old me in Whitehorse, up in front of a huge audience to sing my first and only solo. The piano music started, I opened my mouth, and froze. In spite of hours of practice, I couldn't remember one word to "Under the Lollipop Tree." I'd run from the room crying.

I stared at my three-ringed notebook. What had possessed me to go into education when I had a phobia about public speaking?

"Do you see the symbolism here?"

Grant thumped his big hand on my wooden desk, the one I'd bought for my first attempt at university, after Dan died.

"What are you talking about?" I was hunched over my French essay.

"Well, think about it. Look at your desk. Look at our bed."

I looked around the room. Everything seemed in order. A little cluttered, not much space to move around between the bed, the desk and the dresser, but nothing out of the ordinary.

"Don't you see it?"

I put my highlighter down and sighed. All I wanted was for him to go downstairs and not bug me for the next little while. I had four mid-term exams in the next two weeks and a French essay due in two days.

"The desk is symbolically cutting me off from the bed!" he said, as though he'd just pulled a rabbit out of his hat.

The desk was wedged up against the bed, the first thing you bumped into as you walked into the bedroom. I'd moved it there so I could manoeuvre around the bed and look out the window.

"That's stupid. I just moved stuff where it fits."

Muffled voices rose and fell in the other unit through the wall, followed by thumps up the stairs, like someone dragging a body.

"How do you live like this? Stuck to other people. No windows. Crap everywhere."

"I have a window." I pointed to the window that looked out on the grassy communal area and the sandbox Sam had mistaken for a urinal at first. The view didn't compare to the view of the mountains in the Blaeberry, but it was *my* view and *my* window and *my* house. I could drink water right out of the tap, no more hauling it from town; I could shower for ten minutes and the well would never run dry; I could turn the heat up on a thermostat with one finger instead of dragging the kids out into the snow to chop and haul wood.

That morning, Grant had asked Jenna what *she* thought of her new house and she'd said, "I *love* it!" Grant had just grunted.

Jenna already had a perfect pair of friends, seven-year-old identical twins called Amanda and Cassandra. If one couldn't come over, the other could, and since neither of us could tell them apart, it was like having a best friend who was always at her disposal. A few months earlier their mother, Karen, who was already becoming a good friend, had packed up the twins and their nine-year-old brother in the middle of the night and left in a taxi. When she realized they'd all starve on child support from a guy who filled vending machines for a living, she'd applied to nursing school. We'd be neighbours for the next four years. I was hoping if she could do it with three kids, I could do it with two.

"Yeah, well, I couldn't live like this." He circled around me and went out the door. I shook my head and stared out the window, then shouted at his retreating back, "What the hell is your problem?"

I hunched back over my desk, wrote a couple of sentences, looked a word up in my French-English dictionary, then kept writing, but Grant had messed up my concentration. And now he was banging pots as he rummaged around in the kitchen. I was so primed for his anger I could almost feel it radiate up through the floor like heat from our wood stove.

I reread my paragraph, crumpled the paper and threw it across the room where it landed noiselessly beside a scattering of other balled-up pieces. I needed a computer. I'd calculated that I could buy a second-hand one after Christmas with the hundred dollars a month Mom was giving me out of her old age pension.

Grant started up the vacuum. A few moments later Sam was

tugging on my shirt with an empty bottle in his mouth and his arms out. "Up, Mommy." This was the fourth time Jenna or Sam had interrupted me. Grant had even vacuumed under my feet earlier on. With Sam on my hip, I pounded down the stairs, yanked the plug of the vacuum out of the wall. Jenna looked up from her video.

"You're supposed to watch the kids. I can't get this essay done if you keep letting them come upstairs."

"This place is a pigsty. My feet stick to the floor."

A shiny film covered the linoleum of my tiny kitchen. Sam had chucked his sippy cup of apple juice at the cupboard the other day and I'd wiped it up with a cloth, but our shoes still peeled off the floor like Velcro.

"Can't you take them out to the playground? This paper's due Monday and I still have to get to the library to type it." Actually, I still had to write it.

Grant let the vacuum hose crash to the floor. "Come on, you guys. Let's go outside. Mommy's got more important things to do than look after her kids."

I flinched. "Just give me an hour. And you have to stay with them. You can't just . . ."

"I don't need you to tell me how to look after my kids." He grabbed Sam from my arms. Sam started to cry and reach for me. "See? He needs his mother."

Jenna hopped off the couch and turned up the volume on the TV. The orchestra music swelled, filling the room, as the prince twirled Sleeping Beauty around and around.

"Jenna, turn that down!" Grant roared. He turned back to me. "She shouldn't be watching so much TV."

"She wouldn't be if you'd take them out to play."

"Jenna!" He was losing control, I could hear it in his voice, but Jenna kept her back to her father. He took three giant steps to the TV with Sam under his arm and slammed the power button. The room went quiet except for Sam's crying. Grant put him on the couch with Jenna.

"This is bullshit. How long are you planning to keep this up for?"

"What do you mean?"

"Look at you guys. Sam's always sick from that goddamned day-care. Jenna's stuck to her blanket. You've lost so much weight your clothes are hanging off you."

I looked down at my jeans, pulled them up. I couldn't seem to relax enough to eat. I was always running: from daycare to school to university to home, my metabolism zipping along at a million miles an hour. My face was hollowed out, just like it had been after Dan died.

Sam looked back and forth between me and his father, snot and tears running down his face. Jenna stared at the blank TV, dry-eyed.

It was a struggle to maintain eye contact with Grant, to not cringe and look away. "If you'd just help me," I whispered.

"Help you? All I do is help you. I drive here and clean for two days then drive back to the bush to make more money for you to go to school."

"I need help with the kids, not the house."

"You need to be looking after them yourself."

Sam was howling now. He crawled off the couch and stumbled toward me.

"I *am* looking after them!" I couldn't get any air into my lungs.

Sam wrapped himself around my leg while Grant stepped into the kitchen, picked up a pot with hardened noodles stuck to it. Jenna, Sam and I jumped as he threw it into the steel sink with a crash.

"Look at this fucking place! Every time I come here it looks the same!"

"I don't have time! I don't have time to breathe!" My veins thudded in my ears, in time with my heart.

"Then come home and look after your goddamned family!"

I couldn't believe I'd felt homesick twenty-four hours ago, waiting for him to arrive.

"It's all about you, isn't it? What about us?" His words pummelled me. I fought the urge to duck.

Jenna stood up on the couch, clapped her hands over her ears, squeezed her eyes shut and screamed, "Shut up, shut up, shut up!" She kept screaming. Sam clamped harder around my leg, choking on big shuddering sobs.

"What do you mean 'what about us'? I'm here. I'm still their mother. I pick them up every day at five. I'm with them all weekend, all night, all morning. I'm not the only mother that has a fucking life, you know."

"What kind of mother lets strangers raise her kids, for chrissake?" His voice was quiet, controlled. It sounded like a touché, like he knew the whole community of loggers and back-to-the-land friends in Golden were rallying behind those words. Several couples had voiced their disapproval.

Something let loose inside me. It was too much. Leaving my home. Leaving the mountains. Giving up Gus and Chaba. Being on my own with the kids. Here I was living my dream, but it was more like an LSD-induced psychosis. As though some big hand had just plucked us all up in mid-fight from a living room with a mountain view and plunked us—still squabbling and screaming—into another living room three hours away, one with a red-brick-wall view. Going to school was supposed to transform me, but nothing had changed. And Grant was going to keep putting up roadblock after roadblock until I gave in and came home.

"I hate you!" The words of a trapped teenager burst out of my mouth. I was transported back to Munster, like I'd never left.

I had to get away from this man, but I couldn't move. Sam was clinging to me, sobbing. I shook my leg, like I was shaking off a Jack Russell terrier. I shook until Sam loosened his grip and sat heavily on the floor on his diaper, then I turned and ran up the stairs, away from my family.

By the time Grant came into the bedroom, I was all cried out. He pushed the desk out of the way, sat on the edge of the bed.

"I took the kids over to Karen." His voice was calm, almost gentle.

He lay down beside me, put his hands behind his head. We studied the chart that spanned the whole of my wall, page after page taped together; the semester separated into weeks, the days into columns; my four courses separated into rows. I'd included all my readings, assignments, quizzes, exams and presentations using the kids' markers, a different colour for the level of importance, and I'd calculated the percentage of time I should allot to each. It had taken hours.

"This isn't working," Grant finally said.

"I know."

One month into my first semester and I was wasted, defeated. I knew what he was going to say. He was going to tell me to come home and I didn't have the strength left to fight. Some days I was so homesick for my house, my garden, my mountains, for him, that I wished I could push a rewind button on my life. Sarah had said it wouldn't be easy, but I didn't know it would be this hard.

"I think we should separate. I've been thinking about it for a while," he said.

My breath caught in my throat.

"We're going to kill each other. And we're hurting the kids."

The tears started up again; hot streams coursed down the sides of my face and pooled in my ears. Sobbing, I curled away from him. Wrapped my arms around my knees. "I know, I know." This is what I thought I'd always wanted, to be free, but he wasn't supposed to feel the same way. He was supposed to fight for me.

"I can't think of any other way. Even if you came back to Golden you'd never be happy."

"I know, I know." I squeezed my knees into my chest, doubled in half. I couldn't breathe.

We didn't speak. We didn't touch.

The morning light slanting through the curtains woke me. I pushed through heavy fog, struggling back to consciousness. My head throbbed with dehydration. I was alone in our big bed. Grant's words from the night before settled on me like boulders.

Wrapped in a blanket, I shuffled down the stairs to an empty house. My bare feet hit the linoleum with a cold shock. A sleeping bag was folded neatly on our foamy on the living room carpet. I walked on top of it to turn up the thermostat.

The house was quiet without the kids, without the TV blaring. How had he managed to keep Jenna and Sam out of the bedroom? I must have slept twelve hours. I curled up on the couch, tucking my feet under the blanket. *I should get out my books and study; I should finish my essay; I should do some cleaning; I should eat.* So many *shoulds.* I stared out the window at the wall of bushes.

After a while, it could have been ten minutes or two hours, Grant pushed open the door and the chilly Alberta air followed him into the living room. October was way too early for winter.

"I took the kids to daycare. Looked like you needed to sleep."

"Were they okay?" I pictured Sam, wrapped around my leg, me shaking him off. Jenna screaming. I groaned and curled into a tighter ball. *What am I doing to my children?*

"They'll be fine. Kids are resilient." He sounded like he was quoting from one of my parenting books. "Have you eaten?"

"I'm not hungry."

"You should eat."

I started to say, *Why should you care?* but when my eyes met his I saw genuine concern. "I'll eat later."

He sat on the armrest. "I'm going to head back to Golden."

It was only Friday. He was supposed to stay for two more days. I had four mid-terms to study for.

"This is the best decision for everyone. You know that. We should never have been together in the first place. We've only lasted this long because of the kids."

"I know." I'd always known. But I hadn't thought he knew. It wasn't something to be said out loud. It wasn't something you could take back.

He started rolling up the foamy, cramming the sleeping bag into a stuff sack.

"I've been thinking. I probably shouldn't come back here for a while. We should get used to not being together. Maybe you could meet me in Banff with the kids when I get out of camp. I can take them back to Golden with me for a few days."

My kids and my husband in Golden without me? I dissolved again into big, heaving, hiccuping sobs. I didn't know if I'd ever be able to stop.

Grant sank to the floor, patted my arm as though scared to touch me in case emoting was contagious. "It's okay. I'll stay with you if you want, until you finish this year. We don't have to do this now." He was throwing me a scrap.

"Just go!" The words were barely out before my voice was consumed by sobs. I needed him to go now.

He stood for a moment looking down on me, hesitated, then picked up his bag and pushed open the door.

3 5

ONE LITTLE *"NON"*

I pulled the car up in front of the gate to the playground. We'd decided to meet here so the kids could play, but I'd forgotten how close it was to Dan's old place. The grey walls of his townhouse peeked through the trees.

While I pushed the kids on the swings, Grant pulled the battered Dodge truck up beside the Tercel. We hadn't seen him in three weeks because he'd gotten his dream job in Port Hardy. He was now in big wood, making big money. A faller's dream. Three weeks on, one week off.

As he walked toward us, my throat squeezed shut. He was wearing a new, expensive-looking black leather jacket. He looked cool, self-assured, like an older version of James Dean. Or like he was sleeping with someone.

The kids raced toward him yelling, "Daddydaddydaddy!" I hung back, following slowly, but what I really wanted to do was sidle up to him, put my head on his chest under his chin, feel his heart beat through the black leather. Disappear into him. Quitting him was like quitting chewing tobacco or cigarettes. Needing one more drag, or one more chew, despite the threat of a gruesome assortment of cancers.

"Hey! I missed you two!" He scooped them both up, kissed them.

I edged closer to my little family.

Jenna had drawn a picture at school of her mommy and daddy getting married, with a little blond boy and girl in front of the mom's white wedding dress. She was clinging to her fantasy family, just like I was. She didn't know I'd been married in a twenty-year-old fuchsia-pink silk dress handed down from her grandmother.

"Hi." I was so homesick I could smell the cedar walls of my home.

"Hello. How are you?" His voice was too loud, too formal, like he was talking to the lady behind the counter at the 7-Eleven.

I could tell he didn't really want the truth. He didn't want to know that for three weeks I'd been on the edge of a nervous breakdown during my waking hours, then in my sleep, I'd abandoned the kids in the truck at Emerald Lake in the dark and couldn't get back to them, and lost Sam through a hole in the ice on a river and felt his little fingers slowly slip from mine.

"Fine," I said. *Fake it till you make it.* I forced myself to match the detachment in his voice. "I'd like to have them back by four on Tuesday." A statement, not a question. I was in a women's assertiveness skills training group at the university counselling centre.

"Yeah, I'll be here." It was a full-on competition for who could be the most remote. He switched the car seat and booster seat to the truck, strapped in the kids.

"Say 'bye-bye' to Mommy!" He put on his cute puppy-dog voice, my cue to get lost.

Jenna and I kissed, rubbed noses.

"Butterfly kiss, butterfly kiss!" she said. With my face right up to her cheek, I tickled her with my wet eyelashes.

Sam was quiet, sucking on a bottle with his head resting against the car seat like he'd had enough. Leaning over Jenna, I kissed his cheek. His chin wobbled, and globs of yellow snot peeked from his nostrils, like worms emerging from their holes. He was getting sick, and day-care didn't take sick babies, but I'd have to cross that barracuda-filled moat when I got to it. I wiped his nose with my sleeve. I couldn't imagine being away from him overnight, let alone for four nights.

"Bye-bye, baby." Words from the lullaby I sang to them.

"See you Tuesday." Grant slipped the truck into gear.

Alone for four days. I'd fantasized about this for years: uninterrupted sleeps, long runs on the trails, relaxing glasses of wine. Pure silence. Now here I was, reading the same paragraph in my psychology text over and over with voices from the television filling the long empty room to ward off that silence. Driving back from Banff in an empty car, I'd felt like steering straight into a semi.

The phone rang. Nine o'clock. I had just talked to the kids an hour ago. Maybe Grant couldn't get them settled. Maybe they needed me as much as I needed them. I ran into the kitchen, grabbed the phone.

"Hello, Grant?"

"Hi, Jan. It's your old man."

"Dad. Is everything okay?"

He was on his own in Victoria this week while Mom was visiting Susan in her new house with her new husband in Vancouver.

"I need to talk to you," he said.

Something in his voice sent prickles of fear up the back of my neck, into my scalp.

"Dad, what's wrong? Is Mom okay?" The terror of losing my mother was always there. I could not survive what I was doing without her. She calmed me down every second day over the phone, and she was booking a flight to come help me with the kids.

"I'm sure she's fine. I wanted to talk to you on my own. How are you?" It sounded like he was stalling.

"I don't know. Not great. How are you?"

He cleared his throat, then it sounded like he was taking a sip of a drink, but it could have been my imagination. "There's something I've been wanting to say for a long time." He was slurring, but only slightly. He went quiet.

"Dad. Are you there?"

"Yes, I'm here. I wanted to tell you something. That I'm sorry."

"You're sorry? For what?"

"This stuff with Grant. I feel responsible for your troubles with men."

Was he really saying this? I pulled the phone on its cord around the corner, sank into the couch.

"Dad, are you okay?" He did not sound like himself at all.

"Yes, yes, Jan, I'm fine." His chuckles relaxed me. "But I think I might have something to do with why you can't find a good relationship."

Might? When I didn't answer, he cleared his throat. Once. Then twice, like something was lodged in there. "I wish I'd been a better father to you." His voice cracked.

I didn't know what to say. What *could* I say?

I wish you'd been a better father too.

Or: *You did the best you could.*

Or: *No, Dad, you're a great father.* It was so hard not to try to rescue him.

"Thank you, Dad," I whispered into the phone. "That means a lot to me."

———

The girl sitting two desks ahead of me was reading out loud from the play *Les Belles-Soeurs*. I sat rigid at my desk, hyperventilating. The top of my head tingled. I was so nervous I could barely follow along. The prof had started the readings at the other side of the room, up and down the aisle, which left me last. I wasn't too bad if I got it over with quickly—it was the anticipation that did me in. There was a ringing in my ears like the echo of cymbals clashing. I knew my mind was going to go blank when it was my turn to read, when all those eyes turned toward me.

"Merci beaucoup, Caroline. Julie?"

Julie started reading in the heavy *joual*—Québécois slang—of a bunch of disgruntled, middle-aged housewives who hung out in a kitchen in Quebec licking a million grocery stamps that Germaine had won and would redeem for a lawnmower in the prize catalogue. All the while they complained about *la misère*. Julie's French was perfect; she must have been a francophone.

None of the courses I'd taken by distance, in the safety of my own home, had prepared me for this. I had occasionally talked to a tutor over the phone, but never face to face. Now, thirty students would be eyeing me, judging me, and I knew what they'd see. An imposter. A "mature" student with a grey streak in her hair who wasn't really all that mature, and whose French sucked.

It was almost my turn. I closed my eyes, used my mom's trick on myself: *What's the worst that could happen?* Maybe my voice would shake a bit, but in all likelihood, I wasn't going to throw up or black out just reading a passage from a book.

Julie stopped reading and silence enveloped the room. Someone at the back muffled a sneeze, a couple of people shifted in their seats.

The prof looked in my direction. She was no more than ten years older than I was, already the head of her department. Confident, funny, passionate, and she cursed like a French-Canadian climber. Maybe I could have been on that side of the desk if I'd stayed in school the first time. But then I wouldn't have had Jenna and Sam.

Her brown eyes were friendly. This was not a challenge, I knew that, but I didn't want her to see through me, to that weak, jiggling jelly at my core.

"Janeese?"

The words were doing a little jig on the page, so I pinned them down with my shaky index finger. I started reading softly, slowly. My monotone voice did a disservice to the Quebec housewife, Rose, and her impassioned monologue, loaded with vulgarities.

"We can't hear at the back," someone said.

I stopped.

"*Un peu plus fort*. Just get into the women's lives," the professor said in French. "*C'est le fun.*"

I cleared my throat. This was ridiculous. If I couldn't even read a few paragraphs from a book in front of a small class, I'd never make it as a teacher.

I continued. The prof laughed at a sentence I didn't fully understand and my voice got stronger. After a few more lines, my accent didn't sound so bad after all. When I focused on the women, let their lives unravel, it was hard to focus on my panic attack. The housewives' bitterness was tangible, their isolation in the kitchen complete. Their only hope of escape from *la maudite vie plate*—their miserable, rotten lives—was to score big in a contest. Rose materialized in front of me as she ranted about her husband; how a woman had to tolerate a pig like that for the rest of her life because she had had the misfortune to say *oui* that one time. "*J'aurais dû crier 'non' à plein poumons.*" I should have screamed *no* at the top of my lungs! Regret seeped through her monologue, for the past, for her hopeless future. But she vowed her daughter would never end up like her.

"*Maudit cul!*" The passage ended on a very bad swear word.

A few laughs peppered this room full of twenty-something girls. They probably thought because the play had been written in 1965, these kitchens didn't exist anymore.

"Thank you, we'll stop there."

I put my book down, untangled myself from Rose's life of misery, looked up at the professor.

"You put a lot of heart into that reading."

It always surprised me how much French I understood, like I was slipping into someone else's body. I was only a B student in this class because it was so labour-intensive having to look up every second word in my French-English dictionary, but in my other classes, on every essay, and on every mid-term exam, I'd gotten an A.

"How was the drive?" I asked.

It was Tuesday, back in the playground at Banff, and Grant didn't look quite as in control as he had four days earlier. Instead of his black leather jacket, he was wearing his down coat, the one with duct tape over the holes. Four days with his kids in his rented room in a cabin in the woods and he was haggard.

"Long."

I resisted the urge to apologize. He didn't bother to ask about my drive.

We sat on opposite ends of the bench and watched the kids chase each other through the soft wood shavings. This playground was like a big hamster cage. It even smelled the same. Grant lit up a cigarette. It was hard to see the climber in him. He seemed all logger.

The twins' mother, Karen, had said to me soon after we met, "I can't believe you're a logger's wife. You don't seem the type." And I'd said, "You don't seem like a vending machine filler's wife." We'd agreed we had long, messy stories to compare over a few bottles of wine.

"I read an editorial in the *Calgary Herald* yesterday about how our society is falling apart due to a lack of moral conviction." Grant sounded like he'd rehearsed these lines.

"Yeah, I read it too. The guy that wrote it is from some radical pro-life, pro-family coalition."

"What's wrong with pro-family? Everyone's splitting up these days. There's no commitment, no work ethic."

Sam toddled after Jenna to the slide, his diaper under snow pants making him bowlegged. Jenna squealed as she sailed down, face first. At the bottom she looked over to make sure we were watching, then she put her hands out to catch her brother.

"I think we made a mistake. I think we should get back together," Grant said.

I hadn't seen that coming, even with the pro-family talk. I wrapped my arms around my core and a fog of confusion shrouded my head. We'd split up a month ago. I'd just found out I qualified for student loans as a single mother, and for a daycare subsidy. I was starting to think I could do this.

"I don't think that's such a good—"

"I really miss my family, you know." Grant slumped over with his elbows on his knees, his eyes on the kids. I had a sudden urge to bake him banana bread.

"I know," I said. His sadness stabbed into me, twisted. I had no idea where mine ended and his began. Four days without Jenna and Sam had been like solitary confinement for me. He must have been so lonely without us.

We sat without speaking, only the kids' laughter tinkling through the silence. I forced my breath in and out, pushing tiny puffs of cloud into the cold air. I didn't trust myself to speak. I was scared if I opened my mouth a little *yes* would pop out, just to take away his hurt.

Maybe this meant he was starting to see the benefits of my having a profession. As a teacher I could live in Golden, have the same holidays as the kids, and he could finally get out of logging. And if we got back together I wouldn't have to do this on my own. Mid-terms had almost obliterated me and finals were next, on top of all the assignments, presentations and readings, the volunteering in Jenna's class, and gymnastics on the weekends. Maybe he was right.

Before I could speak, Grant straightened up, as though he'd made a decision. "Look, this is ridiculous. If you quit school, come back to Golden and look after your family, I'll take you back."

His voice worked on me like a hypnotist snapping his fingers. *Poof!* My sympathy was gone. Shrivelled up like a leech laid out on the rocks to dry. I knew this voice. He'd been using it on me for the past six years. Even if I came back to Golden and did everything his way for the rest of my life, it wouldn't change that voice.

Saved by the stupid shit that keeps coming out of your mouth! I jammed my fists deep into my jacket. My anger was back. It inflated me, like a limp balloon filling up with air. It was just what I needed. "Yeah, well, that's not going to happen."

"Look, if it was just the two of us there's no doubt we'd split up, but you're messing up the kids."

"That's your way of trying to woo me back? By telling me *I'm* messing up the kids?"

"Yeah, you are, because I'm willing to work on this. To compromise."

The kids sat at the top of the slide, watching us.

Detach, detach! Don't let yourself get reeled in like a great big tuna fish. I stood up, held my hands in front of me as if to ward off his words. "I can't do this. I can't fight anymore. I just want to go home."

Ultimatum after ultimatum. For years. Each time I received an acceptance letter from the university he'd said, *Tell me where to send the money.* Well, now I had a place for him to send the money.

"Just think about it," he said.

"I've got to go. I don't want to drive in the dark."

Sam landed on his diaper at the bottom of the slide, put both arms in the air. "Up!" I scooped him up, settled him on my hip.

Jenna flew down the slide in a swirl of billowing white lace, pink satin, and gumboots.

Driving along the four-lane highway, I clenched and unclenched my hands around the steering wheel. Flecks of white rushed toward the windshield.

"Oh, look you guys! It's snowing!" I forced my mommy voice, trying to get Grant out of my head.

Jenna and Sam leaned in to look out the front window. Their blond heads touched.

"Ooooh, pretty!" Jenna said.

"Ooooh, pwitty!" Sam parroted.

A soft *thunk!* as Sam's bottle landed beside him on the seat. I adjusted the rear-view mirror to watch him reach for it. It was just beyond his fingertips.

"Bubby!"

My neck muscles tensed up and I turned my eyes back to the road. I was going a hundred kilometres an hour on a highway and my child was about to have a meltdown.

"Shit!" It popped out of my mouth involuntarily, like Tourette's.

"Thit!" Sam said, laughing.

"No, no, Sam, that's not a nice word. Mommy shouldn't say it either."

"Thit! Thit!"

"Shit!" Jenna joined in on the fun.

"Jenna. Give me a break here. You know that's a bad word." I could just imagine some of my less savoury vocabulary coming out of her mouth in kindergarten. That would definitely be cause for another meeting with the teacher.

"You say it. Sam says it. Daddy says it."

I opened my mouth. Closed it.

Sam chewed his fingers. "Bubby!"

Jenna put down her blanket, strained against the seat belt to lean over Sam, plucked the bottle up from where it was wedged beside his car seat. She plugged it in her little brother's mouth and he turned back from a time bomb to a harmless toddler.

I let out my breath. "Thanks, sweetie." I smiled at her in the mirror.

She shoved a corner of her blanket and half her hand into her mouth.

"No pwoblum," she slurred through her fingers.

After all the dips and bends around mountains and lakes, the highway straightened and flattened as we passed through the foothills. I glanced in my mirrors, almost expecting to see Grant following us, like in the movies, the hero barrelling after his one true love in a shiny white pickup, but all I could see were black mountains silhouetted against the fuchsia-pink sky. Grant was driving west, into the sunset, while we were driving away from it. And somehow, no crevasse had opened at my feet to swallow me whole.

I took one more peek at the Rockies as they receded in my rearview mirror, then fixed my sights on the glow of the city to the east.

EPILOGUE: SECOND CHANCES

Mexico, February 2013. With the tip of my purple climbing shoe poised on a foothold, I step up, reach for the edge of a deep hole. The grey limestone is prickly, like everything in Mexico. Even with my eight-year-old climbing shoes, my feet feel secure on this rock. Holes pockmark the wall, some deep, some shallow, providing great handholds, and the rope leads from my harness up to a bomber anchor and my new-ish husband, Dan, a hundred feet above.

Yes. My new husband's name is Dan. Serendipity, if you believe in that shit, which I try not to, but actually do. It's almost as if my first Dan somehow played a part in this. Maybe he got tired of watching me sabotage myself and said, "Enough already!" Picked Dan up and plunked him down in Golden, where I'd returned after university and was working as a grade-three French immersion teacher, living with Jenna and Sam in a white house on a hill not far from my school.

Pulling up with my fingers, I feel the regained power in my forearms from the past two weeks of climbing. From day one I surprised myself with my strength. Here I am, in my fifties, and climbing almost at the level of difficulty I was climbing in my twenties. I'm not sure where the strength comes from—we only climb about half a dozen times a year now. Maybe from gripping the brakes of my mountain bike. Certainly not from my blue rubber doughnut, the one I've been intending to squeeze to strengthen my forearms. It still has the price tag on it.

Mexican pop music pulsates up the long, cactus-filled slope to the base of our climb from the speakers of a row of pickup trucks at the bottom of the canyon. Whole families from Monterrey, an hour south of here, come to El Potrero Chico, a world-class climbing destination, to watch the climbers. It's a noisy weekend ritual. Bring the beer, the tortillas, the BBQ, the kids, the binoculars.

Potrero was not my destination of choice; northern Mexico is not exactly getting the best press these days. As Dan booked the flights to Monterrey on his computer, I googled *Mexico and murder* on mine. The first hit gave me: "Nine bodies hung from bridge in northern Mexico as drug war rages," with a photo of a blindfolded guy hanging right under a big green highway sign that read: MONTERREY.

But I knew my fear of being raped and tortured and murdered and chopped up into little pieces by the drug cartel paled beside my real fear: leading. Lead climbing is the main reason I've traded rock climbing in for mountain biking. My head still can't keep up with my body. But the airline tickets were booked, so off I went to buy a new rope for our trip. At the climbing store, serendipity struck again; the book, *A Rock Warrior's Way: Mental Preparation for Climbers*, almost leapt off the shelf into my hands, and I thought, *Yes! The perfect rubber doughnut for my mind!* At home I opened it up and the first line I read was, "How you live your life is how you climb."

I almost slammed the book shut, but instead I attacked it with my highlighter and vowed to get my butt back on the sharp end of the rope, force myself into that zone where I had to commit or fall. Who would be revealed when I pulled back all my layers of defence? A chickenshit or a rock warrior?

At the top of the pitch, I pull myself up beside Dan, clip into the anchor, and we stand squeezed together on the small ledge partway up a four-hundred-foot pillar, looking out on a canyon flanked by towers of limestone, some as high as two thousand feet.

"That was fun," I say. "Good job."

"You want the next lead?"

Before we left Canada, I asked Dan, "Why am I still such a chickenshit when it comes to leading, but I can do scary stuff on my mountain bike?" and he said, "Probably because you haven't been leading."

Duh. Such simple logic. I can mountain-bike because I mountain-bike. I could lead again if I wanted to lead. Bravery takes practice.

Then he said, "Don't pressure yourself. Plan to just follow for the first few days, don't even consider leading, then you'll be chomping at the bit, needing to lead. Like in the old days."

Like in the old days. He must have been thinking of that first week we were together, about ten years ago. As a single mom and full-time teacher, I hadn't been doing much climbing, but with Dan holding my rope and watching, I pulled off the hardest lead I'd done in years. It was like some bizarre climbers' mating ritual. Other women don makeup and high heels, I show off on the rock. Unfortunately, my newfound courage must have been fuelled by pheromones, because I duly went back to my yo-yoing: two moves up, paralysis, one move down.

"So, Jan. You want the lead?" Dan is handing me the rack of quick-draws, short pieces of webbing with a carabiner in each end. I glance at them, then tilt back my head to study the route.

It's longer than the first pitch, well over a hundred feet. More time to be scared. It's also steeper. I count the bolts, trying to gauge the distance between them. The farther apart they are, the longer the fall. And I've seen some pretty scary bolt placements here. Ones placed by guys over six feet tall with very long arms who gave absolutely no thought to a terrified, middle-aged, short, perimenopausal woman having to make all the hard moves *before* clipping the just-out-of-reach bolt, instead of after.

"The bolts look far apart."

"It's only 5.8. You're not going to die on 5.8."

I glance sideways at Dan, my eyebrow raised. I've heard that one before.

I look back up. *Do I want this lead?* I want to want it. I want to feel like a real climber again.

We're seventeen days into our trip, and I've done only two leads. Leads I would have taken beginners up back when I was working at the cadet camp. Leads that barely produced a ripple of fear. And we only have eight days left for me to test myself.

Dan is still holding the rack out for me to grab. "Are you leading or am I leading?"

"Okay. What the hell. That's what I'm here for, right? To scare the shit out of myself?"

I grab the quickdraws, start clipping them to my harness before I can change my mind. They clink against each other, metal on metal.

"Got me?" I dip my hands in my chalk bag, clap off the excess with a puff of white.

"Yup. You're on belay."

I scramble up the first few feet quickly, pulling on the edges of deep holes, hoping they don't house the red ants, tarantulas, rattlesnakes or scorpions described in the guidebook. The moves are easy, the rock low-angled. I reach the first bolt, clip my quickdraw, then clip the rope. Now I can't hit the ledge if I fall. The second bolt is a good fifteen feet away, but the climbing is still pretty casual. I feel smooth. Balanced and poised. In control. I feel like a climber. I reach the bolt and clip another quickdraw.

"Looking good, Jan." Dan encourages me from twenty feet below.

It was a fluke Dan and I even met. He had planned to go paragliding, then at the last minute changed his mind (he's a Libra) and decided to go climbing near Golden with a friend of mine instead. They invited me along, and when I met him that first time, he felt familiar to me. Like home. Maybe because he has that typical, craggy climber look—fit, weatherbeaten in a good way, after years in the mountains. When I told my friends I'd fallen in love with a stuntman in the film industry, they shook their heads, picturing me with an Arnold Schwarzenegger look-alike. But Dan is no Arnold. He's laid-back, unassuming, calm and calming.

I climb smoothly to the third bolt, clip it. By now I'm starting to feel downright cocky. I've still got it in me! After I clip the fourth bolt, I come back down to a little ledge and study the route. This must be the crux. A pinnacle bulges out for the next thirty feet, more than vertical. There are two cracks on either side. The bolts go up the middle, so I could go either way. Between my clipped bolt and the next bolt is about fifteen feet. If I fall just before that bolt, I'll drop thirty feet.

"The next bolt is really, really far away," I say.

I can still back down. I could lower off the bolt.

"Don't feel like you have to do it, Jan. I can finish if you want."

Of course he could finish it, and with barely a twinge of fear. When I climbed with my first Dan, that knowledge used to vaporize my motivation. But one thing I've figured out over the years is that one woman's molehill is another woman's mountain. This is my

Everest. Besides, I didn't come to Mexico to follow Dan around the mountains. I came to get back in touch with my rock warrior.

So no. I won't lower off the goddamned bolt.

My palms are sweaty so I dip them back in my chalk bag for the umpteenth time. I climb off the ledge, up the left-hand crack in the pinnacle, up to my clipped bolt, then one move past it. I pause. A twinge of the sick *I'm gonna die* feeling roils in my gut. If I make another move I'm committed. It'll be too hard to retreat after that. I waver a good few minutes in that spot, then climb back down to my comfortable little ledge. To the right of the pinnacle looks no easier. I chalk up my hands again.

"This looks fucking hard!" I yell down. "It is not a 5.8."

Dan rubs the back of his neck but doesn't say anything. This Dan is more tolerant of my fear, but that might be because he's made it to fifty-four. My first Dan would have been fifty-three this year, but he never got past twenty-seven.

One more dip into my chalk bag. I look up at the bolt but stay glued to my spot. I don't want to go up and I don't want to go down.

How you live your life is how you climb.

Now here I am, up and down, up and down, waffling, expending my precious energy on stasis. A replica of my first marriage.

My dramatic marital breakdown in that first semester of university was just the first of three. We jumped back into the ring for another brief round while I was still in school, then separated legally, then after four stressful, adrenal-blowing years I returned to Golden, a single mom of a five- and eight-year-old with my long-sought-after degree in a cheap picture frame. We moved into an uninsulated rented house twenty minutes out of town, and I started teaching full-time in my second language, which I had not yet fully mastered. Grant was looking ruggedly handsome, helping me with firewood (I needed eight cords), and the kids and I could see his beautiful house, formerly *our* beautiful house, on the hill above us from our window. I missed him like hell, and the kids missed him like hell and he missed us like hell. Just before the snow came, we were back in that little home on the hill, a family again.

It took less than a week to know nothing had changed, but I stuck around for five more years with one foot in the marriage and one out. What allowed me to leave for good was that hard-earned degree in education. If I could get through four years on my own in Calgary, a full-time student and single mom, I could get through anything.

"Just go for it, Jan!"

I look down at Dan, now lying on his back to ease the strain on his vertebrae. He broke his neck once on an ice climb near Field, in an avalanche that killed his partner. He also broke his back paragliding when his wing stalled. He's seen his fair share of tragedy in the mountains, but it's made him gentle and appreciative of life, not angry.

I shift from one foot to the other. I can't hang out here forever. I climb back up to my bolt, and this time I go one move past it till the bolt is at my feet. The moves feel awkward. The rock wants to push me off, and the holds are tiny, just pinch holds. I now know that this is much harder than 5.8. That I probably should have gone the other way around the pinnacle. But no, as usual, I had to inadvertently choose the hard way up.

Fake it till you make it. My first Dan's motto. Not that I was ever any good at faking it before Alaska. Certainly not after.

I take another step up, and now the bolt is a couple of feet below the soles of my shoes. There's no going back. It'd be too hard to down-climb. I'm committed. The bowel-releasing zone.

My eyes are fixed on the next bolt, well out of reach. The farther I go, the longer the fall, but if I don't climb, the fall's a certainty.

I can climb or fall. It's all up to me.

I reach high, pawing the rock for a positive hold but they're all sloping. There should not be slopers on a climb of this grade. My foot slips slightly, enough to send a sharp sliver of fear through my whole body.

"Watch me!" I yell so that Dan will be prepared in case I fall.

"I'm watching. You're almost there."

I look down, then immediately wish I hadn't. Dan is staring intently. He must see what I now see. The ledge I was just standing on is right below me. If I fall, I'll hit it from twenty feet up. It would be the same as hitting the ground.

Fear settles around me. Not just a tingly fear. This one's cold and heavy. I could end up with a broken neck in a Mexican clinic in Hidalgo. A paraplegic. Quadriplegic. Or worse.

I stretch, trying to reach the bolt, but it's still too far away. Goddamned six-foot-four first ascensionists.

"I can't reach the fucking bolt!"

I'm sucking in little gerbil breaths. Hyperventilating. Fear makes my body instinctively hug the rock, which puts my weight in the wrong place. One foot starts to shake, up and down, up and down like a sewing machine. I grip tighter, and the tighter I grip the more I shake.

Dan doesn't say anything. There's nothing to say. He can't swoop in and rescue me. This is my moment. The one I usually try to avoid. The one I came here looking for.

A deep breath from the belly, not my shallow breaths from the chest. It does what it's supposed to. Brings my heart rate down a couple of beats, just enough to give me courage. I unglue my hand from its hold. Take another small step up.

A couple years ago I watched Jenna do a hard lead. She was high off the ground, unable to get in her first piece of protection, exhausting herself, while I was pacing a groove in the dirt, yelling, "Jenna, get something in!" Dan finally advised her to just blitz through the crux. So she did. I could almost see the change in her body as she made that decision. Her back straightened, her face relaxed, her power returned. She climbed smoothly to a good rest spot. She'd just had to relax and commit.

That's the key. To relax *before* I clip the bolt. To climb as though I've already clipped it. *Fake it till I make it.*

I soften my grip on the rock. Soften my grimace. Breathe. Throw back my shoulders and straighten my spine so my weight is over my feet. My shoes grip the rock again. My thoughts come back to here and now, not to that ledge below me. Not to living out my final years ventilator-dependent in a wheelchair in a nursing home.

If I can control my body, I can control my mind. I always thought it was the other way around. But if I put my body in motion, my mind has to follow. Jocelyn tried to teach me that back when I was fourteen years old: "If the head she goes, the body he follows."

Another hold comes into focus, now that I'm not fixated on the bolt. A good hold. Small, but with a sharp edge. These next moves will take finesse, not force. I reach to my right, high above my head, pull sideways and move my foot up behind me so the sole of my shoe is flat against an outcrop, scrunched under my bum. I could reach the bolt now, but I'm off balance. I have to make another move. I inch my way up the rock till my feet are secure, on two good holds. I take the quick draw from my harness, clip it into the bolt, pull up the rope and clip it into the carabiner.

I let out my breath. When I stop shaking, I look down and grin. "I almost shit myself!"

Dan smiles and it's too far away to see his eyes crinkle in the corners, but I know they do.

What are the odds of marrying a man with the same name as your dead boyfriend? Of getting a second chance? A wave of euphoria courses through me. Is that such a bad thing? To feel comfortable with someone? To feel safe?

Leaning out from the rock, I study the route above. Even though I'm only halfway there, four more bolts to go, I can see the rest of the holds are bigger, the angle more laid-back. I also know whatever I just did on the crux is all mine. It will stick with me to the top.

I dip each hand into my chalk bag, reach high above my head, and continue leading upward.

ACKNOWLEDGEMENTS

I'm indebted to many mentors who have helped me believe in myself as a writer: Wayde Compton (Simon Fraser University's The Writer's Studio), for his unfaltering faith that my next lessons lay in post-publication; and Betsy Warland (SFU's TWS and Vancouver Manuscript Intensive), John Vaillant (Sage Hill Writing), who skillfully nurtured storytelling; Lynne Bowen (UBC), whose teaching skills teased out some of my favourite essays (ie "The Big Sex Talk"); Connie Gault (Banff Wired), who was so unflappable as I plowed through the emotional work of writing my coming-of-age chapters (hopefully part of a future memoir); and Marni Jackson (Banff Mountain and Wilderness Writing), who convinced me that my life, my experiences, and my memories belong to me and that I have a right to tell my story. A special thanks to Marni for introducing me to my wonderful agent and editors.

I wrote most of this book in my very messy office with the buzz of a dozen or so neighbourhood children and dogs in the background, but some of the most emotionally challenging chapters were written in heavenly solitude: on Hornby Island, thanks to Deb McVittie of 32 Books; on the North Bench in Golden, thanks to my mountain-biking buddy Tannis Dakin; and in a cabin on the Sunshine Coast, thanks to Andreas Schroeder and Sharon Brown.

To my SFU Writer's Studio family who had more faith in me than I did and laughed encouragingly at my humping-bunnies story: Eufemia Fantetti, Ayelet Tsabari (who was also instrumental—from Israel!—in connecting me with my agent, Sam), Leslie Hill, Sue Anne Linde, Naz Hazar, Jen Caldwell and Fiona Scott. And to my many other workshoppers and readers: Clarissa Green, Morgan Chojnacki, Sally Halliday, Joan Flood, Julie Okot Bitek, Libby Soper, Cathy Ostlere, Deb McVittie, Barker, Judy McFarlane, Tannis Dakin, my "sista" Theresa Godin and Saul Greenberg, who read multiple drafts, proclaiming each one a finished product (possibly so he wouldn't have to read another one).

About finding one's voice, Tristine Rainer wrote: "Write as you would to that little group of admirers who is really interested in what you have to say and laughs at your jokes." Thank you to Tracey Thatcher for being the little admirer in my head.

A gargantuan thank you to Andreas Schroeder for guiding me through my thesis and not groaning too loudly when I sent him yet another few thousand words, and to Timothy Taylor, my second reader, for recognizing that the focus had to be on the mountains, not on the dysfunctional family. My fellow students at UBC (too many to mention, but you know who you are) gave me courage and confidence, and the amazing instructors in the MFA program helped me become a better non-fiction writer through fiction, screen and journalism: Linda Svendsen, Peggy Thompson, Deborah Campbell and Keith Maillard.

I'm grateful to my kids, Jenna and Sam, for allowing me to write about them, and for charging at life with courage and gumption. And to Dan, for reading everything I write (over and over again), for believing in me as a writer (and climber, mountain biker and person) and for not worrying about my lack of financial viability. You are the calm within my storm. And to my siblings, Eric and Susan, for allowing me to share some of our mutual past (and for helping me survive it).

Since the first words of this book were set to paper, both my parents have passed away: my father soon after my first attempt at a story, and my mother right in the middle of my last rewrite of the whole manuscript. I know they'd be slightly horrified but mostly proud of me. It is my deep regret that my uncle, Dunkin Bancroft, an artist and aspiring writer himself, is not here to see my dream come true. I received word of my book contract days after his death. Thank you for believing in me and laughing out loud at my stories.

Thank you to UBC, the Banff Centre, Sage Hill and the BC Arts Council for your financial support through this and other projects.

And of course, a huge hug of gratitude to Amanda Lewis, my editor and champion at Random House Canada (now freelancing, doing yoga and puttering in her garden). You believed in me from the start. Your e-mail with the subject line "Could we chat?" changed my life. And to Anne Collins, who jumped into the fray toward the end and nipped and tucked so beautifully with her sharp eye. Thank you for your kindness and patience as I kept vigil over my mother. And to my ever-so-supportive agent, Samantha Haywood, with Transatlantic: you so kindly reassure me through my rants that I'm normal, that many writers are afflicted with self-doubt and angst. And to the team at Counterpoint Press, especially my editor, Megha Majumdar, thank you for your constant flexibility, support, and enthusiasm and for bringing my book to a whole new audience.

To the first person to encourage me to get my story down on paper (in third person so I could get much-needed distance and perspective), Elva Mertick, wherever you are, thank you for giving me the courage to move on, and for saying you would read a whole book like the story I wrote about Sam pooping in the bushes in front of our new home in student housing. Well, here it is. A whole book.

And thank you to my climbing family for providing a home that fit, and many stories.

Dan Guthrie and Ian Bult in their element.

JAN REDFORD lives with her family in Squamish, BC, where she mountain bikes, trail runs, climbs and skis. Her stories, articles and personal essays have been published in the *Globe and Mail*, *National Post*, *Mountain Life*, *Explore* and anthologies, and have won or been shortlisted in several writing contests. She is a graduate of The Writer's Studio at SFU and holds a master's in creative writing from UBC.